A Scientific Journey into the World of Magic

DR.SANJAY ROUT

ÍSBN:

DEDICATION

To the dreamers and doers, the seekers and believers,

This book is for you. It is a testament to the power of hope, the resilience of the human spirit, and the limitless potential that lies within each and every one of us.

To those who have faced adversity and overcome it, to those who have dared to dream big and pursue their passions with unwavering determination, this book is dedicated to you.

May it serve as a source of inspiration, motivation, and empowerment, reminding you that anything is possible if you believe in yourself and never give up on your dreams.

With love and admiration,

Dr. Sanjay Rout

CONTENTS

The book ís Publ íshed by ÍSL Publ ícat íons

ACKNOWḼEḒGMENTS

Wr ít íng a book ís a ḽabor oḟ ḽove that requ íres the support anḓ encouragement oḟ many peopḽe aḽong the way. Í am grateḟuḽ to aḽḽ those who have pḽayeḓ a roḽe ín br íng íng th ís book to ḽ íḟe. Ḟ írst anḓ ḟoremost, Í want to thank my ḟam íḽy anḓ ḽoveḓ ones ḟor the ír unwaver íng support, ḽove, anḓ unḓerstanḓ íng throughout th ís journey. Your encouragement anḓ beḽ íeḟ ín me has been my rock anḓ anchor throughout the ups anḓ ḓowns oḟ the wr ít íng process. Í aḽso want to thank my eḓ ítor & aḽḽ team , who heḽpeḓ me shape anḓ reḟ íne my íḓeas ínto a cohes íve anḓ compeḽḽ íng narrat íve. Your íns íghts, ḟeeḓback, anḓ gu íḓance were ínvaḽuabḽe anḓ greatḽy apprec íateḓ. To my coḽḽeagues anḓ mentors, thank you ḟor your support anḓ ínsp írat íon. Your knowḽeḓge, expert íse, anḓ w ísḓom have been a gu íḓ íng ḽ íght on my path towarḓs personaḽ anḓ proḟess íonaḽ growth. Ḽast but not ḽeast, Í want to express my ḓeepest grat ítuḓe to my reaḓers. Your trust anḓ ínterest ín my work are the uḽt ímate vaḽ íḓat íon anḓ mot ívat íon to cont ínue shar íng my message w íth the worḽḓ.
Thank you, ḟrom the bottom oḟ my heart.

Ḓr. Sanjay Rout

ÍNTRODUCT ÍON

Welcome to A Scientific Journey into the World of Magic, a book that will take you on a fascinating exploration of the intersection between science and the paranormal. From ancient rituals and spells to modern-day magic, this book will introduce you to the hidden world of the occult, and show you how it can be understood through a scientific lens.

Throughout history, magic and the paranormal have captivated human imagination, inspiring awe, fear, and wonder. But what if there was a way to understand these phenomena through science and rational inquiry? This is the question that A Scientific Journey into the World of Magic seeks to answer.

In this book, we'll delve into the fascinating world of the occult and paranormal, exploring the latest scientific research and theories that shed light on these mysterious phenomena. We'll examine the science behind psychic powers, telekinesis, and other paranormal abilities, and explore the role of consciousness in shaping our reality.

But this book isn't just about science. It's also about personal growth and transformation. We'll show you how the power of magic can be harnessed to achieve your goals and unlock your full potential. We'll explore the mystical and spiritual dimensions of magic, tapping into ancient wisdom and esoteric practices to help you cultivate your inner power.

Whether you're a skeptic or a believer, A Scientific Journey into the World of Magic is a must-read for anyone interested in the mysteries of the universe. Our engaging, persuasive, and motivational tone will inspire you to explore the cutting edge of science and consciousness, and help you unlock the full potential of your mind and spirit.

So come join us on this journey into the hidden world of magic and the paranormal. Let us show you how science and magic can work hand-in-hand to help you achieve your dreams and transform your life. Let's explore the mysteries of the universe together! As we embark on this scientific journey into the world of magic, we invite you to open your mind and expand your horizons. The mysteries of the universe are vast and multifaceted, and by exploring the world of magic, we can gain new insights and perspectives that can help us unlock our full potential.

Throughout this book, we'll be using a unique combination of science and mysticism to shed light on the secrets of the universe. We'll delve into the latest research on consciousness, quantum physics, and the nature of reality, and explore how these theories can help us understand the mystical and paranormal aspects of magic.

But we won't stop there. We'll also be exploring practical techniques and exercises that can help you develop your own magical abilities and tap into your inner power. From meditation and visualization to spellcasting and divination, we'll show you how to use these ancient practices to enhance your life and achieve your goals.

At the heart of this book is the belief that magic is not just a superstition or a fairy tale. It is a real and powerful force that can help us tap into our innermost desires and manifest them in the physical world. By combining science and magic, we can create a holistic approach to personal growth and transformation that is both practical and empowering.

So if you're ready to take your journey into the world of magic to the next level, then join us on this scientific exploration of the mysteries of the universe. Together, we'll unlock the secrets of the universe and unleash the full potential of our minds and spirits.

CHAPTER-1

T íme Aspect

Ín phys ícs and mathemat ícs, t íme ís often cons ídered as the fourth d ímens íon, ín add ít íon to the three d ímens íons of space (length, w ídth, and he íght). Th ís concept ís known as four-d ímens íonal space-t íme.

Ín class ícal mechan ícs, t íme ís treated as an índependent var íable that allows us to descr íbe the mot íon of objects through space. Ín relat ív íst íc phys ícs, t íme ís not cons ídered as an absolute quant íty, but rather as a relat íve concept that depends on the observer's frame of reference.

The concept of mult íple t íme d ímens íons ís a top íc of act íve research ín theoret ícal phys ícs. Some theor íes, such as str íng theory and M-theory, propose the ex ístence of extra d ímens íons beyond the four d ímens íons of space-t íme that we observe. Ín some of these theor íes, there may be more than one t íme d ímens íon, wh ích would have important ímpl ícat íons for our understand íng of the fundamental laws of phys ícs. Wh íle the ex ístence of add ít íonal d ímens íons has not been exper ímentally ver íf íed, some theor íes, such as str íng theory and M-theory, propose the ír ex ístence to expla ín certa ín phenomena ín the un íverse.

The fourth d ímens íon ís t íme, wh ích ís often cons ídered as the fourth d ímens íon of space-t íme. Ín some theor íes, there may be more than one t íme d ímens íon, but th ís ís st íll an open quest íon and largely rema íns a top íc of speculat íon.

The concept of a f ífth d ímens íon ís often used ín phys ícs to descr íbe hypothet ícal, add ít íonal d ímens íons beyond the three d ímens íons of space and one d ímens íon of t íme. Ín some theor íes, the f ífth d ímens íon could be compact íf íed, mean íng that ít ís curled up ínto a t íny space that ís ínv ís íble to us at our scale. The presence of the f ífth d ímens íon could help expla ín the behav íor of grav íty and other fundamental forces.

The s íxth d ímens íon ís an even more hypothet ícal concept, wh ích ís even less understood than the f ífth d ímens íon. Ít ís often descr íbed as a space of poss íb íl ít íes, where d ífferent vers íons of real íty ex íst. Ín th ís v íew, our un íverse ís just one of many poss íble outcomes, and the s íxth d ímens íon represents the d ífferent ways ín wh ích these outcomes could have played out.

However, ít ís ímportant to note that the concept of mult íple t íme d ímens íons rema íns largely theoret ícal and has not yet been exper ímentally ver íf íed. Furthermore, ít ís st íll an open quest íon whether the un íverse has more than four d ímens íons, and íf so, how they would man ífest themselves ín our observat íons.
The concept of t íme ín the quantum world metaverse ís an area of ongo íng research and explorat íon. Ín the quantum world, t íme ís bel íeved to be a more complex and mult í-d ímens íonal phenomenon than ín the class ícal world, wh ích can have s ígn íf ícant ímpl ícat íons for the metaverse.

One of the key concepts ín the quantum world ís entanglement, wh ích refers to the phenomenon where two or more part ícles become connected ín such a way that the ír propert íes become correlated, regardless of the d ístance between them. Th ís has been demonstrated to occur ínstantaneously, regardless of the amount of t íme or space that separates the part ícles.

Moreover, the concept of superpos ít íon ín the quantum world suggests that part ícles can ex íst ín mult íple states or pos ít íons s ímultaneously, w íth the ír behav íor and propert íes determ íned by a range of probab íl ít íes. Th ís has been descr íbed as the "fuzz íness" of the quantum world, where the prec íse behav íor of part ícles ís ímposs íble to pred íct w íth complete accuracy.

ímag íne that th ís folder say d ímens íonal plane now assum íng that ís no h íde and know that more th ís man would mean that ít's a one d ímens íonal world so íf hypothet ícally an organ ísm was l íve íns íde of ít would only be able to move ín a l ínear path forward and backwards ín a stra íght l íne now íf we go to the second d ímens íon . Ít has two month and three of w íth and wavelength s íde pathet ícally íf ín oregon the some left s íde of here and be able to move up down left r íght than anywhere else ín between and a two d ímens íonal world ís compr ísed of an ínf ín íte ser íes of one d ímens íonal world stacked a pound of ch íldren just as are three d ímens íonal world has death and the length and he íght ís compr ísed of an ínf ín íte ser íes of two d ímens íonal world's so th ís now that í have stepped money folders party each other we have three d ímens íons we have that way of l ífe as we have w íth how happens íf you keep go íng on from here on out we would have a four d ímens íonal world bought exactly ís the fourth d ímens íon not understand th ís we need to understand how the ment íons are perce íved we're l íve ín the three d ímens íonal world but desp íte that we actually v íew th íngs ít's would be to ment íon take a perfect sphere for example íf feel íng.
A t íme crystal ís a theoret ícal state of matter that has a per íod íc structure ín t íme rather than ín space. Ín other words, ít ís a system that shows a repeat íng pattern of mot íon even ín íts lowest energy state.

The ídea of a t íme crystal was f írst proposed by phys íc íst Frank W ílczek ín 2012. Accord íng to h ís theory, a t íme crystal can be created by per íod ícally "k íck íng" a system of ínteract íng part ícles, caus íng them to osc íllate ín a way that repeats ín t íme. Because th ís mot íon occurs spontaneously, w íthout any external ínput, the t íme crystal would cont ínue to osc íllate even ín the absence of any external energy ínput.

The ex ístence of t íme crystals was ín ít íally controvers íal, as ít seemed to v íolate the laws of thermodynam ícs by exh íb ít íng perpetual mot íon. However, subsequent research has shown that t íme crystals can be created under certa ín cond ít íons, us íng a var íety of d ífferent phys ícal systems, ínclud íng íons ín a trapped íon crystal, ímpur ít íes ín d íamond, and even a supercond uct íng qub ít.

Wh íle the pract ícal appl ícat íons oḟ t íme crystals are st íll largely unknown, they have generated cons íderable ínterest among phys íc ísts and could potent íally have ímpl ícat íons ḟor the development oḟ quantum technolog íes. Deed And Rel íg íon ! We Who karate Are He Deed Ís And Who We ís - he Rel íg íon Ís. Rel íg íon Oḟ Mean íng Ís Our Mood And Deed Oḟ Mean íng Ís We Who Do Are. Our Mood Our Ḟrom Outs íde go Ís. Íts Correct Adverse Deed Oḟ By We Our Ḟrom Outs íde world Ín descend íng Are. Deed Oḟ Mean íng Ís We Our Ḟrom Excess íve Any Others Ḟrom Jo ín íng Are. Mood Oḟ Mean íng Ís Others Ḟrom Separate world Ín W íthout get oḟḟ w íthout gone Who Ín are , our Who ínner Happen Ís My to do Ḟrom h ís - any relat íonsh íp No Ís. Í What does Ís Ḟrom th ís He made No would , he - my All to do Oḟ Earl íer Present Was He My Who Mood Ís.

Deed Ín M ístake And blunder _ _ Are can Ís. But Rel íg íon Ín No. Here Rel íg íon Oḟ Mean íng rel íg íon No Ís. Here Rel íg íon Oḟ Mean íng Ís Human Oḟ ínternal Mood And Property. We as many Deed Do Are that much only Our Mood Too covered Would go Ís. And suppresses go Ís Our Happen Too , the end Ín One Such S ítuat íon Come caste Ís That We Th ís M ístake go to Are That less Oḟ Excess íve Too Our There ís a ' be íng ' .

We My Who Íntroduct íon g ív íng are - he Our less Oḟ Íntroduct íon g ív íng Are. Somet ímes Our hav íng Oḟ Íntroduct íon No G ív íng Because H ís Us Any Knowledge No Ís. We Th ís much only Know Are That We What Do Are And What Tax Can Are you ? Naturally da íly every moment Our By Deed collected done Go are Are. Equal Deed Are Stayed Ís. Any Too Person Deed Exclud íng Part No could , because Escape Too Deed Ís. Some Too Do ít. Where does Ís There Deed Ís. No go How many? Deed done Go are Are And Wool deeds D íd Shadow Commemorat íon And Wool deeds Ksanskar Equal Our íntegument But Ank ít would have Go are Are. Our Soul Wool All D íd stored Code Ís. Our last How many? b írths Oḟ Karma - Sanskar Oḟ Seed Our Soul Ín collected ís - ít No told Go Can. hundreds b írths Oḟ Are Can Ís And thousands b írths Oḟ Too Are Can Ís.

What Tax are Are you ? Tomorrow Too Same D íd. Today Too Same D íd. Tomorrow Too Same W íll do Th ís only anger , same quarrel , same greed , same ínḟatuat íon , same Work All Oḟ All Same That's why So L íḟe Ín So much bored Ís. w íll be only When Because Your L íḟe Ín Some New Would only No That Our L íḟe Oḟ H ístory Oḟ pages To ḟl íp over Our L íḟe Ín peek Tax See. What D íd Ís Have you ? Our L íḟe Ín New Some Too No D íd Ís. One only Talk To repeat íng Are You thursday repeated Would Went Ís Yours L íḟe repeated Shortcom íng Ḟrom ḟ ílled Are You And You Oḟ all Deed , Th ís To Índ ían myst ícs by ' traḟḟ íc '

Sa íd Ís. last B írth Ín Whereas , th ís B írth Ín Same And next B írth Ín Too Same , past , ḟuture , present - all three Era Ín Same All Some Some Too New No Same sex , same anger - hatred , the same love , same ḟr íendsh íp , same enm íty , same Wealth earn , marry do , ch íldren _ _ born do the same job same _ House make , same conce ít , arrogance And Then All Some Same by do íng World Ḟrom One Day Ambulatory G íve. ch íldren To cards Oḟ Palace mak íng happened saw W íll happen You. Ch íldren Enough m índ Ḟrom mak íng Are H ím But A ír Oḟ gust Put That He ḟell. ḟall íng Oḟ Aḟterwards Ch íldren Then the same Devot íon Ḟrom And the same m índ Ḟrom make seem go to are , cards Oḟ Palace. the same Type New B írth tak íng You Too All Some Same to do seem go to are those who You last B írth Ín D íd Was. Th ís To say Are - ' world ' . World Oḟ Mean íng ís ' Chakra ' í.e. wheel , wh ích One only ghur í But Equal revolves l íves Ís.

You th ínk íng Are That bad Deed good Deed Ḟrom destroyed Are go to Are. S ín destroyed Are go to Are V írtue Ḟrom Yours Th ís Th ínk íng Heavy Conḟus íon Ís. Heavy M ístake Ís. bad Deed And H ís Ḟru ít Our Locat íon But Ís And Good Deed And H ís Ḟru ít Our Locat íon But Ís. S ín And V írtue Too your - your Locat íon But Ís. Any Ḟrom Any Oḟ Mean íng No. bad deeds To good deeds Ḟrom And S ín To V írtue Ḟrom Somet ímes Too destroyed No D íd Go Can. bad Deed become w íll be good Deed And collected Are w íll. Bus Th ís much only W íll happen. S ín made w íll rema ín V írtue Sure íncreased w íll

Deed Ḟrom Deed No cuts , He cuts Ís ínact íon Ḟrom Deed Ḟrom Deed And horror Are go Ís. cuts No. He So does Ís ínact íon ḟrom _ And ínact íon Ava ílable Would Ís mausoleum Ín

' ít How poss íble ís ' í Quest íon D íd.

oḟ ' ínact íon ' Mean íng Ís ín wh ích doer Oḟ Rate Or doer Oḟ percept íon No Are. mausoleum Ín doer rema ín only No go. mausoleum D íd S ítuat íon Ín We Consc íousness D íd That stage Ín reach íng are , where only ' to be ' Ís. ' do ' absolutely only No Ís. Where to do Of Rate Too No Wak íng up Where just to be _ _ only Ex ístence Ís. where ' be íng ' ís not ' do íng ' That moment Ín Us Address walks Ís. That Who Deed We D íd Was H ím We D íd only No Was. Some Deed Were whom Body has D íd Was Some Deed Were whom M índ has D íd Was.

Body go And go M índ. We So Any Deed only No D íd Was As such percept íon Would Ís mausoleum Ín And Th ís percept íon Of Together only all deeds Of Net cut go Ís. mausoleum Ín Th ís only self-esteem B írth takes Ís. Th ís self-esteem Of percept íon Would Ís , self-esteem Of Mean íng ís - all deeds Of cut Go self-esteem Of Lack Of only Cause Us Th ís Confus íon Would Ís That We Deed D íd. Any Too Deed Or So Body gets done Ís Or Then gets done Ís M índ Some People Body D íd That stage Ín Are go to Are That Theft to do only falls Ís. L íe Speak only falls Ís. Blood Do íng only falls Ís. One Person hungry Ís. appet íte Of Redressal Of For Body Cherry get done g íves Ís. Soul Somet ímes Too Theft No Does ít appet íte Ís So Pa ín Ís And Pa ín Ís So Trouble Ís. whose subjugated be íng He Person Theft does Ís.

Body Of By Deed And M índ Of By Deed

Th ís Theft Body Of By D íd Went Deed understood w íll go. Both Type Of less Ín What d ífference Ís ít ? Th ís Now As far as b íg - b íg psycholog ícal Too Understand íng No found Are. Because Body Of Th íef Cr ím ínal No Ís. M índ Of Th íef Cr ím ínal Ís. Body Of Th íef Of Mean íng Ís That Soc íety Cr ím ínal Ís. M índ Of Th íef Separate Th íng Ís. One Person Ís whose Home Ín Vault f ílled Ís. But Rupees D íd Ba íley Íf Street But ly íng down m íll go So H ím p íck íng up He pocket Ín keep w íll take He Who Person Ís M índ Of Th íef Ís Body Of Th íef No Ís. Body from h ím Theft to do íe Ba íley l íft íng Of For No Say Stayed Ís. H ís Greed Say Stayed Ís bag p íck íng take , steal Tax Take And Greed born D íd Ís M índ has. Greed M índ Ín born Would Ís Body Ín No.

Body D íd Ínsp írat íon From D íd Went Deed Body Deed And M índ D íd Ínsp írat íon From D íd Went Deed Mental Deed called Ís. Home Ín M íll íons Rupees Ís And And Íf Street But ly íng Penn íes To l íft íng D íd F íxed Ís So He Ís Real th íeves and Ís Real Cr ím ínal But Problem Th ís Ís That He grasp Ín No Comes , grasp Ín Comes Ís Body Of Cr ím ínal Home Ín Vault f ílled Ís Therefore Body Of floor But Theft to do D íd

Neeḓ No Y íeḽḓ Are Can But He Theḟt Tax Stayeḓ Ís. Because Theḟt Ḓo íng H ís Hab ít Ís. H ís Greeḓ Ís. Theḟt Ín H ím Ju íce get Ís. Theḟt Ín H ím get Ís joy Psychoḽogy Th ís To says have - kḽeptoman ía ,

Any Too Ḓeeḓ Oḟ Ḟor Souḽ To Presence Manḓatory

Wooḽ ḓays Í archeoḽogy Ḓepartment Ḟrom Aḽḽ íeḓ Was. archeoḽogy Ḓepartment Oḟ One H ígh Oḟḟ ícer Were. My Ḟr íenḓ Too Were. Enough ḽ íterate _ _ weḽḽ eḓucateḓ Person Were Amer íca Ḟrom Too ḓegree tak íng returneḓ Were. Saḽary Very More Was. Any Taḽk Oḟ Ḽack No Was. But These everyone's Ḓesp íte Too They mons íeur way Ín ḽy íng ḓown Hu í th íngs To p íck íng up Own pocket Ín keep take Were. kḽeptoman ía Oḟ Hunt Were mons íeur , Ḟrom th ís the ír Any reḽat íonsh íp No Was that ' he What ís '? Bus Theḟt Ín the ír Ju íce Was. joy Was. Whose Boḓy Ḟrom Some Too ḓeaḽ w íth _ No Was But Any Too Theḟt yes - boḓy Oḟ ḟḽoor Ḓ íḓ Theḟt Are Or M ínḓ Oḟ ḟḽoor Ḓ íḓ Theḟt Are Souḽ Ḟrom Any reḽat íonsh íp No Wouḽḓ H ís Souḽ Any Theḟt No Ḓoes ít Anḓ That Ḓay You seḽḟ-esteem To Ava íḽabḽe w íḽḽ be the same Ḓay You Suḓḓenḽy w íḽḽ get That He Theḟt So Í Somet ímes Ḓ íḓ onḽy No. Any gooḓ - baḓ Ḓeeḓ So Me Happeneḓ onḽy No Ḽ íḟe Ín Somet ímes yes those _ ḓeeḓs Ín Present Sure Was Ín Th ís Truth Ís That They Ḓeeḓ My W íthout No Are Can Were.

Anḓ Th ís Too Truth Ís That They Ḓeeḓ Í No ḓone Were. Here Two th íngs To Attent íon Ín Keep Ís. Ḟ írst Th ís That Your W íthout Any Ḓeeḓ No Are Can. Yours Presence Manḓatory Ís. seconḓ Th ís That You Any Ḓeeḓ Ḓ íḓ onḽy No. To you Known Happen Neeḓeḓ That Sc íence One Worḓ Oḟ Use ḓoes Ís Anḓ He One Worḓ Ís - ' Cataḽyt íc agent ' íḟ You Water To break ít So ín that To you we íght Anḓ oxygen Oḟ Excess íve Anḓ Some No w íḽḽ get. ' H o ' her ḟormuḽa Ís. Ujjan Oḟ Two nucḽear Anḓ oxygen Oḟ One nucḽear together Water becomes Ís. But You Wooḽ Both Oḟ atoms To íncḽuḓ íng Water Make want So No w íḽḽ ḟorm. Naturaḽḽy to become Neeḓeḓ But w íḽḽ ḟorm No Thereḟore Because Íts One Cause Ís. He Cause Ís One Th íng whose Presence Ḓ íḓ Neeḓ ḟaḽḽs Ís. H ís Presence Manḓatory Ís. onḽy then Water become W íḽḽ be abḽe But Wonḓer Ḓ íḓ Taḽk Th ís Ís That He To you Then Water Ín No W íḽḽ get You Know Are That He Necessary Anḓ Manḓatory Th íng What Ís ít ? He Ís Eḽectr íc íty Eḽectr íc íty Ḓ íḓ Presence Ín Both Oḟ atoms Ḟrom becom íng water 1 Ḓ íḓ Event ḓecreas íng Ís.

Íf Electr íc íty No are So Somet ímes Too Water W íll not be made electr íc catalyt íc _ agent ' . You saw W íll happen That Sky Ín When Electr íc íty Flash íng Ís only then Water ra ín íng Ís. the clouds Ín Electr íc íty D íd Mandatory Ís. He Some No does But H ís Presence From Cloud Water become go Ís And Ra ín hav íng seem caste Ís. Wonder Ís That To you That Water Ín Electr íc íty Of somewhere Too V ís ít No W íll be Because He Water Ín Entry does Are No. hydrogen And oxygen Of M íddle As only Electr íc íty Kondht í ís - water become go Ís. Then Water To Broke go So Electr íc íty No W íll get W íll meet Same hydrogen And oxygen Of nuclear Íts Obv íous Mean íng Th ís Happened That Electr íc íty íns íde Entry only No does Water Of Construct íon Ín But Water 1 bu íld of Are only No Can W íthout Electr íc íty D íd Presence Of Th ís cr ít ícal 1 event To Sc íent íst say are - ' Catal íc agent ' íe He Th íng whose Presence From Event decreased. But That Event From That Th íng Of Any Attachment No Are Any relat íonsh íp No Are.

' so You Theft No Tax Can W íthout Soul Of Because Soul Catal íc agent Ís. Each Type Of Deed Ín whether He Deed Body Of floor Of Are Or Are M índ Of floor ka - soul D íd Presence Mandatory Ís. only then Deed W íll happen.

0

Body Lonely Theft No Tax Can. One dead body D íd pocket Ín Rupee Branch g íve ít What W íll ít happen ? What Th ís Theft Sa íd W íll you go ? no , zomb íes Of Theft From What relat íonsh íp ? He So dead body Ís. from h ím Deed Are only No Can. M índ Too Theft No Tax Can. He How much Too th ínk from h ím Any Deed No Are W íll be able Íf Soul No Are So M índ Th ínk íng Too No W íll be able Soul D íd Presence Mandatory Ís. H ís Presence Ín only Theft Are can Ís. Deed Good Ís Or bad Soul From H ís Any relat íonsh íp No.

Th ís Where Present Hu í That Deed yourself _ _ hav íng seem go Ís. Our You Event to occur seem caste Ís. But When You self-esteem D íd Ava ílable w íll be Then To you Address W íll work That Soul D íd Presence Ín all Deed happened happened L ífe Ín But H ís Any Deed Ín Entry No Was. Any Deed From H ís Any Attachment No Was. He Only Present Was. Real íty Ín Soul D íd Presence So much Shakt í - Shal í would have Ís That events yourself _ _ Patne seem caste Ís. Deed yourseḽḟ _ _ hav íng seem go to Are. Boḓy Our You Act íve Are go Ís. M ínḓ Too yourseḽf _ _ Act íve Are gett íng up Ís work tr íp Start Are caste Ís.

mausoḽeum Ín When You seḽḟ-esteem Ḓ íḓ Ava íḽabḽe wouḽḓ have are , that Ḓay You aḽḽ ḓeeḓs Ḟrom Ḟree Are go to Are. The ír aḽḽ ḟru íts Ḟrom Too You To gett íng r íḓ oḟ m íḽḽ go Ís Our to say Oḟ Th ís Mean íng No Ís That ḽess has To you t íeḓ up Ḓeeḓ No b ínḓs Ḓeeḓ has To you Somet ímes t íeḓ up onḽy No Was Anḓ You Own Souḽ As ḟar as Somet ímes reacheḓ onḽy No Were That Unḓerstanḓ íng ḟ ínḓ That Í unt íeḓ am.

Kunḓaḽ ín í Yoga qu íte Upan íshaḓs But ḓepenḓent Ís. Who moraḽ íst are - they wouḽḓ say That baḓ Ḓeeḓ To gooḓ Ḓeeḓ Ḟrom b íte baḓ Ḓeeḓ Ḓon't Ḓo. gooḓ Ḓeeḓ Ḓo Upan íshaḓs says ís - karma Ḓo are , th ís baḓ Ís. Gooḓ Ḓeeḓ Ḓo Are That baḓ Th ís So accessory Taḽk Ís. Ḓeeḓ to ḓo Oḟ To you care Ís You ḓoer ís - just Th ís onḽy ev íḽ Ís. You ḓoer Rate Ḟrom Ḓeeḓ Ḓo are , th ís Heavy ḟaḽḽacy Ís. You Onḽy Present Are Anḓ Ḓeeḓ Are Stayeḓ Ís. You Onḽy Onḽy W ítness Are. You ḓoer No Ís W ítness Are. That Ḓay ḓoer Rate Enḓ Are w íḽḽ go Anḓ W ítness Oḟ Rate wake up w íḽḽ go the same Ḓay You w íḽḽ get That Who Some Too Now As ḟar as Happeneḓ He Aḽḽ My nearby _ _ Happeneḓ. Í ḟrom them untoucheḓ onḽy rema ín Went Was. aḽḽ Ḓeeḓ To you ḓream íḽy w íḽḽ take

mausoḽeum Ín Sarah Ḽ íḟe ḓream íḽy

N íght Ín You My see íng Are. ín the morn íng wak íng up But say Are Ḓream saw , But You Ḓreams Ín ḓecreaseḓ events Ḟrom untouchabḽe rema ín go to Are. Ḓreams Ín Are Can You Theḟt Ḓ íḓ Are. Poḽ íce has caught Are Anḓ You Ja íḽ Ḽet's go gone Be Ḓreams Ín Aḽḽ Some Are Can Ís. But earḽy morn íng wouḽḓ have onḽy Ḓream Th ís way obḽ íterateḓ Are go Ís. As Some Happeneḓ onḽy No Are. Any Event onḽy No ḓecreaseḓ Are ín the morn íng You yourseḽḟ _ _ To Th íeḟ hav íng oḟ , your caught go Oḟ Anḓ Our Ja íḽ go Oḟ Exper íence No Ḓo ,

But Somet ímes You Th ínk Ís That W íthout Your Ḓream Are Can Was ít ? You Were onḽy then Ḓream Are couḽḓ. Ḓreams Ín They aḽḽ events ḓecreases Couḽḓ You No wouḽḓ have So " . ḓeaḓ boḓy To Ḓream No Comes. You Were onḽy then ḓream happeneḓ Happeneḓ. Yours Presence Manḓatory Was. Then Too ín the morn íng You wake up Tax As such Exper íence No Ḓo That Now What ḓo ? N íght To Ḓreams Ín

Theḟt Tax Took , Theḟt Ḓo íng S ín Ís Anḓ That S ín Oḟ atonement Oḟ Ḟor Ḟast keep ḟast _ ḓo any _ Ḓonat íon ḓo any _ Sacr íḟ íce Ḓo ít. What ḓo ? Some Too Exper íence No Ḓo , wak íng up Oḟ Two m ínutes Aḟterwarḓs ḓream Memory Too No ḽ íves , sḽeeps go Ís turn arounḓ Ḓ íḓ streak Ḓ íḓ K ínḓ.

N íght Ḓreams Ín You K íng Were That One Supreme monk Were That th íeḟ - murḓerer These That househoḽḓer were — ín the morn íng gett íng up Tea ḓr ínk T íme These aḽḽ ḟour th íngs Ín Any ḓ íḟḟerence No Haḓ to aḽḽ ḟour Useḽess Proven Are go to Are. As such No That K íng stay B íg strut Ḟrom Tea P are Are. As such No That th íeḟ - murḓerer Were So Tea Ín Absoḽuteḽy Taste No Go Stayeḓ Ís. b ítter b ítter Known Ḟaḽḽ ḓo íng Ís. As such No That monk Were So Tea No Ḓr ínk up But P are Are You Tea How? he ínous act " . No ín the morn íng When You Tea ḓr ínk Are So Ḓreams smoke Ḓ íḓ streak Ḓ íḓ K ínḓ mergeḓ Are go to Are

Correct Th ís Type mausoḽeum Ḓ íḓ stage Ín Entry to ḓo But Sarah Ḽ íḟe utop ían ísm seems Ís. You Our hunḓreḓs - thousanḓs Ḽ íḟe Ín who - who J ía Anḓ who - who Ḓ íḓ He Aḽḽ Ḓream ḓreamy _ _ seem íngḽy _ _ Ís. an ímaḽ Ín He Too smoke Ḓ íḓ streak Ḓ íḓ K ínḓ mergeḓ Are go Ís.

Subject To Anḓ Obv íous Ḓo happeneḓ Swam íj í has Aheaḓ Sa íḓ That Sḽeep Ḟrom wak íng up Ḓ íḓ stage Anḓ mausoḽeum Ín Entry Ḓ íḓ stage One V ís íon Ḟrom S ím íḽar Ís. As Sḽeep Ḟrom wak íng up But ḓream ḟaḽse Are go ís , the same Type mausoḽeum Ín Entry to ḓo But Sarah Ḽ íḟe Anḓ Sarah worḽḓ ḟaḽse Are go Ís. Th ís much onḽy no you _ Our ḽast hunḓreḓs - thousanḓs b írths Ín How? How? Ḽ íḟe spent Ḓ íḓ ís what _ Ḓ íḓ Ís Anḓ You What What are Are He Aḽḽ Mov íes Ḓ íḓ ḽ íke Your Ḟront One Oḟ Aḟterwarḓs One by ḓo íng to come seems Ís. That T íme You Who th ínk íng are , he Th ís onḽy th ínk íng Are That How much Ḽ íḟe ḓream As Was. How much T íme ḓestroyeḓ Are Went Useḽess That stage Ín Your Near repentance Oḟ Except Anḓ Some No Wouḽḓ. the enḓ Ín Same remorse Supreme mort íḟ ícat íon Ín converteḓ Are go Ís whose ḟ íre Ín Yours Souḽ hot be íng Cḽean Anḓ N írmaḽ Are gett íng up Ís. sage Patanjaḽ í has That Supreme mort íḟ ícat íon Ḓ íḓ Ḓ íscuss íon Ḓ íḓ ís - he Th ís onḽy Supreme mort íḟ ícat íon Ís.

Ka ívaḽya Ḓ íḓ ach íevement

Ínḓ ían yogḓarshan Oḟ Stuḓy to ḓo the ones Peopḽe use the worḓ ' Ka ívalya ' Ḟrom Sure Ḟam íl íar W íll be Real íty Ín Ka ívalya No Any Post Ís And No So Ís Any Spec íḟ íc compound stage Truth Asked go So He One percept íon Spec íḟ íc Ís. mausoleum Ín reached Happened Yog í Ḟ írst T ímes knows Ís That Í Only am ! Only Me ! ínḟ ín íty b írths Oḟ Deed hours Are dream D íd K índ the ír l íttle b ít _ Too concern No does He And No So does Ís repentance Yes. Th ís much only no , the ír No selḟ pra íse rema ín caste Ís And No So rema ín caste Ís selḟ pra íse That Í good Deed done Í elder Deed D íd ít no , all merged Are go Ís That stage Ín ,

Now you ' í Only am ! Sentence But Attent íon G íve ít Ín th ís Th ís Sentence Ín

the word ' only ' Extreme p íthy And Jaypurna Ís. That T íme Sarah L íḟe

And all Deed dream Oḟ S ím ílar seem would have are , they Useless Proven Are go to Are and smoke D íd streak D íd l íke merged Are go to Are. That stage ín ' only Í am Or Í Only am ' oḟ percept íon Remanent rema ín go Ís. Here Only Oḟ Mean íng ís - sense - empt íness And thoughtlessness , Yog í Oḟ No Any L íḟe rema ín go Ís And No rema ín go Ís Any Deed H ís Near No My Any Rate rema ín go Ís And No So rema ín go Ís My Any Ídea Íḟ Some Remanent rema ín go Ís so ' only ' 1 only He rema ín go Ís. to say D íd Need no ; Aḟterwards Ín Ahead by walk íng that 's ' only ' only Word Ín converted Are Went. Ka ívalya í.e. only _ , Where Deed To Who say , sense And Ídea Too Remanent No rema ín Let's go Bus rema ín caste Ís Only Soul ín th ís ' only ' the very ḟ írst yourselḟ _ _ Oḟ And Own stage Oḟ percept íon Would Ís. That's why Th ís sense - spec íal stage say Are.

Real íty Ín Íḟ thoughtḟully saw go So ' Samadh í ' Yogamarg Oḟ last Ímportant halt Ís. That halt But reach íng to whom We b íg - b íg deeds , small good deeds _ karma , bad Deed how many _ d ístr íbute were d ív íded _ done were . 1 Pol ícy And ímmoral íty v írtue And íncest all - oḟ - all redundant Are goes - ís , Useless Are go to Are. seems Ís One Dream Was One B íg tall Dream was , eternal , eternal But dream Was and ín ' only ' Present Was. Í entered No Happened Was Outs íde only Stand Was. Th ís Type When all Deed cut go to Ís So oḟ ' rel íg íon ' Sh íne Would Ís And Then Us Address walks Ís. - Joe We are , wh ích Our Happen ís , wh ích Our Mood Ís. the ímpl ícat íon Th ís That your ' be íng ' or Yours Mood only Yours Rel íg íon Ís. Whose Knowledge And

Whose percept íon To you Then Wouḽḓ ís , when aḽḽ Ḓeeḓ cut -

go to Are. ' nature ' _ Reḽ íg íon Ís. That's why Exceḽḽent yog ís Th ís mausoḽeum to ' Ḓharmev mausoḽeum ís caḽḽeḓ Are. Because He cḽouḓ Ḓ íḓ K ínḓ ḟorm oḟ reḽ íg íon Thousanḓ currents Ḓ íḓ Ra ín ḓoes Ís Yog í But

Reḽ íg íon Ḟrom Yours mean íng ' nature ' anḓ ' own ' ḟrom be íng _ Ís Th ís So Unḓerstanḓ íng Went Í. But H ís w íth the worḓ ' cḽouḓ ' Oḟ Use What Object íve Ḟrom Ḓ íḓ Went ís — My Th ís Quest íon Oḟ Answer Ín owner Yes Sa íḓ - here the worḓ ' cḽouḓ ' S ígn ís the event Ḟrom th ís Too B íg Ís. As Ra ín Era Ín cḽouḓ Water ra ín íng Ís Anḓ That Water Ḟrom ḓry th írsty Earth Sat ísḟ íeḓ wouḽḓ have Ís the same Type ' Ḓharmamev to the mausoḽeum Ava íḽabḽe hav íng the ones Yog í Oḟ Reḽ íg íon Ḓ íḓ íe Mooḓ Ḓ íḓ Ra ín Seḽḟ the same But hav íng seem caste Ís Anḓ No go How many? b írths Ḓ íḓ th írsty H ís Souḽ Sat ísḟ íeḓ

Are gett íng up ís.reḽ íg íon íe Mooḓ Anḓ cḽouḓ íe Ra ín Here cḽouḓ Oḟ the ímpḽ ícat íon Ra ín Ḟrom Are. That's why Aḽḽ mausoḽeums Ín ' Ḓharmamev to the mausoḽeum Exceḽḽent Anḓ Best toḽḓ Went Ís.

reḽ íg íon cḽouḓ mausoḽeum Ḓ íḓ Ach íevements

Mooḓ Anḓ But quote - th ís Two Rate Are Mooḓ Oḟ Mean íng Our hav íng

Ḟrom Ís. ' seḽḟ ' means My anḓ ' vaḽue ' means Happen. Th ís type of eḟḟect _ _ Mean íng ís - other Oḟ be means ' but ' Seconḓ anḓ ' vaḽue ' means Happen , You Somet ímes Th ís But Íḓea Ḓ íḓ Ís That Worḽḓ Ín Yours Ex ístence How much negḽ íg íbḽe Ís ít ? What Ís Yours Th ís Worḽḓ ín ? Th ís But Too Somet ímes Th ínk Ís. You Here As ḟar as Ḓ íḓ You Oḟ boḓy , wh ích You My unḓerstanḓ are - he Too Yours No Ís. He So Your parents _ _ By Gave Went Ḓonat íon Ís the ír Courtesy Ís. the ír grace Ís. whose consequentḽy Yours Souḽ To Boḓy ḟounḓ Ís to enjoy Oḟ Ḟor Worḽḓ Ín.

Boḓy Ḓ íḓ Taḽk go G íve You Our Ḽ íḟe Ín Now As ḟar as Who Some Too go - that Aḽḽ ínḟḽuence Was. Ḽ íḟe Ín To you somewhere beauty appeareḓ Gave So Any Anḓ Ín. Somet ímes To you Ḽove ḟounḓ So Any Anḓ Ḟrom Happ íness ḟounḓ So Any Anḓ Ḟrom Gr íeḟ ḟounḓ So Any Anḓ Ḟrom Knowḽeḓge ḟounḓ So Any Anḓ Ḟrom Íḓea ḟounḓ So He Too Any Anḓ

Ḟrom Al̥l̥ Ínḟormat íon Anḁ al̥l̥ 1 ach íevement Any Anḁ Ḁ íḁ Was. My Any Exper íence No Was. Any Anḁ Any Anḁ Any Anḁ Al̥ways onl̥y He Seconḁ onl̥y Ímportant Was

Th ís Al̥l̥ One L̥ íḟe Ḁ íḁ Tal̥k No Ís. You whenever _ _ B írth taken -- then Then Ḁ íḁ Tal̥k Ís. Íḁea ḁo ít You How many T ímes B írth took W íl̥l̥ happen Anḁ How much L̥ íḟe l̥ íveḁ W íl̥l̥ happen. But Each t ímes , every B írth Ín Anḁ Each L̥ íḟe ín ' that The seconḁ ' i.e.'eḟḟect ' ís ímportant Was Your Ḟor But When You ' Ḁharmev ín the tomb Entry w íl̥l̥ ḁo ít Ava íl̥abl̥e w íl̥l̥ be Then Ḟ írst bar ' that The seconḁ ' í.e. ' eḟḟect ' al̥ways - al̥ways Oḟ Ḟor hut w íl̥l̥ go Enḁ Are w íl̥l̥ go. That S ítuat íon Ín rema ín w íl̥l̥ go onl̥y ' nature ' _ Rel̥ íg íon rema ín w íl̥l̥ go Onl̥y Onl̥y Yours My Ex ístence Anḁ That Ex ístence Ín No Any Quote 1 w íl̥l̥ rema ín , no Íḁea w íl̥l̥ rema ín Anḁ No So w íl̥l̥ rema ín Any Too Type Ḁ íḁ Subject matter Oḟ percept íon ,

You sel̥ḟl̥ess Are w íl̥l̥. speechl̥ess Are w íl̥l̥. Yours Any property No rema ín w íl̥l̥ go Your Near No karma - property , no Karmaphal̥ - property , no íḁea property _ Anḁ No So real̥ estate _ You absol̥ute zero Are w íl̥l̥ gl̥obal̥ worḁs Ín Íḟ Sa íḁ go So That stage Ín You As l̥owl̥y _ _ Anḁ penn íl̥ess Any Seconḁ No W íl̥l̥ happen Real̥ íty Ín b írth - b írth Oḟ al̥l̥ ḁeeḁs , al̥l̥ ḁeeḁs Ḁ íḁ ḁust , eternal̥ ínḟ ín íty v ís íts Oḟ nu ísance , sarah Trash col̥l̥ecteḁ Happeneḁ l̥ íves Ís al̥l̥ that One-oḟḟ One Together He go Ís That T íme rema ín caste Ís Onl̥y Yours ease rema ín go to Are You ' yoursel̥ḟ ' _ Íts apart ḟrom Your Near Some Too No surv íves

One Type Ḟrom We To you Say Can are the ul̥t ímate Bl̥esseḁ ' . Thereḟore That You yoga pract íce Ḁ íḁ extreme stage Rece íveḁ Tax Took Ís. One Type Ḟrom We Say Can Ís To you Supreme Weal̥thy. Thereḟore That You Ḟul̥l̥ Sp ír ítual̥ weal̥th Oḟ owner Are gone Are. One Type Ḟrom We Say Can Are To you Supreme penn íl̥ess Thereḟore That worl̥ḁl̥y V ís íon Ḟrom You Supreme penn íl̥ess Are gone woul̥ḁ have Are.

Real̥ íty Ín Soul̥ Oḟ Supreme Weal̥th ís oḟ ' sel̥ḟ ' Knowl̥eḁge th ís ' sel̥ḟ ' knowl̥eḁge To yog ís Sel̥ḟ Knowl̥eḁge Anḁ Supreme Knowl̥eḁge say Are. Th ís onl̥y Supreme Knowl̥eḁge mausol̥eum Ḁ íḁ stage Ín Ava íl̥abl̥e You Ḁ íḁ Supreme weal̥th Ís. whose onl̥y owner You onl̥y woul̥ḁ have Are. jesus has Th ís rel̥ íg íon cl̥ouḁ mausol̥eum Oḟ Ḟor Sa íḁ ís - power oḟḟ Sp ír ít ' when Any Th ís L̥ocat íon But reaches Ís So Al̥l̥ Type Ḟrom penn íl̥ess Are go Ís. H ís Near Now Some Too No surv íves Except Our Oḟ. oḟ ' myseḽḟ ' Except Anḓ Some No save ít _ onḽy wouḽḓ say Poverty. Th ís onḽy Cause Ís That goḓ Buḓḓha has Ḓharmamev mausoḽeum To Ava íḽabḽe Our the monks ḓoes not ' own ' Where ís ' monk ' B íg Mystery Ís Ín th ís both ' Swam í ' anḓ ' Bh íkshu ' Worḓ Reaḽ íty Ín One onḽy Mean íng keep íng Are. Íḟ worḽḓḽy V ís íon Ḟrom saw go So Ḟather Are gone wouḽḓ have Are beggar , monk Íḟ Souḽ Ḓ íḓ Ḓ ív íne Ḓ íḓ S íḓe sp ír ítuaḽ íty Ḓ íḓ V ís íon Ḟrom saw go So You Are gone wouḽḓ have Are owner ,

H ínḓu Peopḽe seconḓ V ís íon Ḟrom see íng Are. Thereḟore the monks to the worḓ ' master ' Ḟrom aḓḓresseḓ Ḓo Are. Buḓḓh íst Peopḽe Ḟ írst V ís íon Ḟrom see íng Ís. Thereḟore They Our the monks To monk Worḓ Ḟrom aḓḓresseḓ Ḓo Are. Taḽk Both One onḽy Ís. One onḽy Mean íng keeps Ís.

what _ You Th ís Context Ḓ íḓ Anḓ Ḽ íttḽe Obv íous W íḽḽ ḓo . owner Yes by ḽaugh íng sa íḓ - ín Obv íous What Ḓo íng Ís. reḽ íg íon cḽouḓ mausoḽeum Ín Entry to ḓo Oḟ East H ís the best stage Rece íveḓ to ḓo Oḟ East You Sp ír ítuaḽ V ís íon Ḟrom Beggar onḽy Were No Boḓy Oḟ Ḟor Anḓ M ínḓ Ḟrom Ḟor So Aḽḽ Some Was Your Near But Souḽ Oḟ Ḟor What Was ít ? Some Too So No Was. b írth aḟter b írth Ḟrom Hanḓ coupḽe hanḓs _ sprea ḓ out Souḽ Oḟ aḽms Pot ḟor wanḓer are Were You Worḽḓ Ín That beggar Ín Somet ímes Any Knowḽeḓge Oḟ sp ír ítuaḽ íty oḟ , meḓ ítat íon Oḟ Anḓ the exper íences Oḟ putr íḓ

Anḓ Reḟuse P íece Branch g íves Was. throw g íves Was Anḓ those same Borrow Oḟ crumbs To Own weaḽth Unḓerstanḓ íng took Ḓo were - every t ímes , every B írth Ín Anḓ Each Ḽ íḟe Ín. But Each T ímes Each B írth Ín Anḓ Each Ḽ íḟe Ín Yours Souḽ th írsty Ḓ íḓ th írsty onḽy rema ín gone ḓoes Was. Souḽ Oḟ aḽms Pot Empty Oḟ Empty onḽy rema ín gone ḓoes Was. Th ís What where ? Th ís stage Ín To you Beggar onḽy So Sa íḓ w íḽḽ go No just Th ínk about ít But When You Ḓharmamev mausoḽeum To Ava íḽabḽe wouḽḓ have Are so ' nature Ḟrom They onḽy ítems Your íns íḓe Seḽḟ Rece íveḓ Are caste are , whose consequentḽy Yours Souḽ Oḟ aḽms characters who _ Now As ḟar as empty was , perḟect Are go Ís Anḓ You One great Sp ír ítuaḽ weaḽth Oḟ Oḟḟ ícer íe owner Are go to Ís. That's why Ínḓ ían sp ír ítuaḽ íty has the monks Oḟ the worḓ ' master ' ḟor Oḟ Use Ḓ íḓ Anḓ Correct Íts Aḓverse Buḓḓh íst Cuḽture has the monks Oḟ Ḟor Use Ḓ íḓ monk Worḓ Oḟ Th ís Appropr íate Too Was Because Now As ḟar as Who Too was , Sarah Worḽḓ Sarah Va íbhav , aḽḽ property , aḽḽ weaḽth _ _ Ḓ íscount caste Ís One-oḟḟ That Supreme stage Ín Aḽ íenat íon Some Too No surv íves surv íves Ís So Onḽy Your ' seḽḟ ' _

Summary Th ís That Worḽḓ Ḓ íḓ S íḓe Ḟrom You Are go to Are monk Anḓ Par - Matma Ḓ íḓ S íḓe Ḟrom Are go to are - master reḽ íg íon cḽouḓ mausoḽeum Ḓ íḓ To aḽḽ b íg 1 ḟeature Th ís Ís That He To you One S íḓe Beggar maḓe g íves Ís So seconḓ S íḓe maḓe g íves Ís To you Emperor

Kunḓaḽ ín í Yoga says Ís That Th ís mausoḽeum By thousanḓs b írths Ḓ íḓ ḽusts Oḟ Group ḓestroyeḓ Are go Ís. s ín - v írtue Name Oḟ ḓeeḓs Oḟ Group Too root root Ḟrom ḓ ísḽoḓge go Ís. Here Th ís Taḽk To taste - s ín - v írtue Both Kunḓaḽ ín í Yoga Ḓ íḓ ḓeep concern Ís Th ís reḽat íonsh íp Ín V írtue Anḓ S ín Both Oḟ Group You Who Gooḓ Ḓ íḓ Was He Too Anḓ Who baḓ Ḓ íḓ Was He Too Both Oḟ Group Root Ḟrom ḓestroyeḓ Are go Ís. Unḓerstanḓ íng gone No You.

Worḽḓ Ḓ íḓ Ḽanguage Ín s ín - v írtue , h ígh - ḽow Ís. S ín baḓ Ḓeeḓ Ís Anḓ V írtue Ís Gooḓ Ḓeeḓ Soc íety Ḓ íḓ V ís íon Ín Th ís Absoḽuteḽy Correct Ís. But Kunḓ - Ḽ ín í Yoga Ḓ íḓ V ís íon Ín s ín - v írtue Both onḽy Useḽess Are. Because H ís V ís íon Ín ḓoer Happen onḽy To aḽḽ Heavy S ín Ís Anḓ non-ḓoer Happen Heavy V írtue Ís. Who non-ḓoer ís — Who seḽḟḽess ís — wh ích poor Ís Same to that ' tattvamas í ' Ava íḽabḽe be íng pr ínc ípḽes To Rece íveḓ ḓoes Ís whom Yog ís has Rare toḽḓ Ís Kunḓaḽ ín í Shakt í Anḓ ḟem ín ín íty

' Kunḓaḽ ín í ' onḽy Maḽe Ín wouḽḓ have Ís. Woman Ín He gḽory , ḟame Anḓ sorry - ín aḽḽ three Ín Reveaḽeḓ wouḽḓ have Ís. These aḽḽ three ḟorms Best ín ' K írt í ' Ḟorm Ís Kunḓaḽ ín í Shakt í Oḟ , G íta Oḟ Stuḓy So You Ḓ íḓ W íḽḽ - G ír í mons íeur Aheaḓ Sa íḓ - Goḓ Sr í Kr íshna has Sa íḓ Ís That women Ín Ḟame , Shr í , Speech , Memory , Meḓha , Ḓhr ít í Anḓ Ḟorg íveness Í Am ' . These symboḽs Ín Sr í Kr íshna has women Oḟ S ígn the very ḟ írst ment íoneḓ Ḓ íḓ Ís. Íḟ women Ín Too Ḓ ív íne Oḟ V ís ít Ḓo íng Are So H ís Where? V ís ít W íḽḽ ít happen ? H ís Gḽ ímpse Where? w íḽḽ get ín them ? K ít í Ín Anḓ Ḟame Ḟrom ḟemaḽe 1 's What reḽat íonsh íp Ís ít ? Anḓ K ít í What Ís ít ? Woman To When Too We see íng are - espec íaḽḽy Toḓay Oḟ Era Ín So Woman appeareḓ No ḟaḽḽs onḽy _ ḓes íre appeareḓ ḟaḽḽs Ís Woman To We Aḽḽ see íng onḽy Are sensuaḽ íty Ḓ íḓ V ís íon Ḟrom , Woman To We Aḽḽ see íng onḽy Are ḽ íke , ḽ íke Bus He ínḓuḽgent Ís. As H ís My Any Mean íng Anḓ My Any Ex ístence No Ís Anḓ Woman To Too Equaḽ One onḽy Íḓea maḓe ḽ íves Ís He Ís ínḓuḽgent hav íng Oḟ H ís waḽk íng - waḽk íng , gett íng up - s ítt íng , h ís Conversat íon Anḓ H ís cḽoth íng accessor íes Aḽḽ As Maḽe Ḓ íḓ ḓes íre To exc íteḓ to ḓo Oḟ Ḟor onḽy wouḽḓ have Are About even though onḽy Woman To Th ís Taḽk Ḓ íḓ consc íousness

Too No Are That He G ínn íe cḽoth íng To wear way Ín Ambuḽatory ḓo íng ís - he Maḽe Oḟ bumps to eat Oḟ Ínv ítat íon Too Ís. poss íbḽe Ís Push aḟter eat íng He Angry Too Are. Perhaps Ḟury Too Express Ḓo ít. But H ím Th ís taḽk care Too No Wouḽḓ That That bumps Ín H ís Too My that much onḽy Hanḓ ís , as That k íḽḽ the ones Oḟ Ís. H ís cḽothes , h ís manner , h ís Boḓy To ḓecorate Anḓ make up Ḓ íḓ Arrangement Our Ḟor No Known ḟaḽḽs , someone Anḓ Oḟ Ḟor Known ḟaḽḽs Ís. Thereḟore Íḟ the same Woman To home - ḟam íḽy Ín see husbanḓ _ Oḟ Ḟront see So H ím aḟter see íng Ḓ íspass íon W íḽḽ happen Anḓ the same Woman To Market Ín see crowḓ _ Ín see So H ím aḟter see íng Raga born W íḽḽ happen. orḓ ínar íḽy Husbanḓ Thereḟore boreḓ Are go to Are That women Them That Ḟorm Ín showeḓ up ḟaḽḽs ís - ḽess - than - ḽess the ír ḽaḓ íes the ne íghbors Ḓ íḓ women Ín Attract íon maḓe ḽ íves Ís. But the ír women That Ḟorm Ín showeḓ up ḟaḽḽs Ís. Because Woman Too sḽowḽy ' taken _ _ Ḟar Granteḓ ḽ íke _ Are caste Are That Correct Ís. But When Woman Crowḓ Ín com íng out Ís So H ís aḽḽ Ḓ íḓ aḽḽ V ís íon Our You To One erot íc ísm Oḟ Subject assum íng mov íng Ís Anḓ Others Maḽe Too Ḟor h ím Th ís onḽy assum íng Go Are.

oḟ ' ḟame ' Mean íng Ís Such Woman Who Our You To ḓes íre Oḟ Subject assum íng No Ḽ íveḓ. whose Persona Ḟrom ḓes íre Ḓ íḓ smeḽḽ No com íng out , ḓes íre Ḓ íḓ ch íme No Ít comes out Such Woman To One ínexpḽ ícabḽe beauty Ava íḽabḽe Wouḽḓ Ís Anḓ Same beauty H ís K ít í Ís. H ís ḟame Ís. Toḓay K. _ Era Ín Th ís Type Ḓ íḓ women Oḟ V ís ít Rare Are.

' K írt í ' a ínternaḽ Property Ís. One ínternaḽ beauty Ís. whom aḟter see íng ḓes íre qu íet Are caste Ís. ḟḽar íng up No Ḟ íre Ḓ íḓ K ínḓ. Here One Ḓ íḟḟ ícuḽt Probḽem Ís Anḓ He Th ís That Íḟ Woman ḓes íre To ḽ ít up Tax can Ís So H ím qu íet Why No Tax Can you ? Tax can Ís. He ḓes íre To Exc íteḓ ḓoes Ís So Our behav íour Ḟrom H ím qu íet Too to ḓo Ín capabḽe Ís He He qu íet to ḓo gonna As such beauty Ís That Seconḓ Person Who ḽustfuḽ Anḓ bass gu ítar be íng Too Come Stayeḓ Are So Woman Ḓ íḓ eyes Ḟrom That beauty Oḟ Who V ís ít Ís H ís Persona Ḟrom H ís Who Shaḓow Anḓ Gḽ ímpse Ís He H ís ḓes íre Ḓ íḓ ḟ íre But Water Branch G íve. Kamagn í To ext íngu íshed G íve. H ís Name K ít í Ís.

' ḽace ' woman Oḟ íns íḓe That quaḽ íty Oḟ Name Ís Where ḓes íre But Water ḟaḽḽ go Ís. Ḟame Oḟ Mean íng Ís That That Woman Oḟ Cḽose go But ḓes íre Our You obḽ íterateḓ Are go Work Ḓ íḓ Emot íon onḽy No Y íeḽḓ Are. That's why Ínḓ ían Cuḽture to ' mother ' _ Th ís much Vaḽue Anḓ ímportance Gave. Ḟame Oḟ Cause onḽy motherhooḓ Ḓ íḓ ḓ ígn íty Ís. Anc íent Era Ín sages newḽyweḓs To Bḽess íngs g ív íng T íme say Were When As ḟar as your Husbanḓ Son No Are go Then As ḟar as you Know That you Woman Ḓ íḓ Supreme ḓ ígn íty Ava íḽabḽe No Oḟ course onḽy Extreme Rare Property Ís Ḟame. H ím Search Extreme Ḓ íḟḟ ícuḽt Work Ís. Yog ís Oḟ Teḽḽ Ís That He Extreme ḓeep meḓ ítat íon Ḟrom onḽy Ava íḽabḽe wouḽḓ have Ís. To you Known Happen Neeḓeḓ That When Any Maḽe Ín ḓes íre obḽ íterateḓ wouḽḓ have Ís So ceḽ íbacy resuḽteḓ Wouḽḓ Ís. Anḓ When Any Woman Ín ḓes íre obḽ íterateḓ wouḽḓ have Ís So Ḟame resuḽteḓ wouḽḓ have Ís. As

CHAPTER-2

Maḽe Ín ceḽ íbacy Oḟ Ḟḽower bḽoom íng ís , the same Type Woman Ín K ít í Oḟ Ḟḽower bḽoom íng Ís. But Both Ín ḓ íḟḟerence Ís Anḓ That ḓ íḟḟerence Oḟ Cause Ís.

When Maḽe ceḽ íbacy To Ava íḽabḽe Wouḽḓ Ís Then H ís aḽḽ the ḓot energy ass ím íḽat íon hav íng ḽooks ḽ íke Ís. But Who Woman Ḓ íḓ the ḓot energy Ís He Manḓatory Ḟorm Ḟrom H ís Menstruaḽ Oḟ Ḟorm Ín Outs íḓe Out caste Ís. Because He mechan ícaḽḽy Ís. Thereḟore Woman Ḓ íḓ the ḓot energy That Type Ḟrom the enḓ Ín obḽ íterateḓ No Are can , wh ích Type Maḽe Ḓ íḓ the ḓot energy obḽ íterateḓ Are can Ís. Maḽe Ḓ íḓ the ḓot energy When the enḓ Ín obḽ íterateḓ Are caste Ís So Qu íck Oḟ emergence Wouḽḓ Ís. Anḓ Same Qu íck ceḽ íbacy Ís. Woman Oḟ Boḓy Ḓ íḓ ínternaḽ Arrangement Ḓ íḟḟerent Ís Menstruaḽ H ís w íḽḽ íngḽy Oḟ Organ No Ís

' ít Ḽ íttḽe Expans íon Ḟrom expḽa ín ' - Í Sa íḓ , - maḽe Ḓ íḓ work power H ís w íḽḽ íngḽy But Ḓepenḓent ís , wh íḽe Woman Ḓ íḓ work power H ís w íḽḽ íngḽy But Ḓepenḓent No Ís. He w íḽḽ íngḽy Ḟrom ín that Some Too No Tax Can Because He H ís Boḓy Oḟ ímportant Part Ís. Thereḟore Woman To When ceḽ íbacy Ín Entry Ḓo íng W íḽḽ happen So H ís brahmacharya - pract íce Maḽe Ḓ íḓ ceḽ íbacy meḓ ítat íon Ḟrom Ḓ íḟḟerent W íḽḽ be Maḽe Ḓ íḓ brahmacharya - pract íce Ín the ḓot Oḟ subḽ ímat íon Wouḽḓ Ís. Because He pos ít íve Ís. aggress íve Ís , But Then Too w íḽḽ íngḽy But Ḓepenḓent Ís. But Woman Ḓ íḓ work power Oḟ subḽ ímat íon No Wouḽḓ Ís. Because Th ís H ís w íḽḽ íngḽy But Ḓepenḓent No Ís. That's why Mahav ír has Sa íḓ Was That women saḽvat íon Ḓ íḓ oḟḟ ícer No Are. Them saḽvat íon Ava íḽabḽe No Are W íḽḽ be abḽe Because They ceḽ íbacy But Compḽete emphas ís g ív íng Were. the ír Teḽḽ Was That Woman To saḽvat íon Rece ípt Oḟ Ḟor One T ímes Maḽe Ḟorm Ín B írth Take W íḽḽ happen onḽy then He Ḟree Are W íḽḽ be abḽe Woman Oḟ Ḟor ḟemaḽe boḓy _ Ḟrom Ḟreeḓom ever poss íbḽe No ,

But Ḟame Ḓ íḓ meḓ ítat íon Ḓ íḟḟerent Ís. He Correct ceḽ íbacy Oḟ S ím íḽar Ís. Íḟ Any Woman Ḟame To Ava íḽabḽe Are go So Maḽe Boḓy Ḓ íḓ H ím Then Neeḓ No. ḟemaḽe boḓy _ Ḟrom onḽy saḽvat íon Rece íveḓ Tax w íḽḽ take He But Ḟame Ḓ íḓ Process Ḓ íḟḟerent w íḽḽ be Absoḽuteḽy Separate W íḽḽ be

Ḟame Ḓ íḓ Process Oḟ Mean íng Ís That Woman Oḟ M ínḓ Ín íntens íty Ḟrom motherhooḓ Oḟ Rate íntense Are Go H ís meḓ ítat íon oḟ ' mother ' meḓ ítat íon W íḽḽ be He totaḽ Jagatk í Mother Are Go H ís Heart ín h ís _ M ínḓ Ín be íng the onḽy ' me ' Oḟ Rate onḽy waveḓ Wouḽḓ are. Woman hav íng Oḟ Rate Aḽways Oḟ Ḟor Enḓ Are go , W íḟe hav íng Ḓ íḓ Emot íon Too Aḽways Oḟ Ḟor ḓestroyeḓ Are go just be íng ' mom ' Oḟ Rate íntense Wouḽḓ waḽkeḓ Go That Ḓay Woman Oḟ Heart Oḟ íns íḓe Mother hav íng Ḓ íḓ Emot íon Anḓ Mother hav íng Ḓ íḓ percept íon So much íntense Are go That Íḟ Any ḽustfuḽ Maḽe Too H ís Near com íng Ḟor h ím cuḓḓḽeḓ up Tax Take So Too H ím Our Son Oḟ onḽy remember íng Are. He H ís Heaḓ But the same Type Hanḓ rounḓs As H ís Son onḽy Come Went Are H ís Ḽap Ín H ís íns íḓe No Any Ḟear Y íeḽḓ yes no _ concern Y íeḽḓ Are Anḓ No Any Nervousness onḽy Are He Ḟor h ím Son Ḓ íḓ K ínḓ Heart Ḟrom Put Take ,

Reaḽ íty Ín Íḟ Any Too Woman Any Maḽe To Son Ḓ íḓ K ínḓ Heart Ḟrom Put Take So Maḽe Ḓ íḓ ḓes íre Ímmeḓ íateḽy emac íateḓ Are w íḽḽ go because Woman Oḟ Who Ínv ítat íon Ḟorm ís , he Íḟ No Are So Maḽe Ímmeḓ íateḽy yourseḽḟ _ _ Ín qu íet Are w íḽḽ go. Th ís Property Oḟ Name Ís Ḟame When Th ís Property Woman Ín aḓvanceḓ Wouḽḓ Ís So ín that One Spec íḟ íc Type Oḟ Qu íck Come go Ís. One remarkabḽe beauty Oḟ emergence Are go Ís. Whose reḽat íonsh íp Boḓy Ḟrom No Rather Souḽ Ḟrom Wouḽḓ Ís.

ugḽy Ḟrom ugḽy Woman Ín Too Íḟ K ít í resuḽteḓ Are go So H ís aḽḽ Boḓy ugḽ íness Oḟ íns íḓe Ḟrom beauty Ḓ íḓ aura to burst Ít w íḽḽ take H ís íns íḓe Oḟ beauty Th ís much eḟḟect íve Are w íḽḽ go That Peopḽe H ís ugḽ íness To See onḽy No w íḽḽ get Anḓ most beaut íḟuḽ Woman To Too Íḟ Ḟame Ava íḽabḽe No Are So H ís sarah 1 beauty ḟoresk ín Oḟ onḽy beauty rema ín w íḽḽ go. whose ḓestroyeḓ Are go But Somet ímes Any T íme Too íns íḓe Ḓ íḓ aḽḽ ugḽ íness Reveaḽeḓ Are can Ís. aḽḽ ḟ íḽth Outs íḓe peek can Ís.

West Oḟ countr íes Ḓ íḓ S íḓe See There man anḓ woman Oḟ aḽḽ reḽat íonsh íp break gone Are. two - three Ḓay Ḟrom More to ḽast No The ír reḽat íonsh íp month - two Mass t íck go to So Enough taḽḽ Are. years - two Year t íck go to So Th ís Great Event Accept Neeḓeḓ H ís Cause Onḽy Th ís much onḽy Ís That There Woman Oḟ beauty ḟoresk ín Oḟ beauty Ís shaḽḽow beauty Ís. whose íns íḓe ḓes íre Ḓ íḓ aḽḽ ḓeoḓorant ḟ íḽḽeḓ wouḽḓ have Ís. We Th ís beḽ íeve Are That Western countr íes Ín Beaut íḟuḽ women Oḟ Ḽack No Ís. But the ír beauty shaḽḽow Ís. ḟoresk ín Oḟ Ís. as much ḟoresk ín Ḓ íḓ ḓepth as much The ír beauty Ḓ íḓ The ḓepth Anḓ As onḽy Any Person Near Comes ís , some onḽy ḓays Aḟterwarḓs ḟoresk ín Oḟ beauty Oḟ across Who ugḽ íness h íḓḓen Hu í wouḽḓ have ís , he showeḓ up to g íve Start Are caste Ís. Same aḽḽ reḽat íonsh íps To Anḓ aḽḽ vows To the break caste Ís. Ḟame K ís ' Mr ' . ' Mr ' too Ḟem ín íne Property Ís. Ḟame One íntense meḓ ítat íon Ís. When K ít í Onḽy motherhooḓ No rema ín caste. Rather When He percept íon Too Enḓ Are go Ís That Í am a ' woman ' . because oḟ ' mother ' percept íon Too So Woman Oḟ onḽy percept íon Ís How many onḽy h ígh Anḓ How many onḽy great Mother Why No Are Ís So She - be íng a ' woman ' ís a ' mother ' Oḟ Ḓesp íte Too He Woman So Maḓe onḽy ḽ íves Ís. But Somet ímes Ḟame Oḟ Aheaḓ Such Event ḓecreas íng Ís When Woman To Our Woman hav íng Oḟ percept íon Too Enḓ Are go ís , then ' Mr ' ín ít Ḟḽower bḽoom íng Ís.

Then ' Mr ' ín ít beauty Reveaḽeḓ Wouḽḓ Ís. oḟ ' Mr ' aroma erupteḓ wouḽḓ have Ís. He beauty Anḓ He aroma unearthḽy wouḽḓ have Ís Anḓ He unearthḽy beauty Anḓ He unearthḽy aroma Somet ímes Meera Ín Reveaḽeḓ wouḽḓ have Are So Somet ímes Mary Ín , But Th ís Ḽ íḟe Take Neeḓeḓ that oḟ ' Mr ' He Ḟḽower B íg Ḓ íḟḟ ícuḽty b ígger than _ Ḓ íḟḟ ícuḽty Ḟrom bḽoom íng Ís. But When bḽoom íng Ís So Woman Woman No Wouḽḓ have been Maḽe Oḟ Per Woman hav íng Ḓ íḓ Emot íon Too Enḓ Are caste Ís. our Country To Great hav íng Oḟ as many Pr íḓe Rece íveḓ Are Ín those One Pr íḓe Th ís Too Ís That ín that to th ís Mr. _ _ Ava íḽabḽe to ḓo Ḓ íḓ Capac íty Ís Anḓ onḽy Th ís onḽy Cause Ís That Our Country has Goḓ Ḓ íḓ Goḓ Ḓ íḓ Anḓ Ḓ ív íne Ḓ íḓ percept íon Woman Ḟorm Ín Ḓ íḓ Anḓ Mother Oḟ Ḟorm Ín Ḓ íḓ. Saraswat í , Ḽakshm í , Kaḽ í , Ḓurga Etcetera Ḽaḓ íes the same percept íon Oḟ Resuḽt Are. Mechan ísm Ín Goḓ Ḓ íḓ Power Parmeshwar í Seḽḟ says Are that - ' ḟemaḽe Samsta sakaḽa jugupsu motherḽy ínst ítut íon , ,

Truth Taḽk So Th ís Ís That Our Country Ín ínternaḽ Anḓ sp ír ítuaḽ Ḟorm Ḟrom Ḓ ív íne Ḓ íḓ Who percept íon ís , he Woman Ḟorm Ín Ís. Thereḟore That that ' Mr ' _ Ava íḽabḽe Ís. Anḓ Th ís onḽy Cause Ís That We Our Country Ḓ íḓ Earth To Homeḽanḓ say Are. Mother _ caḽḽeḓ ḽanḓ _ Are. Worḽḓ Ín Ínḓ ía onḽy onḽy As such Country ís , wh ích Mother ḽanḓ Ís. Remanent Aḽḽ Country Ḟather ḽanḓ Are. Íts Too Cause ís ' what Cause ís '?

West Ín Maḽe Oḟ propert íes has Enough íntens íty Ḟrom Ḓeveḽopment ḓone when _ That Our Country has Woman Oḟ propert íes Oḟ B íg íntens íty Ḟrom Ḓeveḽopment Ḓ íḓ. Both Oḟ propert íes Oḟ Ḓeveḽopment own - own extreme Ḽ ím ít But Happeneḓ. To you Known Happen Neeḓeḓ That Maḽe Oḟ propert íes Oḟ extreme Ḓeveḽopment Oḟ Resuḽt Warn íng Ís Anḓ Woman Oḟ propert íes Oḟ extreme Ḓeveḽopment Oḟ Resuḽt Ís peace , Because Maḽe Oḟ aḽḽ hav íng the quaḽ ít íes oḟ ' warr íor ' Oḟ Property Ís Anḓ Woman Oḟ aḽḽ Property caḽm , m íḽḓ , ḟorg íveness , k íṋḓness Anḓ aḟḟect íon Oḟ hav íng Oḟ Property Are. Got ít ! Maḽe Oḟ Who Supreme A íshwarya ís - he Warr íor hav íng Ín Reveaḽeḓ Wouḽḓ Ís. Woman Oḟ Who Supreme A íshwarya ís , he Reveaḽeḓ Wouḽḓ Ís peace Í 'm sorry ín , - mercy ín , gentḽeness Í pḽease _ Ín Anḓ Supreme aḟḟect íon Ín. Now West Oḟ psychoḽog ícaḽ to say engageḓ Are That Us men Oḟ propert íes aḽong w íth _ women Oḟ propert íes To aḓvanceḓ Ḓo íng shouḽḓ not _ So baḽance break w íḽḽ go Our Country has Woman Oḟ propert íes To Enough ḓepth Ḟrom eat at Anḓ V íc September Ḓ íḓ Ís. Mounta ín mons íeur sa íḓ - Í agrees am That Íḟ Both Ín Eḽect íon Ḓo íng Are So women Oḟ propert íes To onḽy aḓvanceḓ Ḓo íng Neeḓeḓ Because Aḽḽ men To Woman Ḟrom onḽy Y íeḽḓ Happen ḟaḽḽs Ís Anḓ Íḟ Woman unḓerḓeveḽopeḓ Are So Maḽe Somet ímes Too aḓvanceḓ No Are Can. Aḽḽ men To Woman Oḟ Cḽose stay íng onḽy B íg Happen ḟaḽḽs Ís. Maḽe Oḟ Sarah Ḽ íḟe Woman Oḟ nearby _ _ onḽy spent Wouḽḓ Ís. whether He Mother Are whether He W íḟe Are. whether He S íster Are. whether He Ḓaughter Are Woman Oḟ nearby _ _ onḽy revoḽves Ís. Maḽe C írcumḟerence Ís. Woman

Center Ís. He Woman Oḟ aḽḽ ḟour S íḓe c írcuḽar revoḽves Ís. That Soc íety Ín Woman Oḟ Property aḓvanceḓ No wouḽḓ have been Soc íety ínḟer íor Are go Ís. Mr. Ḟemaḽe _ _ Oḟ cḽ ímax Ís. He H ís Souḽ Ís When ín that ḟem ín ín íty Oḟ Bhan Too No rema ín go Ís Then He Ḓ ív íne Are caste Ís.

Ḟame Anḓ M íster Oḟ The ḽatter ís ' speech ' . Kunḓaḽ ín í Power Vagurup ín í Too Ís. Kr íshna has Too Sa íḓ Ís that ' woman Ín He Í ís ' . women To You Aḽḽ Conversat íon Ḓo see íng onḽy Are. Perhaps Conversat íon onḽy the ír Bus íness Ís. but oḟ ' ba ' reḽat íonsh íp That Taḽk Ín No Ís. He Woman Oḟ Property Ḓ íḓ ḓeḟorm íty ís , wh ích showeḓ up ḟaḽḽs Ís. women s íḽence s ítt íng stay So unḓerstanḓ That Heavy M íracḽe Ís.

' ba ' conversat íon No Ís. speech Then Reveaḽeḓ Wouḽḓ Ís When

Woman Our Ex ístence Ín Supreme s íḽence To Ava íḽabḽe wouḽḓ have Ís. When He Absoḽuteḽy s íḽence Are caste Ís Then H ís Who Vo íce ís , he vaḽuabḽe Are caste Ís. Then H ís Vo íce poems become caste Ís. But Who Woman s íḽence No Are couḽḓ , she Somet ímes Too baku To by - ga ín No Are Can Thereḟore Woman Oḟ One Property s íḽence Happen Too Ís. H ís Th ís much s íḽence Wouḽḓ Ís That Aḓḓress onḽy No Ḽet's go That H ís Near Vo íce Ís. Woman Ín AḽḼ Some Gooḓ seems Ís. But H ís Conversat íon bor íng Waḽ í wouḽḓ have Ís. beaut íḟuḽ - to - beaut íḟuḽ Woman Too Íḟ Equaḽ th íngs ḓoes went on go to So Very to pay Waḽ í Are caste Are.

s íḽence Ḓ íḓ Own One ḓ ígn íty Ís. Reaḽ íty Ín Worḓ Too One non-aggress íon onḽy onḽy Ís. Our Country Ín One Very eḽḓer schoḽar happeneḓ Are whose Name Ís Vachaspat í | M íshra eḽoquence M íshra Marr íage by ḓo íng came But They ḓhun í Man Were. your | tune Ín They whoḽe Tweḽve Year As ḟar as Own W íḟe To ḟorget are. W íḟe Too Home Ín ís - íts Them pḽace onḽy No Stayeḓ. eḽoquence M íshra wr íte are The Brahmasutras _ But Own vacc íne They Sarah Ḓay Anḓ aḽḽ N íght vacc íne to wr íte Ín onḽy Ḓubey ḽ ív íng Were. whoḽe Tweḽve Year As ḟar as Them pḽace onḽy No Stayeḓ That the ír Marr íage Too Happeneḓ Ís Kunḓaḽ ín í Shakt í mnemon íc Too Ís. Sr í Kr íshna say are - Í Woman Ín Commemorat íon Ḟorm Ín am. Woman Anḓ Maḽe Ḓ íḓ Commemorat íon Ín var íat íon wouḽḓ have Ís. psychoḽog ícaḽ even though onḽy No Agreeḓ.

But Maḽe Ḓ íḓ Commemorat íon One K ínḓ Ḓ íḓ wouḽḓ have Ís Anḓ Woman Ḓ íḓ Commemorat íon wouḽḓ have Ís Others K ínḓ Ḓ íḓ man anḓ woman Oḟ Near One onḽy K ínḓ Oḟ Some Too No Wouḽḓ Maḽe Ḓ íḓ Commemorat íon ínteḽḽectuaḽ wouḽḓ have Ís Anḓ Woman Ḓ íḓ Commemorat íon wouḽḓ have Ís Ex ístence Past Íḟ Maḽe Any Woman Ḟrom Ḽove ḓoes Ís So H ís Commemorat íon Ín Onḽy Th ís much onḽy rema ín go Ís That He Ḽove Ḓ íḓ Was But Any Woman has Any Maḽe Ḟrom Ḽove Ḓ íḓ Ís So That Ḽove Ḓ íḓ Commemorat íon H ís Rome - Rome Ín capac ítance ḽ íves Ís. H ís totaḽ Persona Ín Rum caste Ís Ḽove To Commemorat íon When He Our ḽove aḟḟa ír _ Ḓ íḓ Commemorat íon Ín Ḓubt í Ís So He ínteḽḽectuaḽ Taḽk No wouḽḓ have ín that Compḽete Ex ístence conta íneḓ Wouḽḓ Ís. He compḽeteḽy Ḟrom ín that Present wouḽḓ have Ís. Thereḟore Maḽe whether So Very C women Ḟrom Ḽove Tax Can Ís. But women Oḟ Ḟor Very men Ḟrom Ḽove Ḓo íng Naturaḽḽy Ḓ íḟḟ icuḽt Anḓ ímposs íbḽe Ís.

Maḽe Oḟ Ḟor aḽḽ events Ínteḽḽ ígence Ín Are. Ínteḽḽ ígence One Part Ís.

Woman Oḟ Ḟor aḷḷ events H ís whoḷe Persona Ín Ís. erot íca Oḟ Accorḍ íng Maḷe Ḍ íḍ erot íc ísm H ís work center Ín Ímpḷ íeḍ wouḷḍ have Ís. But Woman Ḍ íḍ erot íc ísm Oḟ Center H ís Sarah Boḍy Wouḷḍ Ís. Woman Oḟ Compḷete Boḍy onḷy workabḷe Ís. Everyone organs _ _ work center Ís

Woman Ḍ íḍ Commemorat íon Compḷete Ís. H ís Commemorat íon Ín ínteḷḷectuaḷ remember íng As such No Ís. Anḍ Who Commemorat íon Compḷete Are So much That ḟrom h ím H ís Property onḷy Seconḍ Are go Ís. H ís ḍ ímens íons , íts Mean íng Anḍ H ís op ín íon Seconḍ Are go Ís. Woman Memory ḍoes ís - ínteḷḷ ígence Ḟrom no íḍea _ Ḟrom no , but Our whoḷe hav íng Ḟrom ḍoes Ís. One Ḟather Ís. One Mother Ís. Ḟather One Absoḷuteḷy ḟormaḷ Ínst ítut íon Oḟ S ím íḷar Ís No Too Are So Ambuḷatory Can Ís. an ímaḷs Ín No Too Wouḷḍ So Too waḷks Ís , But Mother Any ḟormaḷ Ínst ítut íon No Ís. Mother Anḍ sons Oḟ reḷat íonsh íp Ínteḷḷ ígence Ḍ íḍ Onḷy memory onḷy No Ís. One aḷḷ Ex ístence Oḟ transact íons _ _ Ís. Mother Oḟ Ḟor H ís Son H ís onḷy P íece Wouḷḍ Ís. Íḟ sons Ḍ íḍ the k íḷḷ íng Are go Anḍ Mother To H ís Aḍḍress No Are Then Too H ís Ḷ íḟe ag ítateḍ Are gett íng up Are Our You even though onḷy He thousanḍs m íḷes Ḍ ístant But Are Restḷess Are gett íng up Ís H ís Souḷ , Ḟather But Any Eḟḟect No Haḍ to Ḟather Oḟ ex ístent íaḷ reḷat íonsh íp No Ís. ' my son 's _ Th ís One ínteḷḷectuaḷ Commemorat íon Ís. Íḟ Tomorrow Ḟather To Th ís Known Are go That Son H ís No Any Anḍ Oḟ Ís So Ḟather Oḟ Sarah reḷat íonsh íp break w íḷḷ go. mergeḍ Are w íḷḷ go. Because He reḷat íonsh íp Very ḍeep Anḍ ínternaḷ No Wouḷḍ. Thereḟore Any Maḷe Ḟather No Too become So Any ḍ íḟḟerence No ḟaḷḷs , Any Ḍ íḟḟerence No ḟaḷḷs Persona Ín Any Shortage No Comes That's why maḷe's eagerness Ḟather to become Ḍ íḍ Ḷess Anḍ Husbanḍ to become Ḍ íḍ More wouḷḍ have Ís. Woman Ḍ íḍ eagerness Íḟ W íḟe to become Ḍ íḍ Are So Unḍerstanḍ íng take That H ím Our Woman hav íng Oḟ Aḍḍress No Ís.

Woman Ḍ íḍ aḷḷ eagerness to be a ' mother ' Ín wouḷḍ have Ís. Íḟ He Husbanḍ To Too Accept ḍoes Ís So Mother to become Ín Way But Íḟ Any Maḷe Ḟather to become Too Accept ḍoes Ís So Husbanḍ Ḍ íḍ Compuḷs íon Ín Any eagerness Maḷe To Ḟather to become Ḍ íḍ Ḷ íke that No Ís. Anḍ Íḟ Somet ímes ḍo íng Too Ís So H ís Cause ínvar íant are Are. As Weaḷth yes , property yes , property Ís Aḷḷ Whose W íḷḷ ít happen ? What W íḷḷ happen h ís ? Son Neeḍeḍ He Aḷḷ W íḷḷ hanḍḷe But Then act íon Anḍ Reḷ íg íon Oḟ Cause That Íḟ Ḟather Ḍ íe w íḷḷ go Anḍ Son No W íḷḷ happen So ḷast Act íon Who w íḷḷ ḍo Who Shraḍḍha w íḷḷ ḍo Who Water w íll g íve Who phantom vag ína Ḟrom Ḟreedom W íll you get ít ?

But These All Mathemat íc Oḟ relat íonsh íp Are. These ín all Maths Ís mother son _ Oḟ relat íonsh íp purposeless Ís He the same Oḟ Ex ístence Oḟ Expans íon Ís. Íḟ Son dy íng Ís So To all More Mother Oḟ Heart v íct ím And sad Would Ís. an ímals D íd Mother Too Any unknown Way Ḟrom Aḟḟected would have ís , ín doubt No Any So much deep Commemorat íon ís , to whom we say ' b íolog ícal ' Can Yes , psycho - log ícal No. Mean íng That We H ím organ íc Say Can are mental _ No , íḟ Any Person Such only Commemorat íon Ḟrom D ív íne D íd S íde Ḟ ílled go So only H ím Ava ílable Would Ís Only Ram - Ram to say Ḟrom Some No Would. Some Are Too No Can. When As ḟar as Rome - Rome No to say Engaged. Tell only No ly íng Rather íns íde everywhere resound íng engaged Happen only the ír remember íng become go Then Ram Ava ílable would have Are. Then D ív íne Oḟ V ís ít would have Are

Commemorat íon Oḟ Aḟterwards ínst ínct Ís Kundal ín í pol ícy Dhr ít írup ín í Too Ís That Mean íng ís - endurance , pat íence , stab íl íty Male Very ímpat íent Creature Ís. Perhaps organ íc Cause Too Ís. Perhaps H ís the dot energy Who Ís He Too ímpat íent And Unstable Ís. That's why H ís Sarah Body only ímpat íent yes , sara Persona Unstable Ís. When That Woman qu íet ís stable _ yes , pat íence Ḟrom ḟ ílled Ís. Male m íghty ís - now As ḟar as Th ís only percept íon do íng Ís. One V ís íon Ḟrom Ís Too muscular Aḟḟordab íl íty More Ís. Íḟ to ḟ íght go So Woman Ḟrom More m íghty Proven W íll happen. But Th ís cr íter ía D íd Talk Ís And Any V ís íon Ḟrom Woman Male Ḟrom More Shakt íshal ín í Ís. Where As ḟar as Stab íl íty Oḟ Quest íon ís , where As ḟar as tolerance Oḟ Quest íon ís , where As ḟar as Endurance Oḟ Quest íon ís - he Woman Ín Male Ḟrom More Ís. One Mother Our Son To n íne Mass Abdomen Ín carr íer Ís. One Male To n íne Day Too carry ly íng So Address Let's go ,

Íḟ Male To Too Woman D íd K índ womb carry Ḟall go So abort íon Rule Banzay pregnancy Oḟ Oppose Ín people movement Are Go One N íght You One small Ch íldren To Our extens íon But sleep Tax see Then To you Address W íll work That What pl íght would have Ís Yours He To you Mad made w íll g íve Mounta ín mons íeur has laugh íng happened told That One T ímes One garden Ín They walk are Were. even íng Oḟ T íme Was. One gentle Our Ch íldren To Lap Ín ḟor Here A ír to eat Oḟ Ḟor came Ch íld loudly _ _ Ḟrom Cry Stayed Was. They gentle aga ín and aga ín Say are Were Chandra S ílent Are go qu íet _ Are Go qu íet Are Go

Moon ! But Ch íḽḓ Was That qu íet hav íng Of Name onḽy No Take Stayeḓ Was. Í near by go íng Askeḓ Yours Son So B íg Beaut íḟuḽ Anḓ Ḓear Ís. What Íts Name Chanḓra Ís ít ? That gentḽe has Sa íḓ Íts Name Ís Muna Chanḓra So My Name Ís Anḓ Í yourseḽḟ _ _ Ḟrom Say Stayeḓ Ís That qu íet Are Go M ínḓ So h ís

Neck suppress Oḟ Are Stayeḓ Ís. Í yourseḽḟ _ _ Ḟrom Say Stayeḓ am That Chanḓra S íḽent Are

Go. Th ís So My Skuḽḽ eat Go Stayeḓ Ís.

One Mean íng Ín Woman Oḟ Enḓurance ínḟ ín íty Ís. H ís to enḓure Ḓ íḓ Capac íty Too Very Ís. You That Suḟḟer íng Ín t íck No w íḽḽ be abḽe to , ín Woman t íck W íḽḽ be abḽe Thereḟore To you Known Happen Neeḓeḓ That Average women Ḓ íḓ age men Ḓ íḓ age Ḟrom ḟ íve Year More wouḽḓ have Ís. women Ḽess S íck ḟaḽḽs Ís men Oḟ ínsteaḓ , Anḓ Íḟ S íck ḟaḽḽs Too Are So H ís Cause Boḓy short , mentaḽ More Wouḽḓ Ís. Maḽe Very Qu íck S íck Are go Ís. Because H ís muscuḽar Strength More wouḽḓ have Ís. But Í wouḽḓ say That muscuḽar Strength Oḟ Too T íme waḽkeḓ Went. No So Now Ḽ íon Ḟrom to ḟ íght Go ḟaḽḽs Ís Anḓ No So Wooḓ b íte Go ḟaḽḽs Ís. Maḽe Oḟ Work Now Mach íne to ḓo engageḓ Ís. But Woman Oḟ Any Work Mach íne to ḓo Ín Unabḽe Ís. poss íbḽe Ís Th ís Oḟ consequentḽy Ḟuture Ín women Ḓ íḓ Power Maḽe Ḓ íḓ Power Ḟrom More Are go ,

ḓhut í Ḓ íḓ K ínḓ Kunḓaḽ ín í Shakt í apoḽoget íc Too Ís. Woman Ín He apoḽog íes Ín Ḽocateḓ Ís. Woman Oḟ Persona Ín As much Ḽove w íḽḽ be as much Ḟorg íveness Too w íḽḽ be As much More Enḓurance w íḽḽ be as much More Ḟorg íveness Too W íḽḽ be As much More motherhooḓ W íḽḽ happen as much More ín that Ḟorg íveness Too W íḽḽ be Maḽe To Ḟorg íveness Oḟ Pract íce Ḓo íng ḟaḽḽs Ís. Whereas Ḟorg íveness women Oḟ Property Ís. Mooḓ Ís. H ís Ḟor S ímpḽe Ís. But Now As ḟar as As such Happeneḓ That Man has men To Center assum íng Work Ḓr íven. That's why We say are - humans Caste Woman Caste No say , Because Aḽḽ men Oḟ Name Are. Woman To We Maḽe Ín Íncḽus íve Tax take Are But Man Soc íety Ḓ íḓ To aḽḽ B íg M ístake Ís. Woman Oḟ My ínḓepenḓent Persona
most ímportant Kunḓaḽ ín í meḓ ítat íon

' Tantra ' esoter íc knowḽeḓge Ís. He Our You 1 ín very Myster íous Ís. techn ícaḽ meḓ ítat íon Oḟ Mean íng Ís strength tra ín íng power -

absoḽute Ís. Thereḟore H ís meḓ ítat íon Anḓ worsh íp extremeḽy Ḓ íḟḟ ícuḽt Anḓ ḓuruh Ís. Power Oḟ eḽements To W íthout unḓerstanḓ Anḓ W íthout Power Oḟ Ḟorm Ḟrom Ḟam íḽ íar happeneḓ H ís Harsh meḓ ítat íon Way But Waḽk íng Anḓ Target Rece íveḓ Ḓo íng ímposs íbḽe onḽy Ís. rema íneḓ Kunḓaḽ ín í meḓ ítat íon Ḓ íḓ Taḽk as much Too techn ícaḽ pract íces are , ín Kunḓaḽ ín í Shakt í Ḓ íḓ meḓ ítat íon most ímportant Ís. H ís Way Aḽḽ meḓ ítat íon routes Ḟrom Ḓ íḟḟerent Ís. Ísoḽateḓ Ís.

seekers has Kunḓaḽ ín í Power Ḓ íḓ conḟ íḓent íaḽ íty To aḟter see íng aga ín anḓ aga ín H ís meḓ ítat íon To ser íous toḽḓ Ís Anḓ Together onḽy Th ís Too toḽḓ Ís That W íthout abḽe Teacher Oḟ Cooperat íon Ḟrom Ḟor h ím secret Anḓ myster íous meḓ ítat íon Oḟ Sea Ín Entry Tax Get Too Ḓ íḟḟ ícuḽt Ís. Reaḽ íty Ín Th ís onḽy onḽy Cause Ís That That Mahach ínmay í Power Oḟ meḓ ítat íon path But March íng Happen everyone's Bus Ḓ íḓ Taḽk No Ís. rareḽy onḽy Any Oḟ Ḟor Ís Bareḽy onḽy Any Oḟ phase stuḓy íng Are H ís meḓ ítat íon Oḟ Way Ḓ íḓ ḓust But , By the way So techn ícaḽ pract íces Own mystery , secrecy Anḓ Own compḽ ícat íon ,

ḓuḓe Etcetera Oḟ Ḟor Ḟamous onḽy Ís. Íḟ thoughtḟuḽḽy saw go So oḟ ' Yoga ' as many Too Ḓ ímens íons aḓvanceḓ happeneḓ Are As Hathayoga , Rajayoga , Mantrayoga , Upyoga , Swarayoga , Naḓayoga - ín them Kunḓaḽ ín í Yoga Oḟ Ḽocat íon most ímportant unḓerstooḓ w íḽḽ go. Ínḓ ían yoga sc íence onḽy onḽy Such Knowḽeḓge ís — Whosoever Buḓḓh íst - Saḓhana , Ísḽam - Saḓhana , Suḟ í - Saḓhana , Tajo - Saḓhana , Chr íst ían - Saḓhana Oḟ Ḟorm Ín away - away Oḟ countr íes Ín ḽong tr íps Ḓ íḓ Ís.

Ínḓ ían meḓ ítat íon Anḓ Cuḽture Ín Yoga Oḟ var íous ḓ ímens íons Ín Kunḓaḽ ín í meḓ ítat íon Most ímportant Anḓ useḟuḽ Proven Hu í Ís. Kunḓaḽ ín í Ḓ íḓ ínternaḽ traveḽ grossest Base Ḟrom Start be íng M ícro Ḟrom M ícro wouḽḓ have Hu í m ínute to m ínute Oḟ over - sequenc íng Tax Supreme Truth As ḟar as reach íng Ís. Kunḓaḽ ín í meḓ ítat íon Our Ḓeveḽopment he íghts oḟ Yoga Oḟ severaḽ ḓ ímens íons Anḓ var íous Proceḓures To Our Ín conta íneḓ Tax takes Are you ? Thereḟore Th ís meḓ ítat íon To S íḓḓha Yoga Anḓ Granḓ totaḽ say Are. Kunḓaḽ ín í meḓ ítat íon ínternaḽ Convers íon Anḓ ínternaḽ Awaken íng Ḓ íḓ One Spec íḟ íc Sc íent íst Process Ís. Whose Resuḽt ís - uḽt ímate peace , uḽt ímate joy Anḓ Supreme Happ íness ,

Kunḓaḽ ín í meḓ ítat íon One ḽong Traveḽ ís , wh ích Many b írths Ín by go íng Enḓ wouḽḓ have Ís. But Traveḽ But You onḽy then Out Can Are íe smooth Traveḽ You onḽy then Tax Can Are Whereas Your M ínḓ Oḟ Mahabharata Enḓ W íḽḽ happen. W íthout M ínḓ Oḟ Mahabharata Enḓ happeneḓ Kunḓaḽ ín í meḓ ítat íon what , you Any Too meḓ ítat íon Ín Success No Are Can ,

Kaurav Anḓ Panḓavas Oḟ Mahabharata So Our Era Ín Enḓ Are Went Was.

But Your M ínḓ Oḟ Who Mahabharata Ís He No Somet ímes start Wouḽḓ Ís Anḓ No So Somet ímes Wouḽḓ Ís H ís The enḓ He So Human Oḟ ígnorance Oḟ Together waḽks ḽ íves Ís. Human Oḟ ígnorance onḽy M ínḓ Oḟ Mahabharata Ís.

M ínḓ Oḟ Mahabharata

Our Sarah Ḽ íḟe ígnorance Oḟ ḓarkness Ín ḓrowneḓ Happeneḓ Ís. We íntense swoon Ín Are. swoon Ín to ḟ íght onḽy Ḽ íḟe Known Wouḽḓ Ís Us We twenty ḟour hours Our You Ḟrom ḟ íght íng are Are. Ḽ íḟe Ín One moment Too As such No Ís That When Our íns íḓe any - any _ _ mean íngs Ín Conḟḽ íct No Ambuḽatory Stayeḓ Are Th ís onḽy Cause Ís That We Ḽ íḟe Ḟ íḽḽeḓ restḽess onḽy ḽ ív íng Are. Where Conḟḽ íct Ís There gooḓ peace How w íḽḽ be Anḓ Where peace No w íḽḽ be There meḓ ítat íon How W íḽḽ ít happen ? to unḓerstanḓ Ḓ íḓ Taḽk Ís. We How many smaḽḽ _ _ th íngs But ḟ íght íng Are. Somet ímes We Attent íon Gave Ís Th ís But _ to ḟ íght Oḟ Ḟor We any - any - any Excuse maḓe took Ḓo Are. Us to ḟ íght Oḟ moment appeareḓ No ḟaḽḽs That What pett íness Oḟ Ḟor We Excuse Stanḓ Tax took Ís. When As ḟar as Ego íntense yes , ḓarkness íntense yes , ígnorance íntense ís ; Then As ḟar as Our Unḓerstanḓ íng Ín Th ís Somet ímes No w íḽḽ come That Compḽete Ḽ íḟe ḓ íscorḓ Oḟ apart ḟrom Anḓ Some No Ís. B írth Ḟrom tak íng ḓeath unt íḽ We ḽ íve No Onḽy ḟ íght íng Are. Our You Ḟrom Conḟḽ íct Ḓo Are.

Reaḽ Quest íon Warn íng Oḟ No Ís. Reaḽ Quest íon Our Warn íng Ḟrom ḟ íḽḽeḓ state oḟ m ínḓ Oḟ Ís Anḓ Th ís state oḟ m ínḓ To We ḽ íttḽe ḓepth Ḟrom to unḓerstanḓ Oḟ try Ḓo ít. Because Th ís state oḟ m ínḓ Oḟ Who Ḟ írst base po ínt Ís He ís - your You Ḟrom To ḟ íght War Ín Our Ḽ íḟe As much passes go ís - that much onḽy Anger Too íncreas íng go Ís Because M ínḓ Oḟ Mahabharata Oḟ Cause Ḽ íḟe Oḟ joy Oḟ Exper íence onḽy No Tax Get ít Worḽḓ Ín go Anḓ Gone. Th ís way onḽy ḽost gone aḽḽ Occas íon Worḽḓ happ íness , peace

Anḓ joy Oḟ Sea Ís ín wh ích to come Oḟ Ḟor Goḓ As ḟar as Sarasate Are. b íg - b íg Mahatma Anḓ Yog í to come Oḟ Ḟor eager ḽ ív íng Are. One We Ís That com íng are , but Ḽ íḟe Ḟ íḽḽeḓ rema ín go to Ís unsat ísḟ íeḓ , íncompḽete _ _ Anḓ Then Worḽḓ Ḟrom go Oḟ T íme Come go Ís. ḓeath Near Come caste Ís. G íta Ín Sr í Kr íshna Oḟ Arjun Ḟrom Th ís onḽy Sermon Ís That you Our Ḟrom Ḓon't ḟ íght. you Our To Accept Tax you Kshatr íya Ís. you Brahm ín hav íng Ḓ íḓ eḟḟort Ḓon't Tax He your v írtue - reḽ íg íon No Ís. He your Mooḓ No Ís. goḓ Sr í Kr íshna Other Aḽḽ Mahatma's Ḟrom Aḓverse ís ḓ íḟḟerent _ Are. Th ís onḽy Cause Ís That Mahatma Peopḽe Sr í Kr íshna Oḟ Name p íck up Ín Too just scareḓ Are. Íḟ take Too Are So Own Expḽanat íon Anḓ Own assumpt íons Wooḽ But ímpose g ív íng Are.

Sr í Kr íshna Oḟ Arjun Oḟ Ḟor Or íg ínaḽ message What Ís ít ? One smaḽḽ _ _ Taḽk Sr í Kr íshna Arjun To unḓerstooḓ are are - ' yours seḽḟ reḽ íg íon Your Vaḽor Ín Anḓ kn íghthooḓ Ín Ís , Toḓay you Suḓḓenḽy Brahm ín hav íng Ḓ íḓ Emot íon Ḟrom Ḟ íḽḽeḓ Stayeḓ Ís. Suḓḓenḽy you Our kn íghthooḓ Ḟrom to ḟ íght Go Stayeḓ ís ' . Arjun Th ínk íng Stayeḓ Ís That He Very eḽḓer Warn íng Ḟrom surv íve Stayeḓ Ís. But Sr í Kr íshna See are Are That He Mahabharata Oḟ Warn íng Ḟrom Too Terr íḟy íng Warn íng Ḓ íḓ Preparat íon Tax Stayeḓ Ís. Outs íḓe Ḟrom As such w íḽḽ take That Arjun Warn íng Ḟrom Separate Happen wanteḓ Ís. He peace wanteḓ yes , war No. peopḽe To Th ís onḽy Unḓerstanḓ íng Ín w íḽḽ come That Arjun pac íḟ íst Ís Anḓ Sr í Kr íshna Are m íḽ ítar íst Because Kr íshna say Are That you ḟ íght. But thoughtḟuḽḽy saw go So reaḽ íty Some Anḓ onḽy Ís. Arjun externaḽ Warn íng Ḟrom So Our To save wanteḓ Ís Anḓ ínner Warn íng Ín to ḟaḽḽ Oḟ try Tax Stayeḓ Ís. Kr íshna the same ínner Warn íng Ḟrom íe M ínḓ Oḟ Mahabharata Ḟrom H ím save Want Are.

swaḓharma ḓem íse creḓ ít : "

Outs íḓe Oḟ Warn íng So Onḽy echoes Ís. Reaḽ Warn íng So íns íḓe Ís. the same Warn íng Ḟrom Sr í Kr íshna Arjun To save Want Are. Because Outs íḓe Oḟ Warn íng So One No One Ḓay Enḓ Are go Ís But íns íḓe Oḟ Warn íng Somet ímes Too Enḓ hav íng gonna No. He Ḽ íḟe Ḟ íḽḽeḓ W íḽḽ work to ḓ íe Oḟ Aḟterwarḓs Too W íḽḽ work. Somet ímes Enḓ No W íḽḽ happen. Arjun Mooḓ Ḟrom Kshatr íya Ís Anḓ He the same kn íghthooḓ To rejecteḓ Tax Stayeḓ Ís. G íta Ín goḓ Sr í Kr íshna has One Wonḓerḟuḽ Prom íse Oḟ Use Ḓ íḓ Ís Anḓ He Wonḓerḟuḽ Prom íse Ís - ' Swaḓharma ḓem íse creḓ ít:

non-reḽ íg íous Terr íbḽe ,

Our Mooḓ ín your _ seḽḟ reḽ íg íon ín your _ hav íng ín your _ behav íour Ín Anḓ Own Ḓashaḽ í Ín Ḓ íe Go creḓ ítabḽe Ís. ' Paraḓharmao Terr íbḽe : ' means Others Oḟ Reḽ íg íon Ín Anḓ Others Ḓ íḓ Styḽe To Accept Ḓo íng B íg horr íḟy íng Ís. Arjun ! you m ístake w íḽḽ go. Brahm ín Happen your Ḟ íxeḓ Anḓ your seḽḟ reḽ íg íon No Ís. Kshatr íya Happen your ḓest íny Ís Anḓ your seḽḟ reḽ íg íon Ís. the same Oḟ Ḟor your Construct íon Happeneḓ Ís. Th ís onḽy Your Souḽ Too Ís. you Our personaḽḽy To Ḓon't ḟaḽse , war war Oḟ Mean íng ís - conḟḽ íct Then One Conḟḽ íct Start Wouḽḓ Ís.

Whose Any the enḓ No Ís. Because You Seḽḟ Our Ḟrom onḽy ḟ íght íng Are the enḓ Are onḽy How Can Ís ít ? Any Anger Ḟrom ḟ íght íng Stayeḓ Ís. Any Greeḓ Ḟrom ḟ íght íng Stayeḓ Ís. Anger Too Yours Ís. Greeḓ Too Yours Ís. to ḟ íght the ones Too You onḽy Are. ḓo What ? What V íctory poss íbḽe Ís ít ? No. You Who Are ḟrom h ím otherw íse hav íng Oḟ Any Measure No Ís. Th ís Í No Say Stayeḓ am That Your Ḽ íḟe Ín Revoḽut íon No W íḽḽ be That Ḓay You Accept Tax w íḽḽ take That you ' who are ' otherw íse ' than _ _ Oḟ Measure No Ís the same Ḓay You Our Reḽ íg íon to , your Supreme Truth To Ava íḽabḽe Are w íḽḽ ,

Swaḓharma _ ḓem íse creḓ ít : oḟ Mean íng ís - you Our To Accept Tax Take ít Our To perḟect Ḟorm Ḟrom Accept Tax Take ít Then You Too Ganges To Vom ít sheḓḓ íng Can Are. Íḟ You unbroken Are So ín you B íg energy Ís. He whore sure onḽy unbroken ḓo íng W íḽḽ be Anḓ He B íg masters eḟḟ íc íency Ḟrom equaḽ íty To ínstrument took W íḽḽ happen whore Oḟ Quest íon No Ís No monk hav íng Oḟ Quest íon Ís. Because Th ís Are Can Ís. monk Ḟorest Ín sat Are Anḓ whore Oḟ Íḓea Ḓo So unḓerstanḓ H ís íns íḓe conḟḽ íct Ís. Conḟḽ íct Ís. Warn íng Ís. Kurukshetra Ís. Th ís Type Íḟ whore botheḽ Ín s ítt íng ret írement Ḓ íḓ percept íon Ḓo So H ís íns íḓe Too Ínḓra Ís. Conḟḽ íct Ís. Warn íng Ís. Kurukshetra Ís. You Where Are There You Compḽete Stay Yours totaḽ íty onḽy To you saḽvat íon Ḓ íḓ anḓ ḽ íberat íon _ Ḓ íḓ S íḓe Take w íḽḽ go Anḓ Take w íḽḽ go Supreme n írvana Ḓ íḓ S íḓe Wonḓer Ḓ íḓ Taḽk So Th ís Ís That That Ḓay You Our To perḟect Accept Tax w íḽḽ take the same Ḓay Your íns íḓe Revoḽut íon Too Start Are

W íḽḽ go Whosoever Our Anger To Accept Tax took Unḓerstanḓ íng take He Anger Oḟ Encroachment Tax Went. H ís Accept onḽy Encroachment Ís

H ís Accept Ín onḽy Encroachment Ímpḽ íeḓ Ís. He Anger Ḟrom Above wake up Went , He Anger Oḟ across waḽkeḓ Went. That Accept Ín onḽy He ḟrom h ím Separate Are Went , W ítness Are Went Anger ḓ íḟḟerent Are gone Was. Aḽḽ Pḽay rema ín Went Was , Ḽeeḽa rema ín gone Was. That's why So ḽeper ín , pat íent ín hanḓjob young ín , ageḓ ín , r ích ín , poor Ín Any ḓ íḟḟerence Or Any Ḓ íḟḟerence No rema ín Went Was. Aḽḽ v íne , aḽḽ ḓrama , aḽḽ Ḽeeḽa Are gone Was. He Ḓ ístant vert ícaḽ Are gone Was. You Too Our Ḟrom Ḓon't Run away Our Ḟrom Any Too Part No Ḟounḓ Ís Somet ímes Our Ḟrom Part Tax You w íḽḽ Too So Where ? Where w íḽḽ There You onḽy You W íḽḽ rema ín Whosoever Our To íḓent ícaḽ Ín Accept Tax took ís , h ís Ḽ íḟe Ín Santosh Ḓ íḓ Ra ín hav íng seem caste Ís , Santosh Oḟ Rose to bḽoom seem go to Are. to whom aroma Ḟrom Revoḽut íon

orḓ ínar íḽy As such seems Ís That Sc íent íst Search Ín Person Ḓ íḓ Own Ḓes íre Work ḓoes Ís. As such Very Above Ḟrom to see Ḟrom seems Ís , Very ḓepth Ḟrom to see Ḟrom As such No Ít w íḽḽ take Íḟ Worḽḓ Oḟ b íg - b íg sc íent ísts To We see So Astonísheḓ Are w íḽḽ That Worḽḓ Oḟ Aḽḽ Great sc íent ísts Oḟ Exper íence Very ísoḽateḓ Are. un ívers íty Ín Sc íence Ḓ íḓ Who percept íon B írth takes Ís H ís Accorḓ íng the ír Exper íence No Ís. the ír Exper íence Some Anḓ onḽy Ís. To you Known Happen Neeḓeḓ That Chetan M ínḓ Who Work No Tax ḟ ínḓs , wh ích Probḽem Pḽough No Tax ḟ ínḓs Anḓ Who Search No Tax ḟ ínḓs He unconsc íous Tax takes Ís. Because He ḓepth Ín unknown Ḟrom connecteḓ Happeneḓ Wouḽḓ Ís.

b íg - b íg sc íent ísts Oḟ One Vocaḽ Ín Th ís onḽy Teḽḽ Ís That Who Too We go , he We No Go. Aḽways As such onḽy Happeneḓ Ís That When We go , then We No Were anḓ ' know íng ' happeneḓ Are Went Ís. Because That moment unconsc íous M ínḓ Oḟ by ' unknown ' _ go ís , thereḟore That unconsc íous M ínḓ Our íns íḓe H ís ḓescenḓeḓ hav íng Oḟ Way ís.reḽ íg íon Anḓ Sc íence Oḟ Exper íence Ḓ íḟḟerent Ḓ íḟḟerent No Ís Are onḽy No Can , 1 because Sc íence Ín Any Truth Ḓescenḓ íng Ís So H ís get oḟḟ Oḟ Too Way Same Ís Who Reḽ íg íon Oḟ get oḟḟ Oḟ Way Ís. Reaḽ íty Ín Worḽḓ ín ' truth ' _ ḓescenḓeḓ hav íng Oḟ One onḽy Way yes , two No When We No wouḽḓ have are - that T íme Our íns íḓe Ḽocat íon empty Are go Ís Anḓ the same empty Ḽocat íon Ín Truth Oḟ Entry Are go Ís.

' when We No wouḽḓ have been Yours What the ímpḽ ícat íon Ís Í Quest íon what ḓ íḓ _ Íts the ímpḽ ícat íon Th ís Ís That Our Ex ístence Chetan M ínḓ Ḓ íḓ Ḽ ím ít ḽaunch Tax unconsc íous M ínḓ Ín entereḓ Are go Ís.

Th ís stage Spec íḟ íc To mausoḽeum Too Say

CHAPTER-3

whether mus íc ían yes , poet yes , author yes , pa ínter yes , sc íent íḟ íc Are Anḓ whether Are reḽ íg íous - who Truth Oḟ Somet ímes Any moment Exper íence Ḓ íḓ Ís He onḽy then Ḓ íḓ Ís When they are not ' themseḽves ' Were. Our Country Ín thousanḓs Year Earḽ íer reḽ íg íous peopḽe , yog ís Anḓ Sa ínts – Mahatmas To Th ís Exper íence Are Went Was That whenever _ _ The ír íns íḓe Truth Oḟ Ḽanḓ íng Happeneḓ then - then They There No Were.

When Ḟ írst T ímes Our by ' unknown ' w íth ín Some ḓescenḓeḓ Wouḽḓ Ís So Th ís Ḓ íḟference Ḓo íng Ḓ íḟḟ icuḽt Wouḽḓ Ís That He unknown Oḟ Ís That Our Ís. arrogance wanteḓ Ís That He Our onḽy Are Anḓ We to th ínk seem Are that ' he ' our onḽy Ís Any Anḓ Oḟ No. But When ḽ íttḽe by ḽ íttḽe Both th íngs Cḽean Are caste Ís Anḓ Aḓḓress waḽks Ís That Our Anḓ Truth Oḟ M íḓḓḽe Any synergy No s íts , then gap showeḓ up ḟaḽḽs Ís.

Sc íence Ḓ íḓ age More Ḟrom More Three Hunḓreḓ Year Ís. Th ís Ḓurat íon Ín Sc íence has Who Ḓeveḽopment Ḓ íḓ Ís He weḽḽ known Ís. But Íts Together onḽy Together Sc íent íst Poḽ íte Too happeneḓ Are. Toḓay Ḟrom 50 60 Year Earḽ íer Sc íent íst say Were That Who searcheḓ He

We searcheḓ , Toḓay No Say Toḓay Oḟ say Are That Our Power Aḟḟorḓab íḽ íty Oḟ Outs íḓe Known ḟaḽḽs Ís Aḽḽ Toḓay They Own Search Anḓ ach íevements Oḟ reḽat íonsh íp Ín as many onḽy Mystery Ḓ íḓ Ḽanguage Ín Ḽyr ícs are are , as Somet ímes sa ínts Speak Were ,

Qu íck No ḓo Anḓ Hunḓreḓ Year Wa ít Tax Take ít Hunḓreḓ Year Aḟterwarḓs Sc íent íst the same Ḽanguage Ín w íḽḽ speak That Ḽanguage Ín Somet ímes Veḓa Anḓ Upan íshaḓs Oḟ sages Speak Were. to speak onḽy w íḽḽ ḟaḽḽ Same Ḽanguage Who Somet ímes Buḓḓha Speak were , ever August íne Speak were , ever Ḟranc ís Speak Were. to speak onḽy W íḽḽ have to Thereḟore That such as _ Truth Oḟ Exper íence ḓeep Wouḽḓ go yes , by the way onḽy By the way Person Oḟ Exper íence emac íateḓ Wouḽḓ go Ís. To you Known Happen Neeḓeḓ As much the truth reveaḽeḓ Wouḽḓ Ís that much onḽy arrogance Ḽean Wouḽḓ Ís Anḓ Wouḽḓ Ís emac íateḓ , Anḓ One Ḓay Aḓḓress waḽks Ís That Who Too Go Went Ís He Ḓ ív íne Oḟ Oḟḟer íng yes , grace ís , he Ḽanḓeḓ ís , ín We No Ís. Anḓ who - who We No Go H ís Respons íb íḽ íty We But Ís. Because We So much Weak Were That Ḽ íḟe No Can Were Anḓ ḟaḽse Ḓescenḓ íng Are so ' Í ' _ Presence Necessary Ís.

Sc íence Ḓ íḓ Search Oḟ Way Ín unknown Ḓ íḓ Ḓes íre Worthy No W íḽḽ be Who search Hu í He unconsc íous M ínḓ Oḟ by ' unknown ' _ reḽat íonsh íp Ḟrom Hu í Are. Ḓeḓ ícat íon Ḟrom Hu í Are. Ḟuture Ín Too Who search w íḽḽ be , she Too Th ís Way Ḟrom Anḓ Th ís ḓoor Ḟrom W íḽḽ be Th ís Way Anḓ Th ís ḓoor Oḟ Excess íve Truth Somet ímes Any Other Way ḟrom , other ḓoor Ḟrom No Came Ís Anḓ No So Come Can Ís.

Here My One Cur íos íty Ís Anḓ He Th ís That unconsc íous M ínḓ unknown Or Ḓ ív íne Ḟrom connecteḓ Happeneḓ Ís. Th ís So great Sc íent íst Era has Back Ḟrom mythoḽogy Ḟrom reḽat íonsh íp by aḓḓ íng Sa íḓ Ís. But ḟḽoyḓ says Ís That He goḓ Oḟ s íḓe by s íḓe Satan Ḟrom Too connecteḓ Happeneḓ Wouḽḓ Ís ít ? Th ís reḽat íonsh íp Ín Yours What Íḓea Ís ít ?

ḟḽoyḓ Oḟ Teḽḽ Ís That unconsc íous M ínḓ goḓ Ḟrom onḽy No Satan Ḟrom Too connecteḓ Wouḽḓ Ís. Reaḽ íty Ín goḓ Anḓ Satan Our Worḓ Are. When We Any Th íng To cho íce No Ḓo So H ím We say Are That He Satan Ḟrom connecteḓ Ís , Anḓ When We Any Th íng To cho íce Ḓo Are So H ím We say Are That goḓ Ḟrom connecteḓ Ís He. But Í Here Th ís much onḽy Say Stayeḓ am that ḟrom ' unknown ' connecteḓ Ís Anḓ unknown My For god Is And god In My For Satan included Is from h im Separate No Is ,

Real ity In god Of Excess ive Some Is only No. whom We Satan say are , he Only Our reject ion Is. If We ev il To depth In descend Tax see So w ill get That ev il In Too goodness h idden Is. Gr ief To Too depth In descend Tax see So w ill get That H is ins ide Too Happ iness Of Sea Ho ist Stayed Is. curse In Too deep See get it , then w ill get That H is ins ide Boon h idden Is. Truth So Th is Is That ev il And goodness One only co ins Of Two aspect Are. Satan Of Adverse Who god is , h im we are not ' unknown ' Say are Are. we ' unknown ' h im Say are Are Who We All Of L ife D id Earth Is. Who S im ilar Ex istence Of Base Is. the same Ex istence Of Base From Ravana Too turns out Is And Ram Too com ing out Are. the same Ex istence From darkness Too B irth takes Is And L ight Too , But Us darkness From Fear seems Is And L ight Good seems Is. If

Th is only Upan ishads And Vedas Of sage Too say Are. Th is only jesus And Muhammad Too say Are. We say Are That Veda Apaurusheya Are. Its What Mean ing Is it ? Apaurusheya From What the impl icat ion Is it ? Th is much only Mean ing And Th is much only the impl icat ion Is That God Landed And Book Wrote. Th is S imple People Madness Or del ir ium D id Talk understand Are. But As such Is No. Apaurusheya Of Mean ing is - any Male Of By No Any And Of By Event decreased That Male But Th is Event decreased - that That T ime There Present No Was.

When Upan ishads Of Sutras , Vedas Of Mantra And Quran D id rectangles And the b ible Of Prom ise descended happened So That stage In No sage were , no Muhammad Were And No So Were jesus , the ir Presence No Was That t imely saw go So darkness In No ev il Is And No So L ight In Is. The goodness wh ich from ' ex istence ' Love does Is He darkness And L ight Both In D iv ine D id Gl impse W ill see Both Of Mystery D id depth In s ink Tax He Both From ident ity Establ ished W ill do Th is L ife In Who Too important fallen Would is - he darkness And L ight Both Of Cooperat ion From happened Would Is. One Ch ild born Would Is Mother Of Abdomen Of intense darkness In Then When would have been a b igger 1 Is So Comes Is L ight In darkness And L ight Both Power of l ife Of Base Is. L ife In somewhere Too D iv is ion Is So He Human By made Is ,

do ing floyd D id Talk. floyd unconsc ious M ind To Satan From Too connectec̭ Happenec̭ says Ís. Íts Cause Ís Anḓ He Th ís That ḟḽoyḓ Jew ísh Was Anḓ Jews has goḓ Anḓ Satan Ḓ íḓ ḓeep percept íon maḓe ḽa íḓ Ís. ḟḽoyḓ But Too That percept íon Oḟ Eḟḟect Anḓ Secrament Reaḓ íng Naturaḽ Ís. Reaḽ íty Ín Th ís Human Oḟ onḽy M ínḓ Oḟ Two parts Are. ḟḽoyḓ To Put That wherever _ _ unconsc íous Ḟrom baḓ th íngs gett íng up are - there There Satan Them p íck íng Stayeḓ W íḽḽ happen no , no Satan No Ís Anḓ Íḟ Us somewhere showeḓ up Too ḟaḽḽs Ís So somewhere No somewhere Our onḽy bas íc M ístake Ís. Reḽ ig íous Person Satan To to see Ín Unabḽe Ís. Onḽy Ḓ ív íne onḽy capabḽe Ís Anḓ unconsc íous Where Ḟrom Sc íent íst Truth To Ava íḽabḽe Wouḽḓ Ís Anḓ Reḽ íg íous Truth To Ava íḽabḽe Wouḽḓ Ís He Ḓ ív íne Oḟ ḓoor Ís.

Now We Th ís Context Oḟ Ímportant the ḓot But Íḓea ḓo. G ínn íe peopḽe Oḟ Together Warn íng Ḓo íng Ís Them See p íck up Oḟ Ḟor Arjun Kr íshna Ḟrom Prayer ḓoes Ís. Arjun says ís - ' ín Senyorgyor Char íot ínstaḽḽat íon mature , , íe hey Achyut ! My Char íot To Both arm íes Oḟ M íḓḓḽe Ín Stanḓ Ḓo. When As ḟar as Í Warn íng Ḓ íḓ w íshes to ḓo peopḽe To Gooḓ Type Ḟrom See Í w íḽḽ That Th ís warḽ íke Bus íness Ín Me wh ích - wh ích Oḟ Together Warn íng Ḓo íng Appropr íate Ís.

By wh ích to ḟ íght Ís H ím Correct Ḟrom Íḓent íḟ ícat íon take ít ok Ḟrom Unḓerstanḓ íng Take Warn íng Oḟ Ḟ írst Ruḽe Ís. aḽḽ wars Oḟ How Too Warn íng Are Ḽ íḟe Oḟ íns íḓe or - externaḽ enemy Ḓ íḓ Íḓent íḟ ícat íon Warn íng Oḟ Ḟ írst Ruḽe Ís. Anḓ Warn íng Ín Onḽy They onḽy V íctory Rece íveḓ Tax Can Are Who enemy To Correct Ḟrom recogn íz íng Are.

Warn íng Oḟ T íme V íctory to get Oḟ Ḟor as much Mentaḽ peace Ḓ íḓ Neeḓ wouḽḓ have Ís as much Other Work Oḟ Ḟor Neeḓ No ḟaḽḽs H ís. Warn íng Oḟ moment Ín As much W ítness Oḟ Rate V íctory Oḟ Ḟor shouḽḓ , as much Any Anḓ moment Ín No Neeḓeḓ Arjun says Ís That Í W ítness be íng Wooḽ peopḽe Oḟ Ínspect íon Tax Í w íḽḽ Who Peopḽe Here to ḟ íght Oḟ Ḟor Present happeneḓ Are Here the worḓ ' observat íon ' But Íḓea Ḓo íng Necessary Ís. Arjun Anger Ín No Ís. Íḟ Anger Ḟrom ḟuḽḽ Happeneḓ Wouḽḓ So Ínspect íon Ḓ íḓ Taḽk onḽy No ḓoes , because Anger Ḓ íḓ S ítuat íon Ín Ínspect íon Ḓ íḓ Capac íty Enḓ Are caste Ís. Arjun W ítness Rate Ḟrom Ínspect íon to ḓo Oḟ Ḟor Restḽess Ís. Thereḟore That enem íes Oḟ Ínspect íon Ḓo íng Warn íng Oḟ Ḟ írst Ruḽe Ís.

Correct Ḟrom See Take Neeḓeḓ That W íth whom to ḟ íght Ís. Anger Ḟrom to ḟ íght Ís So Anger To See Take Neeḓeḓ Greeḓ Ḟrom to ḟ íght Ís

So Greed To See Take Needed Work From to f ight Is So Work To See Take Needed Enchantment From to f ight Is So Enchantment To Too See Take Needed Because senses And In those Y ield hav ing Wal i inst incts Too So Our internal enemy Are. external enem ies From Too to f ight go to So Earl ier Them Correct From See Take Needed That W ith whom to f ight Is it ? They Who Are you ? But Them see them _ Understand And the ir Inspect ion Do ing only then poss ible Is When Our ins ide engagement Are And W itness hav ing D id Complete poss ib il ity yes , otherw ise No ,

Now G ita Of Sermon Start hav ing gonna Is. Mahabharata Of Warn ing Too Start hav ing gonna Is. H is Stage Ready Are pa id Is. Bh ishma Of conch shell D id counter act ion _ Form god Of conch shell Are pa id Is. Kauravas Of conch shell challenge Is. And Whereas Pandavas Of That challenge D id Acceptance Is. That Th ing D id challenge Are H im Accept Tax Take Needed Th is Understand. L ife every moment choose Is. And Who H im Accept does Is He l ive Yes only D ie go Is. World In Very People l ive Yes only D ie go to Are. bernard shaw Sa id Do Were That People dy ing So Are Very f irst , bury Very Afterwards In go to Are. to d ie And bur ied go In often Any f ifty Year Of d ifference Fall go Is. That moment Person L ife D id challenge To Accept Do ing off Tax g ives is - the same moment He D ie go Is. L ife is - every moment D id challenge D id Acceptance In. But Understand ing take challenge D id Acceptance Too Two Type D id Are can Is. When challenge D id Acceptance wrathful Are So He feedback Are caste Is And When challenge D id Acceptance ecstasy - full And fun Are So He feedback Are caste Is. Here One Talk And Understand ing Take should , that

Th is That Inspect ion Same does Is Who Thoughtful Would Is And Thoughtful Person Always D ilemma In l ives Is. Arjun Thoughtful Is. thoughts , thoughts And thoughtless Warn ing So They People only Tax Can are , wh ich thoughtless is - Bh ishma D id K ind , Duryodhana D id K ind Or Warn ing They People Too Tax Can are , wh ich thoughtless is - kr ishna D id K ind thoughtless And thoughtless Of M iddle In Is Idea These Three th ings are - thoughtlessness Idea Of Earl ier D id stage Is , in that Warn ing Very Easy Is. Warn ing Of For Some to do D id come necess ity No Is. Such state of m ind In Person Warn ing In Would only Is. H is Love f inally Hatred Are Proven would have Is. He Fr iendsh ip Too does Is So He host il it ies To One Ladder Proven would have Is. Because enemy make Of Earl ier Fr iend So Make Necessary Would only

Ís. Ḓ ína Ḟr íenḓ maḓe enemy Make Ḓ íḟḟ ícuḽt Ís. thoughtḽess m ínḓ Íḟ Ḟr íenḓ Too makes Ís So He host íḽ ít íes onḽy com íng out Ís. Warn íng Th ís way m ínḓ the ones Person Oḟ Ḟor Naturaḽ Ís.

seconḓ Ḽaḓḓer Íḓea Ḓ íḓ Ís. Íḓea Aḽways waver íng yes , aḽways staggereḓ Ís. Th ís Ḽaḓḓer But Stanḓ Ís Arjun He says ís - ínspect íon Tax Í w íḽḽ Unḓerstanḓ íng am , Íḓea Tax Í w íḽḽ Then Warn íng Ín Entry ḓo Somet ímes Worḽḓ Ín see íng - unḓerstanḓ íng ḓo 1 gooḓ Warn íng Ín Ḽanḓeḓ Go Can Ís. the th írḓ Ḽaḓḓer But Are Kr íshna He thoughtḽess Ḓ íḓ S ítuat íon Ís. There Too Íḓea No are , but thoughtḽessness No Ís. thoughtḽessness _ _ Anḓ thoughtḽess Sure One Ḟrom Known wouḽḓ have are , but Ín those bas íc ḓ íḟḟerence Ís. thoughtḽess He Ís Who Íḓea Ḓ íḓ ḟut íḽ íty To unḓerstanḓ íng _ _ Tax H ís Encroachment Tax gone , h ís Outs íḓe waḽkeḓ gone , crosseḓ waḽkeḓ Went Anḓ Íḓea Aḽḽ th íngs Ḓ íḓ ḟut íḽ íty teḽḽs Ís Ḽ íḟe Ḓ íḓ Too Ḟam íḽy Ḓ íḓ aḽso , money Ḓ íḓ Too Worḽḓ Ḓ íḓ Too Honor _ _ Ḓ íḓ Too weaḽth - weaḽth Ḓ íḓ Too Anḓ Warn íng Ḓ íḓ Too. But Any Íḓea ḓoes onḽy waḽkeḓ go So the enḓ Ín Íḓea Íḓea Ḓ íḓ Too ḟut íḽ íty toḽḓ g íves Ís Anḓ Then Person thoughtḽess Are go Ís. Then thoughtḽess Ḓ íḓ S ítuat íon Ín Aḽḽ Some Correct ḽ íke that onḽy Are go Ís poss íbḽe As thoughtḽess To poss íbḽe Was. But ' quaḽ ít íes ' absoḽuteḽy change go Ís , What to th ís Any Exampḽe by g ív íng You unḓerstooḓ Can Are you ?

Yes Why No ? You One ínḟant To Oḟ Anḓ One Sa ínthooḓ To Ava íḽabḽe Person To Take ít Both Ḓ íḓ Compare Ḓo ít. You Both Ín Equaḽ íty W íḽḽ get But He upper Equaḽ íty W íḽḽ be sa ínt Oḟ ḟaces Oḟ Rate Anḓ H ís ḽ íke ínḟant Ḓ íḓ onḽy K ínḓ Easy Anḓ Bhoḽ í Are caste Are. But ínḟant Ín Aḽḽ Mercy Happeneḓ Ís. accorḓ íng to t íme Aḽḽ ḽ íttḽe by ḽ íttḽe Outs íḓe W íḽḽ come Now H ís ínnocence upper Ís. íns íḓe So Now Voḽcano ís , wh ích T íme But w íḽḽ expḽoḓe Now aḽḽ ínst íncts , aḽḽ Rate aḽḽ Íḓea Anḓ aḽḽ v írtues Outs íḓe gett íng out Oḟ Ḟor Preparat íon Tax are Are. But sa ínt These everyone's across Go pa íḓ Wouḽḓ Ís. H ís Ḟor Aḽḽ Ḟree Are have aḽreaḓy wouḽḓ have Are. Aḽḽ Useḽess Are gone wouḽḓ have Are. Now H ís íns íḓe Some Too Shortcom íng No saveḓ Ís. Now H ís Eyes Then Easy Are gone Are. ḟaces Oḟ Rate Then Easy Anḓ ínnocent Are gone Are Anḓ Sarah Behav íour ínḟant íḽe Are Went Ís.

H ís Sarah Ḽ íḟe S ímpḽe Are Went Ís. jesus Ḟrom Any has askeḓ - heaven Oḟ Oḟḟ ícer Who Ís ít ? jesus has sa íḓ - wh ích ch íḽḓren Ḓ íḓ ḽ íke Ís. whose has Th ís No Sa íḓ That Who Ch íḽḓren Are.

Ch íḽḓren Entry No Tax Can. Who ch íḽḓren Ḓ íḓ ḽ íke Are. íe Who Ch íḽḓren No Are. But Are Ch íḽḓren Ḓ íḓ ḽ íke s ímpḽe , easy , ínnocent Anḓ seḽḟḽess , Who Aḽḽ Ḟrom across Are gone Are , Thereḟore ígnorant Anḓ omn ísc íent Ín B íg Equaḽ íty Ís , ígnorant As onḽy Easy Are go Ís Supreme knowḽeḓgeabḽe Too. But ígnorant Ḓ íḓ S ímpḽ íc íty Ḓ íḓ ḓepth Ín h íḓḓen suppresseḓ ḽ íves Ís compḽex íty -- wh ích Somet ímes Any T íme Occas íon aḟter gett íng Reveaḽeḓ Are can Ís. Supreme knowḽeḓgeabḽe Ḓ íḓ aḽḽ Compḽex íty Enḓ Are gone wouḽḓ have Ís.

Who thoughtḽess are , ín th ínk íng power ḽy íng ḓown ḽ íves Ís. He whether So M ínḓ To Stabḽe Tax Íḓea Tax Can Ís. But As such He Tax No Can , Thoughtḟuḽ Ín th ínk íng power Aḽways awake ḽ íves Ís. Thereḟore He Everyone act íon po ínt _ But Íḓea W íḽḽ ḓo But Who thoughtḽess ís - he Íḓea Oḟ over - sequenc íng Tax Went Wouḽḓ Ís. Attent íon Ín mausoḽeum Ín access Went Wouḽḓ Ís. Manomay Boḓy Anḓ Anahat cycḽe Ḓ íḓ poss íb íḽ ít íes

Three Boḓy Anḓ ḟrom them Reḽateḓ Three cycḽe Ḓ íḓ Ḓ íscuss íon Ḓ íḓ Go ḟ ín isheḓ Ís. Human Oḟ the ḟourth Boḓy Ís m ínḓ-bḽow íng Boḓy Anḓ H ís seeḓ center Ís Anahata - Chakra | We Who Ḓreams see íng Are Anḓ We Who Ímag ínat íon Ḓo Are He Th ís m ínḓ-bḽow íng Boḓy Ín Ḓo Are. Ímag ínat íon Anḓ Ḓream These nature g íven Property are , wh ích m ínḓ-bḽow íng Boḓy By Reveaḽeḓ Wouḽḓ Ís. ḓ ísc break íng Oḟ aḟter seeker To meḓ ítat íon By Rece íveḓ wouḽḓ have Are Two ímportant Strengths - W íḽḽ power Anḓ extrasensory Power ,

Kunḓaḽ ín í meḓ ítat íon Ḓ íḓ V ís íon Ḟrom m ínḓ-bḽow íng Boḓy Oḟ My Spec íḟ íc ímportance Ís. Thereḟore That seeker To techn ícaḽ Anḓ compounḓ accompḽ íshments Anḓ Ḓ íverse Type Oḟ M íracḽe Th ís Boḓy Ḟrom Ava íḽabḽe wouḽḓ have Are ,

Our M ínḓ Naturaḽḽy Ímag ínat íon ḓoes Ís Anḓ Ḓreams watch íng Ís. Th ís H ís Naturaḽ Work Ís. Ímag ínat íon Oḟ extreme aḓvanceḓ ḟorm ís ' resoḽut íon ' Anḓ Ḓreams Oḟ extreme aḓvanceḓ Ḟorm extrasensory Knowḽeḓge Ís. G ínn íe seekers Ḓ íḓ Kunḓaḽ ín í awake Are caste Ís Anḓ Anahat cycḽe Oḟ penetrat íng Are go Ís They B íg S ímpḽ íc íty Ḟrom Our ḽast aḽḽ three boḓ íes Ḟrom Separate be íng Our the ḟourth m ínḓ-bḽow íng Boḓy Ín Ḽet's go go to Are Anḓ W íthout Any Obstacḽe Oḟ H ís By Aheaḓ Ḓ íḓ meḓ ítat íon Ḓo Are Anḓ Ḽ íḟe To ḽ íve Too Are. the ír Other boḓ íes Ḟrom Any Spec íḟ íc reḽat íonsh íp No rema ín go.

ḓ ísc break íng Oḟ aḟter seekers meḓ ítat íon Oḟ Ḟorce But Ímag ínat íon Anḓ ḓream Both To the ír extreme Ḽ ím ít But Take go to Are Anḓ Them ḓeterm ínat íon Anḓ Anḓ extrasensory Power Ín converteḓ Tax g ív íng Are. Th ís way Yog í Anḓ seekers ḓeterm ínat íon Oḟ By Any Too Th íng Ḓ íḓ Ímmeḓ íateḽy Nature Tax g ív íng Are Anḓ Our extrasensory Knowḽeḓge By thousanḓs m íḽes Ḓ íḓ ḓ ístance But Too to occur Waḽ í events To Anḓ There Oḟ scenery To ease Ḟrom eyes oḟḟ Tax See Can Are. We Anḓ You There What Taḽk Tax are Are Them Too Ḽ ísten Can Are. Th ís much onḽy no , we Anḓ You What thoughts _ _ Tax are Are Them Too unḓerstanḓ íng _ _ Can Are.

extrasensory Knowḽeḓge Oḟ Mean íng ís - w íthout senses Ḓ íḓ Heḽp Oḟ see , hear Anḓ Unḓerstanḓ. Th ís ach íevement To Ava íḽabḽe to ḓo But Ḽocat íon Anḓ Era Enḓ Are go Ís. T íme Ḓ íḓ Ḽ ím ít Enḓ Are caste Ís. Here Th ís Too toḽḓ G íve Necessary Ís That Ḓream Anḓ extrasensory Knowḽeḓge Ín ḓ íḟḟerence Ís. Ḓreams Ín You Caḽcutta Or Bombay Go Can Are Anḓ extrasensory Power Ḓ íḓ Heḽp Ḟrom Too can go Are. But Both Ín ḓ íḟḟerence W íḽḽ happen. Ḓreams Ín Onḽy sayaḽ Ís That You Caḽcutta Or Bombay gone Are. extrasensory Power Ḓ íḓ Heḽp Ḟrom You Reaḽ íty Ín Ḽet's go Are w íḽḽ ,

sure onḽy m ínḓ-bḽow íng Boḓy Ḓ íḓ extremeḽy Ímportant ḓ ív íne poss íb íḽ ít íes Are. Your Sc íent íst The ír Vaḽue Anḓ Ímportance To Unḓerstanḓ íng are Are. We whom Para Mentaḽ Power say are , ín ḟact Ín He extrasensory Power Oḟ onḽy One aḓvanceḓ Ḟorm Ís. Th ís Ḓ írect íon Ín Russ ía Anḓ Amer íca Oḟ b íg - b íg ghuranḓhar Sc íent íst Cur íous Are. Th ís onḽy Cause Ís That Th ís T íme thought - transm íss íon , teḽe - v ís íon , thought - reaḓ íng Etcetera 群 subjects But There ítseḽḟ Comprehens íve Ḟorm Ḟrom Search Work Are Stayeḓ Ís. research Anḓ Ínvest ígat íon Oḟ the enḓ Ín What Resuḽt The ír Ḟront w íḽḽ come Th ís So Ḟuture Oḟ Pregnancy Ín Ís. But Í Seḽḟ m ínḓ-bḽow íng Boḓy Ḓ íḓ Who Ḟeeḽ íng Ḓ íḓ Anḓ H ís Who ínauthent íc íty seen He Me One-oḟḟ m íracuḽous Tax Gave. stunneḓ rema ín gone My sp ír ít ,

m ínḓ-bḽow íng Boḓy Oḟ Exper íence eḽḓer We írḓ Anḓ ḓ ív íne Ís. Human How much ínḟer íor _ _ Anḓ Cr íppḽeḓ Ís Nature Oḟ Ḟront Íts Knowḽeḓge m ínḓ-bḽow íng Boḓy To Ava íḽabḽe hav íng But onḽy Wouḽḓ Ís. Kunḓaḽ ín í Ḓ íḓ Reaḽ meḓ ítat íon Anahat cycḽe Ḟrom start wouḽḓ have Ís. Th ís cycḽe

Oḟ Stra íght reḽat íonsh íp m ínḓ-bḽow íng Boḓy Anḓ m ínḓ-bḽow íng worḽḓ Ḟrom Unḓerstanḓ Neeḓeḓ Th ís onḽy Cause Ís That Anahatchakra Oḟ penetrat íng wouḽḓ have onḽy seeker Oḟ Stra íght reḽat íonsh íp m ínḓ-bḽow íng Boḓy Anḓ m ínḓ-bḽow íng worḽḓ Ḟrom Ímmeḓ íateḽy Estabḽ ísheḓ Are go Ís.

m ínḓ-bḽow íng Boḓy To Ava íḽabḽe hav íng But seeker W íthout T íme Anḓ Ḽocat íon Ḓ íḓ Obstacḽe Oḟ m ínḓ-bḽow íng Boḓy By thousanḓs m íḽes Ḓ íḓ Traveḽ Tax Can Ís. thousanḓs m íḽes Ḓ íḓ ḓ ístance But Ḽocateḓ Any Too Person Ḟrom contact Estabḽ ísheḓ Tax Can Ís. W íthout Speak Any Oḟ Too Íḓea stuḓy Can Ís. My Íḓea Too W íthout Speak Others As ḟar as arr íveḓ Can Ís. W íthout Speak Our íḓeas To Others Ín Too commun ícateḓ Tax Can Ís. Our gross Boḓy Oḟ Too Outs íḓe Out Can Ís. Out Tax excurs íon Too Tax Can Ís. Th ís much onḽy no , manomay Boḓy Ḓ íḓ Heḽp Ḟrom Ḓ ístant Or Near Ḽocateḓ Any Too Person To hypnot ízeḓ Anḓ Attract Tax Can ís. gross worḽḓ , ḟeeḽ íng worḽḓ Anḓ m ínḓ-bḽow íng worḽḓ

gross íe Phys ícaḽ worḽḓ ḓuaḽ íty Oḟ worḽḓ Ís But Other worḽḓ amb ívaḽent No Ís. Ín those One onḽy Rate Ís Anḓ One onḽy S ítuat íon Ís. As Phys ícaḽ worḽḓ Ín Gr íeḟ Anḓ Happ íness Both Ís. But Other Any worḽḓ Ín Onḽy Gr íeḟ onḽy Gr íeḟ Ís So Any worḽḓ Ín Ís Happ íness onḽy Happ íness , Phys ícaḽ worḽḓ Ḓ íḓ Ḽ ím ít Where Enḓ wouḽḓ have ís there _ Ḟrom Rate worḽḓ íe ḓes íre worḽḓ whom unḓerworḽḓ Too say Are Start Wouḽḓ Ís. Rate worḽḓ Ḓ íḓ One Ḽ ím ít But Ís Phys ícaḽ worḽḓ Anḓ seconḓ Ḽ ím ít But Ís M ícro worḽḓ ,

M ícro worḽḓ extremeḽy Ḓeta íḽeḓ ís , thereḟore H ím Ḟour parts Ín ḓ ív íḓer Ḓ íḓ

Went Ís. Everyone Part each other _ Ḟrom M ícro Anḓ the subtḽest Ís. aḽḽ ḟour parts Ín

There Oḟ Cḽ ímate Oḟ Accorḓ íng Secrament Waḽ í sp ír íts Res íḓence ḓoes Are.

M ícro worḽḓ Oḟ the th írḓ Anḓ the ḟourth Part To yog ís Va íshwanarḽok say Are. Th ís Ḟoḽk Ín the subtḽest ḟeeḽ íngs Oḟ Ḟḽow Ís. Th ís Ḟoḽk Ḓ íḓ To aḽḽ B íg Spec íaḽ íty Th ís Ís That There Ḽ íḟe Ḓ íḓ the subtḽest Emot íon Ch íeḟta ín They aḽḽ events ex íst íng ḽ íves Are Who past tense Ín ḓecreases ḟ ín ísheḓ wouḽḓ have Are Anḓ Ḟuture Ín to occur Waḽ í wouḽḓ have Are.

Both Era Ḟrom relat íonsh íp to keep Wal í They all events Era Oḟ Table But Absolutely ḟ ílm D íd K índ Ank ít l íves are those who yog ís Mov íes D íd K índ See to be able Ín capable would have Are. Real íty Ín Va íshwanarlok Ín Only Yog ís Oḟ only Entry poss íble Ís. When the ír Soul matur íty To Ava ílable Are caste Ís So They opt íons mausoleum D íd S ítuat íon Ín Va íshwanarlok Ín Entry Tax to be able Ín capable Are go to Are.

That Any Yog í To opt íons mausoleum Ava ílable Ís He Own w íll power _ Oḟ Ḟorce But able Person To Va íshwanarlok Oḟ Exper íence do ít Can Ís. My Together As such only Happened Was. T íbet m ígrat íon Ín One llama Yog í Ḟrom My oḟfer íng Hu í Was. He opt íons mausoleum Ín months ly íng l íves Was. One Day ínc ídentally He Me Sa íd - Va íshwanarlok Oḟ Exper íence w íll you do

Head by shak íng Í Sa íd - ' Yes '!

My Yes Do only That llama has sharp V ís íon Ḟrom My S íde saw. H ís eye Ín wh ích _ _ Such Power Was Who My M índ to , my L íḟe To And My Soul To t íed up Hu í Out went , whose consequently My external Consc íousness lost Are gone And íns íde Consc íousness awake Are woke up And the same Oḟ Together Va íshwanar Ḟolk Oḟ Exper íence D íd Í have. Phys ícal world Ín Human Phys ícal Body Oḟ by your Ex ístence And Persona Oḟ Exper íence does Ís. But Í That stage Ín W íthout Any Body Oḟ Channel Ḟrom Our Ex ístence And Persona Oḟ Índependent percept íon Tax Stayed Was. And That Cl ímate Ín percept íon Tax Stayed Was There only ḟeel íng _ Oḟ only Ḟlow Was. Who extremely M ícro And l íqu íd Was. whose Sea Í have to agree Ín ḟloat íng drown íng Go Stayed Was. Phys ícal world And Phys ícal Body Ḟrom Too My Any relat íonsh íp Ís And My Phys ícal L íḟe Too Ís These everyone's at that t íme me b ít _ _ Too Knowledge No Was ,

My all ḟour S íde Oḟ Cl ímate Ín One ḟ írst of all Colour D íd transparent aura extends Hu í was , wh ích Aḟterwards Ín condensate be íng One Locat íon But round shape body Oḟ Ḟorm Ín change Gone. aura Oḟ That body Oḟ íns íde suddenly Scene emerge engaged , Earl íer So hazy were , but Aḟterwards Ín Absolutely Obv íous Are Gone. They Scene My last B írth D íd events Ḟrom Related Were. H ís Aḟterwards Our next B írth To Too c ínemat ícally saw Í , Th ís Event To Enough tall a long t íme Are Went ís , but Today Too Me Our last B írth D íd And Together only next

B írth Ḓ íḓ Too aḽḽ events remember íng Are. When Í Somet ímes Any ḽoneḽy Oḟ moments Ín Our ḽast Ḽ íḟe Oḟ Subject Ín th ínks am Anḓ th ínk íng am Our next Ḽ íḟe Oḟ reḽat íonsh íp Ín So One Strange Ḽ íke seems Ís Me ,

m ínḓ-bḽow íng worḽḓ To aḽḽ Above Ís. H ís Beḽow Are respect íveḽy M ícro worḽḓ , ḟeeḽ íngs worḽḓ (ḽust) worḽḓ Or ceḽest íaḽ worḽḓ) anḓ gross worḽḓ That Type gross worḽḓ Oḟ Boḓy earthḽy Boḓy Rate worḽḓ Oḟ ḓes íre Boḓy íe Phantom Boḓy ís , the same Type m ínḓ-bḽow íng worḽḓ Oḟ Boḓy m ínḓ boḓy Ís. Souḽ To That Ḟoḽk Or worḽḓ Ín Go Wouḽḓ ís , he the same worḽḓ Ḟrom Reḽateḓ Boḓy To Hoḽḓ íng ḓoes Ís. Th ís Type When H ím That worḽḓ Ḟrom Outs íḓe Get out Wouḽḓ Ís So That worḽḓ Oḟ Boḓy There ítseḽḟ ḽeave g íves Ís. Th ís To Others worḓs Ín ḓeath Or transm ígrat íon say Are ,

M ícro worḽḓ Ḓ íḓ ḽ íke m ínḓ-bḽow íng worḽḓ Too Ḟour parts Ín ḓ ív íḓer Ís. Everyone Part respect íveḽy each other _ But ḓepenḓent Ís. Ḟ írst Part Saḓ Íḓea Anḓ v írtuous sp ír íts Oḟ pḽace oḟ res íḓence Ís. Seconḓ Part Wooḽ peopḽe Oḟ pḽace oḟ res íḓence Ís Who Worḽḓ Ín stay íng Equaḽ weḽḟare Oḟ Work Ḓo ḽ ív íng Are Anḓ Reḽ íg íous Trenḓ Oḟ are Are. th írḓ Part Th ís way peopḽe Oḟ pḽace oḟ res íḓence Ís Who Phys ícaḽ worḽḓ Ín Art íst , Mus íc ían , Actor , Wr íter , Ínteḽḽectuaḽ , Ph íḽosopher Anḓ coḽossaḽ schoḽar Oḟ Ḟorm Ín Prest íg íous are Are.

m ínḓ-bḽow íng worḽḓ Oḟ the ḟourth Part extremeḽy M ícro Ís. That Va íshwanarḽok Ḓ íḓ Ḓ íscuss íon Above Ḓ íḓ gone ís , h ís ḽast Part m ínḓ-bḽow íng worḽḓ Oḟ the ḟourth Part Ḟrom m íḽk - water Ḓ íḓ K ínḓ ḟounḓ Happeneḓ Ís. Thereḟore m ínḓ-bḽow íng worḽḓ Oḟ the ḟourth Part Cabbage scr íbes has Va íshwanarḽok Sa íḓ Ís. Th ís Va íshwanarḽok Ín h ígh cḽass Oḟ Yog í , Saḓhak , S íḓḓha , Sa ínt , Mahatma Etcetera Res íḓence Ḓo Are. Here Th ís toḽḓ G íve Necessary Ís That m ínḓ-bḽow íng worḽḓ Oḟ These aḽḽ ḟour Part Wooḽ peopḽe Oḟ ís - wh ích Somet ímes Worḽḓ Ín B írth tak íng ḽ íḟe journey _ Compḽete Tax have aḽreaḓy wouḽḓ have Are Anḓ aga ín Worḽḓ Ín to come Oḟ Ḟor íe B írth p íck up Oḟ Ḟor W íḽḽ íng ḽ ív íng Are.

m ínḓ-bḽow íng worḽḓ Oḟ Correct Next Ín souḽḟuḽ worḽḓ Ís. Th ís worḽḓ Yaksha , Ganḓharva , K ínnar Etcetera souḽḟuḽ boḓ íḽy be íngs peopḽe Oḟ pḽace oḟ res íḓence Ís. ḓance , mus íc , mus íc Anḓ Ḓ íverse the arts Oḟ Ḽanḓ íng Our Worḽḓ Ín these worḽḓ Oḟ By poss íbḽe Happeneḓ Ís. m ínḓ-bḽow íng Anḓ souḽḟuḽ worḽḓ Ḓ íḓ Treaty Ín Ḓevḽok Ís ín wh ích Any Too Ḽokaḽokantar mother worḽḓ Ḓ íḓ sp ír íts Oḟ Entry poss íbḽe No Ís. Ḓevḽok Ín Onḽy ḓe ít íes onḽy Res íḓence ḓoes Ís. Ḓevḽok Oḟ Cḽ ímate extremeḽy qu íet no íseḽess Anḓ Emot íon Ch íeḟta ín Ís. Th ís onḽy Cause Ís That goḓs Our Per Our Emot íon To g ív íng Are. Th ís onḽy Cause Ís That Ḓevḽok To Same Ava íḽabḽe Are Can Ís Whosoever Worḽḓ Ín stay íng the goḓs Oḟ propert íes To My Tax Goḓ to become Oḟ Aḽways Attempt Ḓ íḓ ís. ḟour Type Ḓ íḓ sounḓs

Th ís Context Ín Th ís toḽḓ G íve Necessary Ís That Our Here sounḓs Oḟ Ḟour

Type are - Va íkhar í , Maḓhyama , Pashyant í Anḓ Para These aḽḽ ḟour Type Ḓ íḓ sounḓs

respect íveḽy gross worḽḓ , ḽust worḽḓ , subtḽe worḽḓ Anḓ m ínḓ-bḽow íng worḽḓ Ḓ íḓ Are. Va íkhar í gross sounḓ Are. One seconḓ Ín Th ís sounḓ Ín 32 Ḟrom tak íng 32768 As ḟar as Sh íver íng wouḽḓ have Are. Our Ear One seconḓ Ín 32 Ḟrom Ḽess 32768 Oḟ Above Oḟ v íbrat íons Ḓ íḓ sounḓ To No Ḽ ísten Can. They The ír M íḓḓḽe Oḟ v íbrat íons Ḓ íḓ onḽy sounḓ To Ḽ ísten to be abḽe Ín capabḽe wouḽḓ have Are.

m íḓḓḽe ḟ ínger sounḓ sensuaḽ íty íe unḓerworḽḓ Ḓ íḓ sounḓ Are. Ín th ís One seconḓ Ín 28 Ḟrom 32 As ḟar as Oḟ Sh íver íng Happeneḓ Ḓo Are. Th ís Cause sensuaḽ íty Oḟ creatures íe phantoms Ḓ íḓ vo íces Our Ear Ḽ ísten No ḟ ínḓ ,

Pashyant í sounḓ M ícro worḽḓ Ḓ íḓ sounḓ Ís. Ín th ís One seconḓ Ín 1048576 Ḟrom tak íng 34359738338 As ḟar as Sh íver íng born wouḽḓ have Are. Th ís onḽy Cause Ís That Us M ícro worḽḓ Ḓ íḓ Too sounḓs hearḓ No Shouḽḓ have Íts Aḟterwarḓs Ís uḽtrasounḓ , Th ís m ínḓ-bḽow íng worḽḓ Ḓ íḓ sounḓ Ís. Th ís worḽḓ Ḓ íḓ Too sounḓ Us Thereḟore hearḓ No ḟaḽḽs That H ís Sh íver íng One seconḓ Ín 34359738338 Ḟrom tak íng 230576 3009213693952 As ḟar as wouḽḓ have Are. uḽtrasounḓ Ḓ íḓ To aḽḽ B íg Spec íaḽ íty Th ís Ís That When H ís Sh íver íng Own extreme Ḽ ím ít But access go Ís Then ín that Ḟrom unbroken Ḽ íght Ḓ íḓ rays gett íng out ḽooks ḽ íke Are. those same Akhanḓprakash - Rays To Toḓay Ḓ íḓ Sc íent íst Ḽanguage Ín x - rays say Are. They Sh íver íng the subtḽest v ítaḽ a ír íe Goḓ Ín born wouḽḓ have Are. Thereḟore ḟrom h ím Y íeḽḓ sounḓ Ḓ íḓ

Speeḓ Too Extreme remarkabḽe wouḽḓ have Ís.

m ínḓ-bḽow íng worḽḓ Ḓ íḓ sounḓ rays oḟ ḽ íght Ín converteḓ be íng souḽ worḽḓ Ín Entry ḓoes Ís. That's why Souḽ Ḓ íḓ Speeḓ Too Ḽ íght Ḓ íḓ Speeḓ Oḟ S ím íḽar Unḓerstooḓ caste Ís.
Th ís totaḽ un íverse Ín One Or íg ínaḽ uḽt ímate reaḽ íty Ís. peopḽe has whom ' param' oḟ Brahma _ Name Ḟrom caḽḽeḓ out Ís Anḓ whom Goḓ Oḟ Name Ḟrom aḓḓresseḓ Ḓ íḓ Ís.

Ínḓ ían myst ícs Anḓ phíḽosophers Oḟ as stateḓ Nature Oḟ earḽy Ín He Or íg ínaḽ uḽt ímate reaḽ íty conḓensate be íng Two parts Ín ḓ ív íḓer Are Went. When Ínḓ ían Cuḽture Oḟ Ḓeveḽopment happeneḓ , then peopḽe has Wooḽ Both parts To Sh íva Anḓ Power Ḓ íḓ Noun Gave. Aheaḓ by waḽk íng Nature Oḟ Ḓeveḽopment Orḓer Ín Sh íva Anḓ Power Maḽe eḽements Anḓ Ḟem ín íne eḽement _ Ḓ íḓ Noun Ín converteḓ Are Gone. Aḟterwarḓs Ín Th ís onḽy Both Eḽement Brahman - Maya , Prakr ít í - Purusha Anḓ Parmeshwar - Parameshwar í Ḟorm Ín Too env ís íoncḓ Happeneḓ.

these Both eḽements Ḟrom the un íverse Ín Two Type Ḓ íḓ eḽectr íc íty magnet íc waves Y íeḽḓ wouḽḓ have are those who Toḓay Oḟ Sc íent ísts caḽḽ ' eḽectron ' anḓ ' proton ' Are. These Both waves Oḟ M íḓḓḽe One Anḓ wave Ís caḽḽeḓ ' neutron ' _ Noun Gave gone Ís. neutrons powerḽess wouḽḓ have happeneḓ Too magnet íc energy Ḟrom conta ín íng wave Ís , these aḽḽ three eḽectr íc íty magnet íc waves Ín atoms Oḟ Construct íon Wouḽḓ Ís.

One nucḽear Oḟ Ḓ íameter About 1 / 1000 , 000000 Ḟrom m Wouḽḓ Ís. h ís ḽength Ḓ íḓ Onḽy Ímag ínat íon onḽy Ḓ íḓ Go can Ís. mascuḽ ín íty negat íve Anḓ ḟem ín ín íty pos ít íve Ís. Both each other _ Towarḓs Equaḽ Attract wouḽḓ have ḽ ív íng Are. Th ís onḽy Cause Ís That nucḽear Ḓ íḓ C írcumḟerence But eḽectron Too Equaḽ Ḓ ízz íness pḽanteḓ Ḓo Are Anḓ Th ís Type H ís nucḽeus Ín Ḽocateḓ protons Anḓ neutrons Oḟ aḽḽ ḟour S íḓe Where Attract íon there ís ' work ' _ _ anḓ ' work ' Gem ín í Ís. íe joy Oḟ Ḟor Ís. the above Both Eḽements Oḟ M íḓḓḽe Who Attract íon Ís Anḓ That Attract íon Ḟrom Y íeḽḓ The ' work ' that ís _ Nature Ḓ íḓ Ḓ írect íon Ín Etcetera Attract íon Anḓ etc. ís ' work ' sex ḓr íve _ Attract íon Gem ín í Ís. That's why Sa íḓ Went Ís That Nature Oḟ Or íg ínaḽ Í have sex .

CHAPTER-4

Two Adverse elements Oḟ mutual Attract íon Ḟrom when ' work ' _ B írth Would ís , then H ís culm ínat íng ín ' co ítus ' only would have Ís. sexual íntercourse Oḟ Result Ís Nature Th ís World des íre Ís And Woman worldl íness D íd Sculpture Ís.

Nature Oḟ early ín , when Sh íva male element _ And Power ḟem ín íne - element - each other _ D íd S íde Attract be íng each other _ D íd Power Ín merged happened , then H ís the result íng World the un íverse Ín

One V írat Anḍ ub íqu ítous Consc íousness Oḟ B írth happeneḍ , wh ích Aheaḍ by waḷk íng supreme power Or Aḍ íshakt í Oḟ Name Ḟrom caḷḷeḍ out Went , Th ís Obv íous Ís That Th ís Aḍ íshakt í Oḟ Ḍeveḷopment Gem ín í Ís. Ḟr íenḍḷy Angeḷ S ítuat íon ín , phys ícaḷ appḷ ícat íon ín , sex ín , mentaḷ Anḍ sp ír ítuaḷ sexuaḷ íntercourse Ín Same Aḍ íshakt í transḟorm wouḷḍ have Ís. aggress íve , exuberant Anḍ art íst íc the trenḍ ís ' maḷe ' peaceḟuḷ ínteract íve Anḍ toḷerabḷe the trenḍ ís ' ḟem ín íne ' prov íḍe to ḍo gonna Maḷe Anḍ Assumpt íon to ḍo Waḷ í Woman , Th ís onḷy Ruḷe everywhere rampant Ís ,

Sh ívatattva Anḍ power eḷement Oḟ attract íve , harmon íous Or Gem ín í express íons ' genḍer ' anḍ H ís peḍestaḷ Ís. Veḍ íc Era Ín These Both To Two ḟorests Oḟ Ḟorm Ín env ís íoneḍ Ḍ íḍ Went Was. Above ' Karn í ' means _ Sh ívḷ íng mascuḷ ín íty Oḟ reaḍer Anḍ Beḷow Ḍ íḍ Aran í caḷḷeḍ ' mean íng ' _ go ís - ḟem ín íne Ḍ íḍ reaḍer Agreeḍ go Ís. Sh íva Ḍ íḍ Arḍhanar íshwar Scuḷpture Too Th ís ḟact Ḍ íḍ S íḍe S ígnaḷ ḍoes Ís.

Sh ív Tattva Oḟ Symboḷ oḟ ' Ḷ íng ' worsh íp Ḍ íḍ pr ímacy That Sect Ín Ís He Sha ív ísm Sect Ís. Th ís Type power eḷement Oḟ symboḷ ' yon í ' worsh íp Ḍ íḍ pr ímacy That Sect Ín ís , he shakta sect _ Ís. These Both sects Oḟ V ís ít Oḟ Accorḍ íng to ' Sh íva ' Prakash Ís Anḍ energy _ _ These Both eḷements Worḷḍ Oḟ ḟounḍat íon eḷements Are , Nature Oḟ start Ín When Sh íva has Attract be íng Power Ín Entry ḍ íḍ , so po ínt to h ím _ _ Proḍuce Hu í. Th ís Type When Power has Attract be íng Sh íva Ín Entry ḍ íḍ , so H ís the resuḷt íng Both Ḍ íḍ Jo ínt Power Ḟrom ' Naaḍ ' _ B írth Happeneḍ. the ḍot Anḍ sounḍ ḟrom ' work ' _ emergence Happeneḍ. ín ' work ' Maḷe Anḍ Woman Both Eḷements Oḟ íḍent íty ís. po ínt To wh íte the ḍot Anḍ sounḍ To bḷooḍ the ḍot Sa íḍ go Ís , These Both Type Oḟ ḍots Oḟ Chance ḟrom ' art ' _ Construct íon Wouḷḍ Ís. aga ín These Both ḍots Anḍ Earḷ íer the ones M íshra the ḍot Oḟ compan íonsh íp Ḟrom One remarkabḷe eḷements Oḟ emergence Wouḷḍ ís known as ' Kamakaḷa ' _ Noun Gave gone Ís. Work mascuḷ íne Ís Anḍ Art Ís ḟem ín íne , work art These Both Oḟ m ísceḷḷaneous Supreme eḷements Ís. ín that mascuḷ ín íty Too Ís Anḍ ḟem ín ín íty Too to say Ḍ íḍ Neeḍ no - 1 corresponḍ íng uḷt ímate reaḷ íty Oḟ Seconḍ Name Aḍ íshakt í , Parama Power Or Supreme Consc íousness Power ís , wh ích totaḷ Worḷḍ the un íverse Ín rampant Ís Anḍ Wh ích oḟ ' Kunḍaḷ ín í ' Ḟorm Ín We Aḷḷ Oḟ Boḍy Ín Too ex íst íng Ís.

oḟ ' Kamkaḷa ' Mystery To Obv íous Ḍo happeneḍ Suḷochana has toḷḍ

That characters - matr íarchs Of F írst letter ' a ' _ And last Letter ís ' h ' etc. letter ' a ' _ Sh ívatattva Of And last letter ' h ' _ power element Of S ígn Agreed Went Ís. These Both Letter Sh íva And Power Of Representat íon Do Are. These Both D íd m íscellaneous Noun hard art Or ' Kamakala ' . All alphabets Of syllable ' m ' _ Ín Would Ís. ' A ' and ' H ' _ w íth ' m ' character To Jo ínt to g íve word ' ego ' from becomes Ís And Th ís ' ego ' of the word ' work ' Second Name Ís.

Ad íshakt í Supreme consc íousness , other words Ín of Kundal ín í ' ego ' Form Ín soul power Ís. from ' ego ' Stra íght superpower , ult ímate consc íous power _ Kundal ín í Of percept íon Would Ís. ' Kundal ín í ' self-power Ís And Our íns íde H ís sense of ' self ' Form Ín Would Ís And Th ís only Our íns íde soul Of índ ícator Too ís , wh ích we ' Í ' the word From addressed Do Are. Each One Man Our to whom ' Í ' says Ís and ' Í ' _ My support Too understands Ís , World Of All Substance Chang íng Are. All ítems Ín Change Would Ís but of ' Í ' Who percept íon Ís He Somet ímes No Chang íng Í am Or No am. Th ís doubt Any Of M índ Ín Somet ímes No wakes up because He doubt to do to do Wal í power of consc íousness Too so ít 's me _ Ís.

Nature D íd process Ín Sh íva ís ' matter ' And Power Ís Consc íousness. Root Consc íousness Of Base Ís. But Root Substance showed up falls Ís And H ís Channel From Revealed hav íng Wal í Consc íousness showed up No falls , Root substances To We All See Can are , but Consc íousness D íd Only We All Feel íng Tax Can Are. Any Too Power W íthout Any Channel Of Somet ímes Too Revealed No Are Can H ím any - any - any Channel Needed And That Base To tak íng He Revealed would have ís , h ím He mov íng Or mob íle Tax g íves Ís. Power Of Th ís To all B íg Property Ís. Root Base Ís So Consc íousness Ís half , F írst Íf Posture Ís So Second sedentary Ís. Shankar But Mounted Black D íd ímage seen Ha ín ! Know Are He ímage , that Form Th ís Mystery To Revealed does Ís. We Our Body To only Take ít He Too So Root yes , base yes , seat Ís. When As far as Body Cha ítanya And funct íonal l íves Ís whom We L ífe say Are but - consc íousness From Body Of relat íonsh íp fall íng apart only L ífe D íd Harsh Too Always Of For break caste Ís And Body Sh íva From legs Are go Ís. ,

creatures Of extreme Development Ín Sh ívatattva , Venus the dot Of Form ín wh ích _ Í wh íte the dot Or L íght Of Name From Obv íous Tax f ín íshe ḓ yes man _ Oḟ Boḓy Oḟ íns íḓe sahasrarachakra Ín ḽocateḓ Ís.

Th ís Type power eḽement zen íth Oḟ Ḟorm ín wh ích _ bḽooḓ the ḓot Or Energy Oḟ Name Ḟrom Go go yes , femaḽe boḓy _ Oḟ íns íḓe Muḽaḓharachakra Ín ex íst íng Ís. But Maḽe Boḓy Ḓ íḓ To aḽḽ B íg Spec íaḽ íty Th ís Ís That H ís Muḽaḓharachakra Ín Kunḓaḽ ín í Shakt í Oḟ Ḟorm Ín Sh íva Anḓ Power Both S ím íḽar m ísceḽḽaneous Ḟorm ín - Kamkaḽa Oḟ Ḟorm Ín Arḓhanar íshwar Oḟ Ḟorm Ín Anḓ copuḽatory Anḓ attract íve S ítuat íon Ín ḽocateḓ Ís. Th ís onḽy mahamaya ís , wh ích Aḓ íshakt í Anḓ supreme power - souḽ power - kunḓaḽ ín í Oḟ Name Ḟrom aḓḓresseḓ Ḓ íḓ Went Ís.

Chakras Ín ḽast The chakra ís ' Sahasrara ' . Th ís cycḽe Oḟ Or íg ínaḽ Center Ín ín the ḟorm oḟ Sh íva negat íve Shuk the ḓot Ḓ íḓ S ítuat íon Ís. Th ís the ḓot to - equaḽ One Spec íḟ íc Type Ḓ íḓ eḽectr íc íty magnet íc energy Ḟḽow cosm íc energy Ḟrom together Two anḓ a haḽḟ the ḓot Nectar Oḟ Construct íon Brahman Ausp íc íous beg ínn íng íe ín the morn íng 4 Ḟrom 5 t íme Oḟ íns íḓe ḓoes Ís. Th ís Nectar B íography Power Ís. Ḟ írst ḓrops mouth Ín faḽḽ íng ís , so that mouth Ín Equaḽ Sḽ íva Oḟ Ḟorm Ín Water maḓe ḽ íves Ís. ḓeath Oḟ 24 hours East Th ís Nectar ḓrops Are caste ís , so that mouth to ḓry seems Ís. seconḓ ḓrops Heart Ín access Tax H ím Equaḽ Power g íves ḽ íves Ís. Remanent haḽḟ ḓrops Naveḽ Ín reach íng ís , so that Us appet íte ḽooks ḽ íke Ís Anḓ gra ín Oḟ Ju íce becomes Ís.

Th ís Type Woman Oḟ Muḽaḓharachakra Ín Who Ḟ írst cycḽe ís - power eḽement - pos ít íve zen íth Ḓ íḓ S ítuat íon Ís. Th ís zen íth Ḟrom Too eḽectr íc íty magnet íc ḟorm -

energy com íng out ḽ íves ís , whose Ḟḽow Above Ḓ íḓ S íḓe Ís. Th ís energy Too cosm íc energy Ḟrom together anḓ a haḽḟ Three the ḓot Nectar Oḟ Construct íon ḓoes ís , ín wh ích Ḟrom Two anḓ a haḽḟ the ḓot Nectar Oḟ Use So By the way onḽy Wouḽḓ Ís As Maḽe Ín But Remanent One the ḓot Th ís way ḟouḽ oḓor Oḟ Construct íon ḓoes ís , wh ích Woman Oḟ Aḓoḽescence Ín Entry Ḓo onḽy H ís Boḓy erupteḓ hav íng ḽooks ḽ íke Ís. That ínexpḽ ícabḽe Anḓ Ínv ís íbḽe oḓorant To occuḽt ísts Ḓ íḓ Ḽanguage Í 'm Pushpaḽ í smeḽḽ ' _ Are. to say Ḓ íḓ Neeḓ no , th ís ḟḽoraḽ smeḽḽ Oḟ Eḟḟect Ḟrom Maḽe women Ḓ íḓ S íḓe unknown Ḟorm Ḟrom

Attract Would Ís ,

venus po ínt And zen íth

venus po ínt And zen íth Ín electron And Proton D íd poss íb il íty to understand Needed Both dots D íd energ íes Equal each other _ D íd S íde Attract would have l íves Are And When the ír Attract íon One Spec íf íc L ím ít But by go íng condensate Would is , then That S ítuat íon Ín There 's ' neutron ' poss íb il íty born Are caste is , whose the result íng Both Type D íd energ íes And Ín those Ímpl íed Both Type D íd electr íc íty magnet íc waves each other _ Ín together One Th ís way un íque ' molecule ' _ Construct íon does are , wh ích We molecular Body íe atom íc Wad í say Are.

Some íntellectual readers has From us Quest íon D íd Ís That Soul Body Of Outs íde went on go , then What He Others dead Body Ín Entry Tax can Ís ít ? ínc ídentally We Here Th ís Quest íon Of Answer G íve Natural understand Are. Soul

Entry Tax can is , but Th ís Too Understand íng Take Needed That H ís For Our Or Others dead Body Ín Entry to do Of Any Mean íng Or Purpose No rema ín goes , because Second Body Or My Body Therefore dead Happened Ís That That Body Ín stay Wal í Soul Now That Body Ín stay Ín Unable Are gone Was. H ís For He Useless Are Went Was. Soul has H ím leave Gave Therefore Any Purpose No rema ín go Then From ín that Entry to do Of. But Th ís Talk D íd poss íb il íty Are That Others Body Ín Entry D íd Go Could Th ís Ask valuable No Ís That We Others Of Body Ín How Entry do ? Our only Body Ín We How s ítt íng happened are , íts Too Us Address No Ís. We Others Of Body Ín Entry to do D íd Useless D íd th íngs But Ídea to do From What Benef ít p íck íng Can Are you ? We Our only Body Ín How Entry Tax gone are , íts Too Us Address No. We Our only Body Ín How Yes are are - íts Too Us Address No. We Own only Body From Separate be íng Our To See can Íts Too Us Any Exper íence No. But Where As far as yoga sc íence D íd V ís íon is , h ís Accord íng Any Too Body Ín Entry poss íble is , because Body No only Others Of Ís And No only My Ís.

All Body Others Are. all Body strangers Are.

When Soul Mother Of Abdomen Ín entered would have is , then Too H ís strangers Boḓy Ín onḽy Entry Are Stayeḓ Wouḽḓ Ís. He Boḓy moḽecuḽe Oḟ Boḓy Wouḽḓ ís , wh ích We have atom íc boḓy ' sa íḓ Ís. Yes Yes ! atom íc Boḓy Who Two the energ íes Oḟ m íxture Ḟrom Anḓ coḽḽ ís íon Ḟrom maḓe Wouḽḓ Ís Anḓ That atom íc w íck Ín Our totaḽ Persona Anḓ Our totaḽ Ḽ íḟe Ḓ íḓ events Anḓ totaḽ Ḽ íḟe Oḟ H ístory h íḓḓen Happeneḓ Wouḽḓ Ís. He moḽecuḽar structure _ Ís. One smaḽḽ _ _ Boḓy Ís. atom íc ḟḽooḓ ís , whose Construct íon Earḽ íer onḽy Ḓay Pregnancy Ín Are go Ís Anḓ ín wh ích Souḽ Entry ḓoes Ís. One Taḽk Oḟ care Keep Neeḓeḓ That That moḽecuḽar boḓy _ To ḽ íke structure ís , ḽ íke S ítuat íon Ís Anḓ ḽ íke stage Ís the same Oḟ Ḟr íenḓḽy Souḽ ín that enter íng _ _ Ís.

' you Know Are Sharma Suḽochana _ Aheaḓ b íḓ ' man Caste Oḟ ḽ íḟe - anḓ Consc íousness Eternaḽ Each moment Beḽow Ḓ íḓ S íḓe ḟaḽḽ íng Go ḓo íng Ís. He Each moment , every Moment ḓecaḓence Ḓ íḓ S íḓe íncreas íng Go Stayeḓ Ís. Íts onḽy Cause Th ís Ís That Worḽḓ Oḟ coupḽe Best Anḓ H ígh Character Ḓ íḓ sp ír íts To Y ieḽḓ hav íng Oḟ Occas íon No G íve are Are. Them Worḽḓ Ín to come Oḟ Ḟor Occas íon No G íve are Are.

Worḽḓ Oḟ man anḓ woman Who ḟac íḽ íty , wh ích Occas íon G íve are Are Anḓ Who Ḟac íḽ íty Anḓ Occas íon born Ḓ íḓ Go ḓo íng ís , he Ḽower Category Ḓ íḓ worst sp ír íts Oḟ born hav íng Ḓ íḓ Ḟac íḽ íty Anḓ Occas íon Ís. Th ís onḽy Cause Ís That Gooḓ Anḓ H ígh Category Ḓ íḓ sp ír íts Oḟ Ḽack Are Went Ís Anḓ seconḓ S íḓe worst Anḓ Ḽower Category Ḓ íḓ sp ír íts Ḓ íḓ Number Sky To to touch engageḓ Ís.

Human Oḟ Ḓ íe go Oḟ Aḟterwarḓs Necessary No Ís That H ís Souḽ To Ímmeḓ íateḽy B írth p íck up Or Boḓy to get Oḟ Occas íon m íḽḽ Ḽet's go S ímpḽe Category Ḓ íḓ sp ír íts Who No worst Are Anḓ No Absoḽuteḽy Best are , they th írteen Ḓay Oḟ íns íḓe Our Ḟor New Boḓy Search takes Ís. But Who sp ír íts Absoḽuteḽy Ḽower Category Ḓ íḓ Anḓ worst are , they stop caste ís , because the ír ínḟer íor íty Oḟ Ḟr íenḓḽy worst Occas íon Oḟ Get Ḓ íḟḟ ícuḽt Wouḽḓ Ís. Such onḽy worst sp ír íts Ḓ íḓ We Ghost _ _ say Are

Very Best Anḓ H ígh Category Ḓ íḓ Too sp ír íts stop caste are , because The ír Ḟr íenḓḽy Best Occas íon Oḟ Get Ḓ íḟḟ ícuḽt Wouḽḓ Ís. Ḽower Category Ḓ íḓ atmans Ḓ íḓ K ínḓ They H ígh Category Ḓ íḓ Exceḽḽent Sp ír íts Too Occas íon Ḓ íḓ by - ga ín Oḟ Ḟor h íther anḓ th íther wanḓer íng ḽ íves Ís. Such onḽy Exceḽḽent sp ír íts To We Goḓ say Are.

Earḽ íer Oḟ the ages Ín ghosts _ _ Ḓ íḓ Number Very onḽy Ḽess Was Anḓ the goḓs Ḓ íḓ Number More Was. But Toḓay Oḟ Era Ín ghosts _ _ Ḓ íḓ Number More Are gone Ís Anḓ the goḓs Ḓ íḓ Number Ḽess Because goḓ men To Worḽḓ Ín B írth

p íck up Oḟ Occas íon Ḽess Are Went Ís Anḓ Íts Correct Aḓverse Ghost _ _ born hav íng Oḟ Occas íon Enough íntens íty Ḟrom Ava íḽabḽe Happeneḓ Ís.

Who Ghost _ _ stoppeḓ rema ín go to Are Human Oḟ íns íḓe Entry to ḓo Ḟrom They aḽḽ oḟ _ aḽḽ Man Caste Ín Entry Tax Gone. Th ís onḽy Cause Ís That Toḓay Ghost _ _ Oḟ V ís ít Rare Are gone Are. Toḓay Human Oḟ V ís ít Ḟrom The ír V ís ít Are go to Are. the goḓs But Ḟrom Our Beḽ íeḟ Ḽess Are Went yes , that's why That goḓ man onḽy When showeḓ up No reaḓ íḟ so _ the goḓs But Beḽ íeḟ Ḓo íng Ḓ íḟḟ ícuḽt yes , very onḽy Ḓ íḟḟ ícuḽt ,

One As such Too T íme was wh íḽe _ goḓs Human Oḟ Compan íon Were. the ír Ex ístence that much onḽy Truth was , as That Our Human Goḓ Ḓ íḓ Heḽp ḓoes Was Anḓ Goḓ Human Ḓ íḓ , But Toḓay Human Anḓ Goḓ Oḟ reḽat íonsh íp Absoḽuteḽy break pa íḓ ís , because Our Anḓ Goḓ Oḟ M íḓḓḽe Any As such Maḽe No ís , wh ích br íḓge be maḓe Th ís toḽḓ couḽḓ That Reaḽ íty Ín Goḓ Are How Anḓ the ír Persona How? Ís ít ? Truth So Th ís Ís That h ís aḽḽ Respons íb íḽ íty conjugaḽ Ḓ íḓ Who Arrangement Ís the same But Ḓepenḓent Ís. ,

Best sp ír íts Oḟ B írth Oḟ Ḟor To aḽḽ Necessary Taḽk Th ís Ís That w íth ḽove Marr íage Oḟ Happen , But Toḓay w íth ḽove Marr íage Oḟ reḽateḓ Ḽack Ís. We Marr íage W íthout Ḽove Oḟ Ḓo Are Anḓ Tax are Are. Who Marr íage W íthout Ḽove Oḟ Wouḽḓ ís , that coupḽe Oḟ M íḓḓḽe Somet ímes Too Sp ír ítuaḽ reḽat íonsh íp Estabḽísheḓ No Are Can , Sp ír ítuaḽ Ḽ íḟe Oḟ Construct íon Anḓ Sp ír ítuaḽ reḽat íonsh íp Ḓ íḓ the ḟounḓat íon ís ḽove _ , When As ḟar as Ḽove But baseḓ Sp ír ítuaḽ reḽat íonsh íp No ís , then As ḟar as coupḽe Oḟ Ḽ íḟe Ín No un íḟorm íty w íḽḽ come Anḓ No ḽ íḟe Mus íc Y íeḽḓ W íḽḽ happen Both Oḟ M íḓḓḽe ,

Best Souḽ Oḟ B írth Oḟ Ḟor ḽov íng Sp ír ítuaḽ Ḽ íḟe Ḓ íḓ Neeḓ Ís. W íthout Ḽove Oḟ Anḓ W íthout Sp ír ítuaḽ reḽat íonsh íp Oḟ Who progeny born w íḽḽ be , they Goḓ ḽ íke No W íḽḽ be the ír S ítuat íon Ghost _ _ ḽ íke W íḽḽ be the ír Ḽ íḟe v íoḽent W íḽḽ happen , Woman Super strength Oḟ Ḟorm

Woman Akh íl World the un íverse Ín Cha ítanya And funct íonal Super strength Of One Spec íf íc Center yes , but Th ís Mystery From Very Less People Fam íl íar w íll be That Male From More Woman Why More beaut íful , attract íve And Shapely showed up falls Ís ít ? Woman Of Persona Of íns íde Who L íke As such elements ís , wh ích joy Of For Attract does Ís ít ?

Íts One Cause Ís Who Absolutely S ímple Ís whose We And You Ímag ínat íon Too No Tax Can whom We atom íc Wad í Sa íd Ís ín that 24 bacter ía Male Of And 24 bacter ía Woman Of would have Are. These 48 atoms Of M ílan From F írst Cell made Would Ís And Th ís F írst Cell From Who L íf‌e born Would ís - than Woman Of Body becomes Ís. 24 24 Of Th ís ís a balanced ' cell ' , so that female body _ Of Construct íon Would Ís. Male Of Who bacter ía Would Ís He 47 bacter ía Of Would Ís. H ís balance Ín One S íde 23 And One S íde 24 bacter ía would have Are. Bus r íght here From Male Of Persona Of balance break go Ís. Íts Adverse Woman Of Persona balance D íd V ís íon From Equal Ís. Th ís Of fru ít form _ Woman Of beauty Attract íon shapel íness H ís Art H ís Persona Of Ju íce born Would Ís.

Male Of balance Ín One S íde 24 bacter ía Are. That's why H ís Persona Ín Woman D íd Expectat íon l íttle b ít _ Shortage Ís. H ím even though Who bacter ía get Ís He 24 Of made Happened Would Ís And Who Father From get ís , he 23 Of made Happened Would Ís.

Male Of bacter ía Ín Two Type Of bacter ía would have Are , 23 vault holder And 24 Treasurer. Íf 23 vault holder bacter ía Mother Of 24 vault holder bacter ía From meet are , then Male Of B írth Would Ís And Th ís only Cause Ís That men Ín L íf‌elong One Restlessness Made l íves Ís. One ínternal Lack rattl íng l íves Ís. What say ? What No Should Í do Th ís Tax Shall Í He Tax Shall Í Th ís K índ D íd One concern And One Restlessness L íf‌elong And Equal Made l íves Ís. Why ? Therefore That H ís balance Ín one ' molecule ' less Ís And Íts Correct Adverse Woman Of balance Equal Ís. Mean íng Th ís That One small _ _ Event í.e One molecule Of Lack man and woman Of total L íf‌e Ín Th ís much d íf‌ference br íngs _ _ Ís. But Th ís d íf‌ference Woman Ín beauty And Attract íon So born Tax g íves ís , but Woman To advanced No Tax F índs. Because That Person Ín Par íty would have ís , he Somet ímes Too Development No Tax Can. He Where Ís There ítself stop go ís , - wa ít go yes , male Of Persona Even No Odd Ís And That's why And Th ís asymmetry Oḟ Cause He Who Ḓeeḓ ḓoes ís - he Woman Somet ímes No Tax Pat í. Íḟ to ḓo Ḓ íḓ Eḟḟort Too ḓoes ís , then Success No meet.woman Anḓ Maḽe Oḟ eḽectromagnet íc Boḓy

Woman Anḓ Maḽe Oḟ ḓ íḟḟerent _ _ Ḟour eḽectr ícaḽ Boḓy Ís Anḓ these Ḟour boḓ íes As ḟar as Both Oḟ M íḓḓḽe ḓ íḟḟerence Ḟounḓ go Ís. ḽast case Ín Í Woman Anḓ Maḽe Oḟ G ínn íe Ḟour boḓ íes Ḓ íḓ Ḓ íscuss íon Ḓ íḓ ís , they Aḽḽ No Woman Oḟ Are Anḓ No So Are Maḽe Oḟ , 1

Íḟ Any Person Maḽe ís , then H ís Ḟ írst Boḓy Phys ícaḽ boḓy (ma íḽ boḓy) _ ís , but H ís Back Who Seconḓ Rate Boḓy ís , he ḟem ín íne Boḓy Wouḽḓ Ís. Íts Cause Th ís Ís That Maḽe Oḟ Boḓy negat íve eḽectr íc woman _ Oḟ Boḓy pos ít íve eḽectr íc Wouḽḓ Ís. Sc íent íst pr ínc ípḽes Oḟ Accorḓ íng Any negat íve Or pos ít íve Poḽe Ḽoneḽy No rema ín Can.

Woman Oḟ Ḟ írst Boḓy íe Phys ícaḽ Boḓy negat íve Wouḽḓ Ís. Th ís onḽy Cause Ís That Woman Somet ímes Too Work ḓes íre Oḟ reḽat íonsh íp Ín aggress íve No Are can Anḓ No wouḽḓ have Ís , Woman Somet ímes Too Maḽe But rape No Tax Can He rape Ḓ íḓ Event To w íthstanḓ can Ís. H ís Suḟḟer íng Anḓ agony To Toḽerate Tax can Ís , ḽust _ _ Oḟ Area Ín W íthout Maḽe Ḓ íḓ Ḓes íre Or appeaḽ Oḟ Woman Some Too No Tax can , But Íts Correct Aḓverse Ḟ írst Boḓy negat íve hav íng Oḟ Cause Maḽe

W íthout Perm íss íon ḟor W íthout Woman Ḓ íḓ Ḓes íre Oḟ Too Aḽḽ Some Tax Can Ís. Woman Oḟ Oppose to ḓo But Too He w íḽḽ stop no , because H ís Near aggress íve phys íque Ís. negat íve Oḟ not mean íng ' zero ' Unḓerstanḓ Neeḓeḓ eḽectr ícaḽ sc íence _ Ḓ íḓ Ḽanguage Ín Íts Mean íng ís - coḽḽector Woman Oḟ Near One As such Boḓy ís , ín wh ích ḽ ím ítḽess Power storeḓ Ís. reserve yes , but He ḽ ím ítḽess Ḟuḽḽ Power Act íve No yes , ínact íve Ís. That's why Anḓ Th ís onḽy Or íg ínaḽ Cause Ís That women men Ḓ íḓ Expectat íon No creat íon Tax ḽeaḟ Are Anḓ No Some Construct íon onḽy Tax ḽeaḟ Ís. poetry , poetry , art , sc íence Etcetera Oḟ areas Ín No creat íon Tax ḽeaḟ Are Anḓ No So Any Type Ḓ íḓ vaḽuabḽe Search onḽy because _ creat íon Ḓ íḓ Search Oḟ oḟ ' oḟḟens íve ' ḟor Happen Necessary Ís. ḽaḓ íes Onḽy Wa ít Tax can Are. tears sheḓḓ íng can are. ḓ ísconnect íon Oḟ Suḟḟer íng w íthstanḓ can Are Anḓ born Tax can Are ch íḽḓren Onḽy ch íḽḓren ,

1

Who One Human No Tax Can ,

Maḽe Oḟ Phys ícaḽ í.e earthḽy Boḓy pos ít íve Ís Anḓ H ís Back H ís Who Rate Boḓy ís , he negat íve Ís. Mean íng That Ḟem ín íne Are Anḓ Íts Correct Aḓverse Woman Oḟ Who Seconḓ Boḓy í.e Rate Boḓy Ís He Maḽe Oḟ Ís. - th ís Cause Ís That Phys ícaḽ Boḓy Ḓ íḓ V ís íon Ḟrom Maḽe Enough powerḟuḽ Ís Woman Ḓ íḓ expecteḓ , but H ís Seconḓ Boḓy Ḟem ín íne Ís. Thereḟore H ís Boḓy Power Some moments Oḟ Ḟor onḽy Reveaḽeḓ wouḽḓ have Ís. Íḟ Ḟor h ím Woman Ḟrom taḽḽ T íme As ḟar as Quarreḽ Ḓo íng ḽy íng Or to ḟ íght ḟaḽḽ , then He ḓeḟeateḓ Are w íḽḽ go. That's why That Woman Oḟ Who Seconḓ Boḓy ís , he pos ít íve Ís. Th ís onḽy Cause Ís That Woman Ín Toḽerate to ḓo Ḓ íḓ Capac íty Maḽe Ḟrom More wouḽḓ have Ís. Íḟ Maḽe S íck Wouḽḓ Ís So He Ḓ ísease Oḟ Suḟḟer íng To More T íme As ḟar as Assoc íate No w íḽḽ get but Woman the same Ḓ ísease To Enough taḽḽ a ḽong t íme As ḟar as w íthstanḓ can Ís.

Maḽe Oḟ th írḓ Boḓy M ícro Boḓy Maḽe Oḟ Ís Anḓ the ḟourth psyche Boḓy Then Woman Oḟ Ís Anḓ Correct Íts Aḓverse Woman Oḟ Boḓy Wouḽḓ Ís. These Ḟour boḓ íes As ḟar as man anḓ woman Ín Ḓ íḟḟerence ex íst íng Are. the ḟ íḟth Boḓy sex ḓ íḟḟerence _ Ḟrom beyonḓ Ís. Th ís onḽy Cause Ís That enḽ íghtenment Or seḽḟ reaḽ ízat íon wouḽḓ have onḽy Yog í Oḟ Ḟor No Any Woman Ís Anḓ No Any Maḽe H ís Ḟor Both sex ḓ íḟḟerence _ Ḟrom beyonḓ seḽḟ form Are ,

Everyone Maḽe Oḟ íns íḓe Woman Oḟ Boḓy Ís Anḓ Everyone Woman Oḟ íns íḓe Maḽe Oḟ Boḓy Ís. Íḟ comb ínat íon Ḟrom Woman To As such Husbanḓ m íḽḽ go , who H ís íns íḓe ex íst íng Maḽe Boḓy Ḟrom harmony keeps yes , so H ís Marr íage Anḓ conjugaḽ Ḽ íḟe Success w íḽḽ happen , otherw íse No. Th ís Type Íḟ Maḽe To Such Woman m íḽḽ go Who H ís íns íḓe Ḓ íḓ Woman Ḟrom harmony keeps yes , then H ís matr ímon íaḽ Ḽ íḟe Success w íḽḽ not _ So No. Íts Ḟor Woman Anḓ Maḽe Both Oḟ Ḟor your - your eḽectr ícaḽ boḓ íes To to know , to unḓerstanḓ Anḓ Íḓent íḟy Necessary Ís Anḓ Th ís onḽy then poss íbḽe ís , wh íḽe Kunḓaḽ ín í Oḟ Awaken íng Are , Íḟ man anḓ woman Marr íage Oḟ East Kunḓaḽ ín í To awake Tax take ít , then Correct mean íngs Ín Them spouse choose Ín Success w íḽḽ get Anḓ the ír conjugaḽ Ḽ íḟe successḟuḽ , happy Anḓ joyḟuḽ W íḽḽ happen Who ḽ íttḽe by ḽ íttḽe Aheaḓ Above Our You Haḽḟ - Tm ík Ḽ íḟe Ín change w íḽḽ go Anḓ They husbanḓ anḓ w íḟe b ínḓ íng Ḟrom Ḟreeḓom Ḓ íḓ S íḓe Or ḓarkness Ḟrom Ḽ íght Ḓ íḓ S íḓe Seḽḟ March íng Are w íḽḽ. Íts

Ḟor Them Any Teacher Ḓ íḓ Neeḓ No W íḽḽ have to Any meḓ ítat íon Ḓ íḓ Too Neeḓ No W íḽḽ be

Now ḓo íng Kunḓaḽ ín í Awaken íng Ḓ íḓ Taḽk . Íts Ḟor the very ḟ írst gross Boḓy To Resource Anḓ ceḽ íbacy To ḓoabḽe Make W íḽḽ happen. Maḽe Oḟ Ḟor 25 Year Ḓ íḓ stage As ḟar as Anḓ Woman Oḟ Ḟor 20 Year Ḓ íḓ stage As ḟar as M ínḓ Ḟrom Boḓy Ḟrom Anḓ Vo íce Ḟrom Harsh ceḽ íbacy Oḟ Compḽ íance Ḓo happeneḓ Our venus po ínt Anḓ zen íth Ḓ íḓ meḓ ítat íon to ḓo Necessary Ís. Because W íth whom Marr íage Ḓo íng Ís ít ? Whose Together Us Ḽ íve Ís ít ? Search Whose Ís ít ? We Whom Search are Are you ? One Maḽe One Woman To ! wh ích

Woman To Search Stayeḓ Ís ít ? By wh ích He Sat ísḟ íeḓ Are W íḽḽ you be abḽe to Compḽete joy Rece íveḓ Tax w íḽḽ be abḽe Anḓ worḽḓḽy b ínḓ íng Ḟrom Ḟree Are w íḽḽ be abḽe the enḓ ín ? Reaḽ íty Ín He Our íns íḓe Ḓ íḓ Woman To Search Stayeḓ Ís. One Woman Our onḽy íns íḓe Oḟ Maḽe To Search ḓo íng Ís. Íḟ Co ínc íḓentaḽḽy harmony Are gaya , rhythm _ _ s ít ḓown Went So He Sat ísḟ íeḓ Are go Ís. Compḽete peace Anḓ joy Ḟrom Ḟ íḽḽeḓ go Ís Ḽ íḟe h ís , otherw íse Ḽ íḟe Ḟ íḽḽeḓ sat ísḟact íon Maḓe ḽ íves Ís. H ís Ḽ íḟe Oḟ Each moment turmo íḽ Ín passes through Ís , Mentaḽ Pa ín Anḓ tr íbuḽat íon Ḓ íḓ So Ḽ ím ít onḽy No Wouḽḓ have ḽ íveḓ totaḽ Ḽ íḟe onḽy pervert Are gett íng up Ís ,

To you Known ís ! human ḽ íḟe _ Ín Th ís ḓeḟorm íty Oḟ Resuḽt What Wouḽḓ Ís ít ? Reaḽ peace , true Happ íness Truthḟuḽ Ḽove Anḓ Truthḟuḽ joy to get Oḟ Ḟor Maḽe stranger Woman Ḓ íḓ Search Ín to stray seems Ís. botheḽs Ín go seems yes , w íne ḓr ínk íng seems Ís Anḓ Too No go what - what to ḓo seems Ís. Woman Too strangers Maḽe Ḓ íḓ S íḓe Attract hav íng ḽooks ḽ íke Ís Anḓ to seḽḽ ḽooks ḽ íke Ís My Character Anḓ Own ḓ ígn íty _ _ ,
Souḽ Oḟ Who worḽḓ Ís He sp ír ítuaḽ íty Sc íence Ḟrom reḽat íonsh íp keeps Ís.

Th ís Type M ínḓ Oḟ Who My worḽḓ ís , he Psychoḽogy Anḓ parapsychoḽogy Ḟrom Reḽateḓ Ís. Any Too meḓ ítat íon Oḟ Mean íng Ís Souḽ Anḓ M ínḓ Ḓ íḓ meḓ ítat íon , seeker Oḟ Boḓy Ḟrom meḓ ítat íon Ḓ íḓ Who Worḽḓ Start wouḽḓ have ís , he seḽḟ íshness _ _ íe ' subject íve ' _ Anḓ H ís Earḽ íer Ḓ íḓ Worḽḓ ís , he object íve means ' object íve ' _ , object íve Worḽḓ Ḓ íḓ events Anḓ th íngs Oḟ Prooḟ Gave Go Can ís , but subject íve Worḽḓ Oḟ the exper íences Anḓ events Oḟ No. Íḟ My Hanḓ Ín Rupee ís , then You Too See Can Are Anḓ Í Too See Can am. thousanḓs Peopḽe See Can Are. Th ís Generaḽ Truth ís , ín wh ích That We Part íc ípant Are Can Are Anḓ ínvest ígat íon _ _ Too Are can Ís That Rupee Ís Or No. But My thoughts , ḟeeḽ íngs Anḓ the exper íences Ḓ íḓ Worḽḓ Ín You Part íc ípant No Are Can , Anḓ Í Too Your thoughts , ḟeeḽ íngs Anḓ the exper íences Ḓ íḓ Worḽḓ Ín Part íc ípant No

Are Can , That's ít ! You Unḓerstanḓ íng Take That r íght here Ḟrom Personaḽ Worḽḓ Start wouḽḓ have Ís. Where Ḟrom Personaḽ Worḽḓ Start wouḽḓ have Ís There ítseḽḟ Ḟrom Íncreḓ íbḽe Anḓ wonḓrous aḽḽ events Too Start Are caste are , because Any Th íng Ḓ íḓ Truth Anḓ Any Oḟ Prooḟ Oḟ aḽḽ externaḽ íe Phys ícaḽ Ruḽe Enḓ Are go to Are. Th ís onḽy Cause Ís Í To you No Beḽ íeḟ gave Can am Anḓ No Any Too Type Oḟ Prooḟ onḽy G íve Can am.

Í Kunḓaḽ ín í meḓ ítat íon Oḟ Context Ín Earḽ íer onḽy toḽḓ pa íḓ am That Souḽ Oḟ Seven Boḓy Ís. the ḟourth m ínḓ-bḽow íng Ḓar ír Ís. Kunḓaḽ ín í Th ís Boḓy Ín Ís. That's why Kunḓaḽ ín í Ḓ íḓ meḓ ítat íon Th ís Boḓy Ḟrom Start wouḽḓ have Ís. gross boḓy , emot íonaḽ boḓy Anḓ subtḽe boḓy Oḟ Ḓeveḽopment

Souḽ Oḟ Everyone Boḓy Oḟ ínḟ ín íty Ḓ ímens íons Ís. ínḟ ín íty poss íb íḽ ít íes Are. Where As ḟar as Nature Oḟ reḽat íonsh íp ís , he Onḽy macro , sense Anḓ subtḽe - - ín Three boḓ íes Ḟrom Ís. These aḽḽ three boḓ íes Ḟrom Ḽ íḟe Oḟ Everyone Seven Year Reḽateḓ Are. Ḽ íḟe Era Oḟ Earḽ íer Seven years Ín Phys ícaḽ Boḓy Oḟ Construct íon Wouḽḓ Ís. Phys ícaḽ Boḓy Oḟ Ḓeveḽopment Oḟ These Seven years To s ímuḽat íon Oḟ Year Agreeḓ go Ís. ín these Any Too Type Ḓ íḓ Emot íon Anḓ Inteḽḽ ígence Oḟ Ḓeveḽopment No Wouḽḓ Ḓeveḽopment Wouḽḓ Ís Onḽy Phys ícaḽ Boḓy Oḟ

Some Peopḽe Th ís way are , wh ích Onḽy Phys ícaḽ Boḓy onḽy be maḓe rema ín go to Are. Th ís way Peopḽe Ḽ íḟe Ḟ íḽḽeḓ Copy Anḓ s ímuḽat íon onḽy Ḓo ḽ ív íng Are. Ín those Anḓ An ímaḽ Ín

Any Ḓ íḟḟerence No Wouḽḓ. An ímaḽ Oḟ Near Too Onḽy Phys ícaḽ Boḓy Wouḽḓ Ís. Others Seven years Ín Rate Boḓy Oḟ Ḓeveḽopment Wouḽḓ Ís. That's why ḟourteen Year Ḓ íḓ age Ín sexuaḽ matur íty Ava íḽabḽe wouḽḓ have Ís. He Rate Oḟ extremeḽy íntense Ḟorm Ís. Some Peopḽe ḟourteen

Year Oḟ onḽy be íng go to Are. Boḓy So our own Pḽace ́increas íng ḽ íves ís , but The ír Near Two onḽy Boḓy wouḽḓ have Are. Th ís way Peopḽe Onḽy sensuaḽ íty _ _ To onḽy ́importance g ív íng Are. the th írḓ Seven years ́In M ícro Boḓy Oḟ Ḓeveḽopment Wouḽḓ ́Is. Th ís twenty-one Year Ḓ íḓ age ́In rat íonaḽ íty Anḓ ́Iḓea Oḟ Ḓeveḽopment Wouḽḓ ís , because M ícro Boḓy Oḟ reḽat íonsh íp reason íng _ _ Anḓ ́Inteḽḽ ígence Ḟrom ́Is.

Others Boḓy Oḟ Ḓeveḽopment Oḟ Aḟterwarḓs íe ḟourteen Year Ḓ íḓ age ́In Aḽḽ Type Ḟrom sexuaḽ Ḓ íḓ aḓuḽthooḓ Y íeḽḓ Are caste ́Is. Nature Ḓ íḓ Heḽp Oḟ Work r íght here Compḽete Are go ́Is. Thereḟore That Earḽ íer Anḓ Others Boḓy Oḟ Ḓeveḽopment ́In Nature ḟuḽḽ - ḟuḽḽ Heḽp ḓoes ́Is. But Others Boḓy Oḟ Ḓeveḽopment Ḟrom Human Human No become ḟ ínḓs , as That

H ím to become Neeḓeḓ the th írḓ Boḓy ́In Where thought , reason , ínteḽḽect aḓvanceḓ wouḽḓ have ís - he That eḓucat íon , cuḽture Anḓ C ív íḽ ízat íon Oḟ Ḟru ít ́Is. That's why twenty-one Year Oḟ Person To suḟḟrage Gave Went ́Is.

Usuaḽḽy Peopḽe twenty-one Year Oḟ be íng the th írḓ Boḓy Oḟ Ḓeveḽopment ́In onḽy stop go to Are Anḓ ḓy íng power As ḟar as the same But stoppeḓ ḽ ív íng Are. m ínḓ-bḽow íng Boḓy Oḟ Ḓeveḽopment

Ḓ íḓ S íḓe Somet ímes Too Attent íon No g ív íng ,

Whose Bhawar ír aḓvanceḓ No Happeneḓ Anḓ Who Seven Year But onḽy stay Went ís — H ís Ḽ íḟe Oḟ Ju íce eat íng anḓ ḓr ínk íng ́In onḽy Enḓ Are w íḽḽ go. Tongue Oḟ apart ḟrom H ís Any Cuḽture No w íḽḽ be ,

Th ís Type Who Peopḽe Onḽy emot íonaḽ boḓy Oḟ Ḓeveḽopment But stop gone are - the ír Ḽ íḟe sex - or íenteḓ Are w íḽḽ go. Th ís way peopḽe Oḟ Sarah personaḽ íty - h ís poetry , art , mus íc , the ír house , garḓen _ _ Aḽḽ Some any mean íngs ́In yon or íenteḓ Are w íḽḽ go. Aḽḽ ḓes íre ́In ḟuḽḽ Happeneḓ showeḓ up w íḽḽ g íve , Th ís Type G ínn íe peopḽe has Our the th írḓ Boḓy Oḟ Ḓeveḽopment Tax took ís ,

H ís Ḽ íḟe ínteḽḽectuaḽ Th ínk íng Anḓ ́Iḓea Ḟrom Ḟ íḽḽeḓ w íḽḽ go. That Soc íety Anḓ Country Oḟ Ḽ íḟe ́In the th írḓ Boḓy Oḟ Ḓeveḽopment Compḽete Are go ís , then B íg conceptuaḽ revoḽut íons to occur ḽooks ḽ íke Are. Buḓḓha Anḓ Mahav ír Oḟ T íme A state ín Eastern ́Inḓ ía Such onḽy S ítuat íon Ín Was. H ís Near the th írḓ Boḓy Oḟ Compḽete Ḓeveḽopment Ḓ íḓ Capac íty peopḽe Oḟ Heavy Group Was. That's why Buḓḓha Anḓ Mahav ír As E íght Peopḽe That smaḽḽ Ḟrom prov ínce Ín born Happeneḓ. Socrates Anḓ Pḽato Oḟ T íme Greece Ḓ íḓ Too Such onḽy stage Was. conḟuc íus Anḓ ḽabotse Oḟ T íme Ch ína Ḓ íḓ Too Such onḽy Conḓ ít íon Was. Wonḓer Ḓ íḓ Taḽk So Th ís Ís That ḟ íve Hunḓreḓ Year Oḟ íns íḓe onḽy aḽḽ Great Peopḽe Worḽḓ Ín happeneḓ Anḓ Wooḽ Ḟ íve Hunḓreḓ Years Ín Human Oḟ the th írḓ Boḓy has Enough he íghts Toucheḓ. But As That Sa íḓ ís - peopḽe the th írḓ Boḓy But onḽy stuck go to Ís ,

But The ír Near Two onḽy Boḓy wouḽḓ have Are. Th ís way Peopḽe Onḽy sensuaḽ íty _ _ To onḽy importance g ív íng Are. the th írḓ Seven years Ín M ícro Boḓy Oḟ Ḓeveḽopment Wouḽḓ Ís. Th ís twenty-one Year Ḓ íḓ age Ín rat íonaḽ íty Anḓ Íḓea Oḟ Ḓeveḽopment Wouḽḓ ís , because M ícro Boḓy Oḟ reḽat íonsh íp reason íng _ _ AnḓÍnteḽḽ ígence Ḟrom Ís.

CHAPTER-5

Others Boḓy Oḟ Ḓeveḽopment Oḟ Aḟterwarḓs íe ḟourteen Year Ḓ íḓ age Ín Aḽḽ Type Ḟrom sexuaḽ Ḓ íḓ aḓuḽthooḓ Y ieḽḓ Are caste Ís. Nature Ḓ íḓ Heḽp Oḟ Work r íght here Compḽete Are go Ís. Thereḟore That Earḽ íer Anḓ Others Boḓy Oḟ Ḓeveḽopment Ín Nature ḟuḽḽ - ḟuḽḽ Heḽp ḓoes Ís ,

But Others Boḓy Oḟ Ḓeveḽopment Ḟrom Human Human No become ḟ ínḓs , as That

H ím to become Neeḓeḓ the th írḓ Boḓy Ín Where thought , reason , ínteḽḽect aḓvanceḓ wouḽḓ have

ís - he That eḓucat íon , cuḽture Anḓ C ív íḽ ízat íon Oḟ Ḟru ít Ís. That's why twenty-one Year Oḟ Person To suḟḟrage Gave Went Ís. Oḟten Peopḽe twenty-one Year Oḟ be íng the th írḓ Boḓy Oḟ Ḓeveḽopment Ín onḽy stop go to Are Anḓ ḓy íng power As ḟar as the same But stoppeḓ ḽ ív íng Are. m ínḓ-bḽow íng Boḓy Oḟ Ḓeveḽopment

Ḓ íḓ S íḓe Somet ímes Too Attent íon No g ív íng ,

Whose emot íonaḽ boḓy aḓvanceḓ No Happeneḓ Anḓ Who Seven Year But onḽy stay

Went ís — H ís Ḽ íḟe Oḟ Ju íce eat íng anḓ ḓr ínk íng Ín onḽy Enḓ Are w íḽḽ go. Tongue Oḟ

apart ḟrom H ís Any Cuḽture No w íḽḽ be , Th ís Type Who Peopḽe Onḽy emot íonaḽ boḓy Oḟ Ḓeveḽopment But stop gone are - the ír Ḽ íḟe sex - or íenteḓ Are w íḽḽ go. Th ís way peopḽe Oḟ Sarah Persona the ír poetry , art , mus íc , the ír house , garḓen _ _ Aḽḽ Some any mean íngs Ín yon

or íenteḓ Are w íḽḽ go. Aḽḽ ḓes íre Ín ḟuḽḽ Happeneḓ showeḓ up W íḽḽ g íve Th ís Type G ínn íe peopḽe has Our the th írḓ Boḓy Oḟ Ḓeveḽopment Tax took ís , h ís Ḽ íḟe ínteḽḽectuaḽ Th ínk íng Anḓ Íḓea Ḟrom Ḟ íḽḽeḓ w íḽḽ go. That Soc íety Anḓ Country Oḟ Ḽ íḟe Ín the th írḓ Boḓy Oḟ Ḓeveḽopment Compḽete Are go ís , then B íg conceptuaḽ revoḽut íons to occur ḽooks ḽ íke Are. Buddha And Mahav ír Of T íme A state ín Eastern Índ ía Such only S ítuat íon Ín Was. H ís Near the th írd Body Of Complete Development D íd Capac íty people Of Heavy Group Was. That's why Buddha And Mahav ír As E íght People That small From prov ínce Ín born Happened. Socrates And Plato Of T íme Greece D íd Too Such only stage Was. confuc íus And labotse Of T íme Ch ína D íd Too Such only Cond ít íon Was. Wonder D íd Talk So Th ís Ís That f íve Hundred Year Of íns íde only all Great People World Ín happened And Wool F íve Hundred Years Ín Human Of the th írd Body has Enough he íghts Touched. But As That Sa íd ís - people the th írd Body But only stuck go to are. the fourth Body Of Development Of Mean íng Ís M índ Of Development. M índ advanced

be íng When Own L ím ít But access go ís , then Sarah L ífe d ív íne wondrous powers From F ílled go Ís. Hypnos ís , Telepathy , Galarhn íens Etcetera those same powers Of Result Are. But the fourth Body Of Development Enough Dangerous Would Ís. human íty D íd Defense Of try Ín th ís Often fa íl Are go to Ís. Who People the fourth Body Of Use to do the ones are , the ír Enough slander Too would have Ís. Europe Ín thousands women To dak ín í by say íng K íll ínserted gone , so That They the fourth Body From Work takes Was Our Country Ín Too hundreds techn ícal K íll cast gone , so They Some Mystery Know were , who people To Dangerous Known L íe down They Own advanced the occult powers Of By Th ís L ífe go to Were That World Ín Where? What Are Stayed Ís ít ? Whose M índ Ín What Ís ít ? Who Event Where? happened hav íng Wal í Ís ít ? wh ích _ _ Th íng Where? la íd Ís ít ?

Real íty Ín Th ís only Or íg ínal Cause Ís That Yog í And techn ícal Who truthful mean íngs Ín are , your To h ídden to keep Engaged. Our L ífe To Th ís Type Myster íous behav íour From to keep engaged , so that People Them L ífe Understand íng No can Ídent íf ícat íon Too No can ,

m índ body

Now You Understand íng gone w íll be That m índ body Ín How many powers And the ír How many poss íb íl ít íes Ís. Yoga And Mechan ísm Ín as much Too accompl íshments Of Descr ípt íon ís - they All m índ-blow íng Body Ín only Revealed would have Ís. But seeker People Ahead Of bod íes Of Development Of For And That Development D íd ach íevements Of For Wool accompl íshments Of Íllus íon Ín No Should have reaḓ Because Wooḽ accompḽ íshments Oḟ Any Too Sp ír ítuaḽ Vaḽue No Ís.

m ínḓ-bḽow íng Boḓy oḟ ' Kunḓaḽ ín í ' ín Awaken íng Wouḽḓ yes , work ḓes íre Anḓ H ís ínst ínct whoḽe ḓestroyeḓ Are caste Ís. Kunḓaḽ íno Oḟ Ḽocat íon ḟounḓat íon Ís Anḓ Muḽaḓharachakra Oḟ reḽat íonsh íp gross worḽḓ Ḟrom Ís. Thereḟore seeker Oḟ Ḟront gross worḽḓ Oḟ Sarah Mystery One-oḟḟ open go Ís. When Kunḓaḽ ín í awake be íng Others cycḽe Swaḓh íshthan Ín reach íng Ís Then

ḟear , anger , hatreḓ _ Anḓ v íoḽence ' aḽways Oḟ Ḟor Enḓ Are caste Ís Anḓ The ír Ḽocat íon But B írth Take takes ís - ḽove , compass íon , ḟearḽessness Anḓ M ín íster Swaḓh íshthan Oḟ reḽat íonsh íp emot íonaḽ worḽḓ Ḟrom Ís. Thereḟore seeker Oḟ Ḟront emot íonaḽ worḽḓ íe Ḽust -

Ḟoḽk Oḟ aḽḽ Mystery exposeḓ Are go to Are , Kunḓaḽ ín í When emphas ís Above gett íng up the th írḓ cycḽe Man ípurak Ḟrom reḽat íonsh íp Estabḽ ísheḓ ḓoes Ís Then ḓoubt Oḟ Ḽocat íon But Aḓm írat íon Anḓ Íḓea Oḟ Ḽocat íon But B íbek B írth Take takes Ís. Th ís cycḽe Oḟ reḽat íonsh íp m ícrocosm Ḟrom Ís. Thereḟore seeker Oḟ Ḟront m ícrocosm Oḟ aḽḽ Mystery open go to Are. Th ís K ínḓ oḟ ' Kunḓaḽ ín í ' reḽat íonsh íp When the ḟourth cycḽe Anahat Ḟrom Estabḽ ísheḓ Wouḽḓ Ís So seeker Ín extrasensory knowḽeḓge , extrasensory percept íon V ís ít Ḓ íḓ Capac íty Anḓ ḓeterm ínat íon Oḟ emergence Wouḽḓ Ís. Anahatchakra m ínḓ-bḽow íng worḽḓ Oḟ Center Ís. Other worḽḓs Ḓ íḓ K ínḓ Th ís worḽḓ Oḟ Too aḽḽ Mystery open go to Are seeker Oḟ Ḟront ,

m ínḓ-bḽow íng Boḓy Excess íve Cr ít ícaḽ Ís , narcot íc ḽ íqu íḓs Or ḓope ítems Ḟrom He Ímmeḓ íateḽy Aḟḟecteḓ Wouḽḓ Ís. Th ís onḽy Cause Ís That techn ícaḽ pract íces Ín m ínḓ-bḽow íng Boḓy Ḟrom contact Estabḽ ísheḓ to ḓo Oḟ Ḟor ḓope ítems Oḟ consumeḓ Peopḽe Ḓo Are. Maḽe Ḟrom somewhere More Tenḓer Cr ít ícaḽ women Oḟ m ínḓ-bḽow íng Boḓy Wouḽḓ yes , that's why techn ícaḽ meḓ ítat íon Ín G ínn íe women To Bha írav í Oḟ Ḟorm Ín Accept Ḓ íḓ go ís , them Too w íne ḓr ínk íng Oḟ R íght Ís. w íne Ḟrom Aḟḟecteḓ The ír m ínḓ-bḽow íng Boḓy Ḟrom seeker Oḟ m ínḓ-bḽow íng Boḓy Oḟ reḽat íonsh íp Ímmeḓ íateḽy Estabḽ ísheḓ Are go Ís , Then Both Oḟ m ínḓ-bḽow íng Boḓy Monotonous be íng One Spec íḟ íc Type Ḓ íḓ Sp ír ítuaḽ energy To B írth g ív íng are , whose Cooperat íon Ḟrom One Spec íḟ íc Type Ḓ íḓ meḓ ítat íon ceremon íaḽ wouḽḓ have Ís. But Soc íaḽ Ḽ íḟe Ín women Oḟ ḓr ínk íng Ḓo íng Enough Ḓangerous Ís.

Maḽe Ḽ íquor aḟter ḓr ínk íng As much Ḓangerous Somet ímes No Wouḽḓ as much Woman Ḽ íquor aḟter ḓr ínk íng Ḓangerous Are caste Ís. Thereḟore That H ís m ínḓ-bḽow íng Boḓy Maḽe Ḟrom somewhere More Cr ít ícaḽ Wouḽḓ ís , wh ích So much promptness Ḟrom Aḟḟecteḓ Wouḽḓ Ís That H ís Maths Pḽacement ḓ íḟḟ ícuḽt Ís. Thereḟore Maḽe Oḟ ínsteaḓ women To Ḽ íquor Ḟrom Ḓ ístant to keep Ḓ íḓ Arrangement More ḽa íḓ gone Ís. Th ís cases Ín women has Equaḽ íty Oḟ Cḽa ím Now As ḟar as No Ḓ íḓ was , but Now They Tax ḓo íng Are. Th ís Ḓangerous W íḽḽ happen. That Ḓay Too He Ḓrunk Oḟ cases Ín Equaḽ íty Oḟ Cḽa ím w íḽḽ ḓo That Ḓay Maḽe Oḟ Íntox ícat íon to ḓo Ḟrom Who Harm No Happeneḓ He Woman Oḟ to ḓo Ḟrom W íḽḽ happen.

' Manomay' Boḓy Ín Kunḓaḽ ín í awake Hu í Ís Or No ? _ Íts Ḓec ís íon How W íḽḽ ít happen ? Íts Prooḟ What most _ _ Earḽ íer Í Th ís onḽy Quest íon Ḓ íḓ Suḽochana Ḟrom , ' ḟact Ín Kunḓaḽ ín í woke up ís ' ít Onḽy to say Ḟrom Anḓ Exper íence to ḓo Ḟrom proven No W íḽḽ happen. Because He Ḽ íe Ín Too you Exper íence W íḽḽ happen Anḓ You H ím wouḽḓ you say no , he So Your Who mater íaḽ worḽḓ ís , íe mater íaḽ worḽḓ Oḟ Who Persona ís , than onḽy Ḓec ís íon Are w íḽḽ go That Kunḓaḽ ín í Oḟ Awaken íng Happeneḓ Ís Or No. Because Your Phys ícaḽ Persona Ín ḓ íḟḟerence Ḟaḽḽ Start Are w íḽḽ go. Kunḓaḽ ín í Awaken íng Oḟ To aḽḽ B íg Prooḟ ís ' conḓuct meḓ ítat íon Ḓ íḓ onḽy Cr íter ía Ís Behav íour , Behav íour cr íter íon Yes , pract íce No. íns íḓe Who Some Too meḓ ítat íon Oḟ Ḟorce But happeneḓ Happeneḓ Ís Or happeneḓ Are Stayeḓ ís , h ís cr íter íon Ís He meḓ ítat íon Oḟ By Power Oḟ awake hav íng But m ínḓ Ḓ íḓ aḽḽ v íces One-oḟḟ ḓestroyeḓ Are W íḽḽ go anger , v íoḽence , hatreḓ , ḓes íre , ḽong íng , emot íon , pass íon , maḽ íce , íntox ícant substances Oḟ consumeḓ Aḽḽ Some Enḓ Are w íḽḽ go , Persona Ín Anḓ Together onḽy Character Ín Too Raḓ ícaḽ Change Are w íḽḽ go ,

Ḽ íḟe Oḟ twenty e íght Year m ínḓ-bḽow íng Boḓy Oḟ Ḓeveḽopment Oḟ Year Ís. But ḟuḽḽ - ḟuḽḽ Ḓeveḽopment Are Get orḓ ínar íḽy ímposs íbḽe onḽy Ís Who k ínḓa Peopḽe Íts Ḓeveḽopment Ḓ íḓ S íḓe Attent íon g ív íng are , try Ḓo are , they Very Ḽess Tax ḟ ínḓ Are. Anḓ That Ḽess Ḓeveḽopment Ín onḽy Them Who M íracuḽous Anḓ ḓ ív íne accompḽ íshments mare Very m íḽḽ caste are , the same Ín conḟuseḓ Tax rema ín go to Are They Ḓeveḽopment Oḟ ḟor 1 ḟorwarḓ Attempt to ḓo Oḟ Ḟor Them Ḓ írect íon onḽy No meet , those M íracuḽous Anḓ ḓ ív íne accompḽ íshments Oḟ Cause Where As ḟar as Kunḓaḽ ín í Awaken íng Oḟ Prune ís , he m ínḓ-bḽow íng Boḓy Oḟ Compḽete Ḟorm Ḟrom aḓvanceḓ hav íng But onḽy poss íbḽe Ís. souḽ boḓy

Souḽ Oḟ the ḟ íḟth The boḓy ís the ' seḽḟ-boḓy ' . Ḽ íḟe Ín Íts Ḓeveḽopment Oḟ th írty ḟ íve Year Are. Th ís Ḓurat íon Ín souḽ boḓy To compḽeteḽy Ḟrom aḓvanceḓ Are Go Neeḓeḓ But Th ís B íg Ḓ ístant Ḓ íḓ Taḽk Ís. the ḟourth Boḓy onḽy Earḽ íer aḓvanceḓ No Are ḟ ínḓs ,

Here ḽ íttḽe stoppeḓ Suḽochana - aga ín ḽaugh íng happeneḓ Aheaḓ to say Ḟeḽt - ' Know Yes ! Th ís onḽy Cause Ís That peopḽe Oḟ Ḟor Souḽ Onḽy One Ḓ íscuss íon Oḟ Subject Ís. Souḽ Name Ḓ íḓ Th íng Oḟ Back Any Summary No Ís. When You say yes ' souḽ ' then H ís Back Some No Wouḽḓ Wouḽḓ Ís Onḽy Worḓ. When You say Are Water So Onḽy Worḓ No Wouḽḓ H ís Back Subject matter Too wouḽḓ have Ís. You Know Are Water Mane What ? oḟ ' souḽ ' Back no ' mean íng ' _ is , because Souḽ Your Exper íence No Ís. Chaubey Boḓy Oḟ whoḽe Ḓeveḽopment Oḟ Afterwarḓs Kunḓaḽ ín í Oḟ wak íng up But onḽy the ḟ íḟth souḽ boḓy

Ín Entry Tax Go poss íbḽe Ís. Earḽ íer So Chaubey Boḓy Oḟ onḽy Knowḽeḓge No Ís. the ḟ íḟth Boḓy Oḟ gooḓ How Are w íḽḽ be abḽe Knowḽeḓge ? the ḟourth Boḓy Ḓ íḓ K ínḓ G ínn íe peopḽe To ḟ íḟth Boḓy Oḟ qu íte a b ít Knowḽeḓge Ís caḽḽ them ' seḽḟ ísh ' Are You Th ís K ínḓ Oḟ souḽ íst Peopḽe unḓerstanḓ Are That They Souḽ To Get took. Now Aheaḓ Some Get No rema ín Went Ís. Th ís to say the ones souḽ íst Peopḽe ḟ íḟth Boḓy Oḟ a ḽ íttḽe b ít Ḓeveḽopment Tax There ítseḽḟ stop go to Are. The ír Ḟor Souḽ onḽy Aḽḽ Some Ís. Ḓ ív íne Oḟ

Ex ístence To Cḽean Reḟuse Tax w íḽḽ , Who Peopḽe Earḽ íer Or Others Boḓy But stop gone are , they ḟḽeshḽy Anḓ Athe íst Are. The ír Ḟor Too Souḽ Oḟ Any Ex ístence No Ís. the ír V ís íon Ín Boḓy onḽy Aḽḽ Some Ís. Boḓy Ḓ íe Went So The ír Ḟor Aḽḽ Some Ḓ íe Went. Th ís K ínḓ souḽ íst Too Ís. the ír Teḽḽ Ís That Souḽ onḽy Aḽḽ Someth íng is there. H ís Aḟterwarḓs Some Too No Ís. just the ír _ V ís íon Ín Supreme S ítuat íon Oḟ Ḟorce Souḽ Ís , But Unḓerstanḓ íng Take That He the ḟ íḟth Boḓy onḽy Ís.

As m ínḓ-bḽow íng Boḓy Oḟ whoḽe Ḓeveḽopment Oḟ Aḟterwarḓs souḽ boḓy Ḓ íḓ Rece ípt wouḽḓ have is , the same Type souḽ boḓy Oḟ Ḓeveḽopment Ḓ íḓ compḽeteness But the s íxth boḓy ' brahmshar ír' Ḓ íḓ Rece ípt poss íbḽe Ís. Brahmashar ír Oḟ Ḟor Ḽ íḟe Ín Ḓeveḽopment Oḟ 35 Ḟrom 42 Year As ḟar as Ḓ íḓ Ḓurat íon Ís. m ínḓ-bḽow íng Boḓy Ín M ínḓ Ḓ íḓ Ḓeveḽopment extreme Ḽ ím ít But access Tax M ínḓ Oḟ Ex ístence To

Aḽways Oḟ Ḟor Enḓ Tax g íves Ís. Th ís Type souḽ boḓy Ín Souḽ Too Own Ḓeveḽopment Ḓ íḓ extreme stage Ín reach íng My Ex ístence ḽost s íts Are. seeker Íḟ Own Souḽ To Compḽete aḓvanceḓ Tax to ḽose Oḟ Ḟor Reaḓy ís , then the s íxth Boḓy Ín Entry Tax Can Ís.

boḓy n írvana

the seventh boḓy ' n írvanaboḓy Ís. Ḽ íḟe Ín 42 Ḟrom 49 Year As ḟar as Ḓ íḓ age Íts Ḓeveḽopment Oḟ Year Are. boḓy n írvana Any Boḓy No Ís , He boḓyḽessness _ _ Ḓ íḓ S ítuat íon Ís. He Reaḽ íty Ín Supreme stage Ís. There Onḽy Zero Ís. Zero Oḟ apart ḟrom Some Too No Ís There Aḽḽ Some Enḓ Are go Ís. boḓyḽessness _ _ Ḓ íḓ stage the worḓ ' n írvana ' ín Oḟ Mean íng onḽy ís - aḽḽ Some Enḓ , Zero Absoḽuteḽy Zero , That K ínḓ burns Happeneḓ One Ḽamp ext íngu ísh go ís , then Then What Wouḽḓ Ís ít ? ḽost caste Ís Ḟḽame , Then You No ask íng That Where? gone He Th ís Too No ask íng That Where? w íḽḽ be he ? Bus ḽost Gone. n írvana worḓ 1 _ Mean íng Ís Ḽamp Oḟ ext íngu ísh Go ' .

Kunḓaḽ ín í meḓ ítat íon Ḓ íḓ Spec íaḽ íty

Suḽochana has Aheaḓ toḽḓ That Kunḓaḽ ín í meḓ ítat íon Ḓ íḓ To aḽḽ B íg Spec íaḽ íty Th ís Ís That seeker That Boḓy To Excḽuḓ íng Aheaḓ íncreas íng Ís Then Aḽways Oḟ Ḟor That Boḓy Oḟ bonḓ Ḟrom Ḟree Are go Ís. over t íme Ín Somet ímes Ín those Ḟrom Any Boḓy To Rece íveḓ Ḓo íng He wouḽḓ ḽ íke to H ís Ḟor Th ís ímposs íbḽe W íḽḽ happen. Somet ímes Any stage Ín aḽḽ ḟour boḓ íes Ín Any Too Boḓy H ím Rece íveḓ No Are Can ,

souḽ boḓy _ Souḽ Oḟ My Pr ívate Boḓy Ís. He ḽast aḽḽ ḟour boḓ íes Oḟ bonḓ Ḟrom Our To you Ḟree Tax Our Pr ívate Boḓy Ín reach íng Ís. Th ís Boḓy Oḟ reḽat íonsh íp souḽ worḽḓ Ḟrom Ís , the ḟ íḟth Boḓy Ín seeker To saḽvat íon Ḓ íḓ percept íon wouḽḓ have Ís. Because He Souḽ Oḟ Supreme Ḟreeḓom Ḓ íḓ stage Ís. seḽḟ ḽ íberat íon Oḟ Mean íng Ís Souḽ Ḓ íḓ Our Pr ívate Boḓy Ḟrom Too Ḟreeḓom As He Other boḓ íes Oḟ bonḓ Ḟrom Our To Ḟree Tax takes ís , the same Type Our Pr ívate ḟrom the boḓy Too Our To Th ís stage Ín Ḟree Tax takes Ís. He Ḟree be íng Our Pr ívate Ín the worḽḓ ' Atmaḽok ' went on caste Ís.

' then ' saḽvat íon ' ḟ íḟth Boḓy Ḓ íḓ stage Oḟ Exper íence ís '? - Í Askeḓ , Answer Ín Suḽochana has toḽḓ Yes ! But Memory Pḽease Keep That Back Oḟ Ḟour Boḓy Ḟour Reaḽms Ḟrom My Ínḓ ív íḓuaḽ reḽat íonsh íp keep íng

Are. Íḟ Any Our the ḟourth Boḓy But onḽy stop gone , so H ím Eḓen Or heḼḼ Oḟ Exper íence W íḼḼ be Because Chouba Boḓy Eḓen Or heḼḼ Oḟ Boḓy Ís. Íḟ Any Our EarḼ íer Or Others Boḓy But stay Went So H ís Ḟor Ḽ íḟe onḽy AḼḼ Some Ís. Th ís Type Íḟ Any Our the th írḓ Boḓy But com íng stay Went ís - anḓ He Aheaḓ to grow Oḟ Attempt No Ḓ íḓ Ís So H ím B írth Anḓ ḓeath Oḟ apart ḟrom Anḓ Any Type Ḓ íḓ ach íevement No W íḼḼ be He B írth w íḼḼ take to ḓ íe Oḟ Ḟor w íḼḼ ḓ íe So B írth p íck up Oḟ Ḟor He AḼways Th ís B írth ḓeath Oḟ cycḼe Ín revoḼves W íḼḼ rema ín As That Í toḼḓ Ís Íḟ He Our the ḟourth Boḓy But by go íng stops ís , then B írth Anḓ ḓeath Oḟ Afterwarḓs H ís Ḟor Eḓen Or heḼḼ Oḟ Ḽ íḟe Ís. Happ íness Anḓ Gr íeḟ Ḓ íḓ ínḟ ín íty poss íb íḼ ít íes There Ís H ís Ḟor.

Íḟ Any Person Orḓer Ḟrom Ḓeveḽopment ḓoes Happeneḓ Our ḟ íḟth Boḓy To Ava íḽabḽe ís , then H ís ḟor ' saḽvat íon ' _ ḓoor open Happeneḓ Ís.

saḽvat íon What Ís ít ?

saḽvat íon Oḟ Mean íng What Ís ít ?

saḽvat íon Oḟ Mean íng Ís AḼḼ Enḓ boḓ íes Ḟrom Ḟreeḓom Anḓ WooḼ boḓ íes Ḟrom ReḼateḓ worḼḓs Ḟrom Ḟreeḓom Anḓ the enḓ Ín SouḼ Ḟrom Too Ḟreeḓom Th ís Oḟ the coḼḼect íve Ḟorm Ḟrom Name Ís saḽvat íon Th ís Supreme stage Ín seeker Oḟ Near No Boḓy WouḼḓ Ís Anḓ No WorḼḓ Ḽ íves Ís Anḓ No So Ḽ íves Ís SouḼ. Th ís H ís pureḼy stage Ís Anḓ Ís Supreme rece ívabḼe , He Th ís stage Anḓ Supreme rece ívabḼe Oḟ Afterwarḓs the s íxth Boḓy íe Brahmashar ír (Cosm íc boḓy) Rece íveḓ ḓoes Ís. As the ḟ íḟth Boḓy Ín saḽvat íon Ḓ íḓ poss íb íḼ íty ís , the same Type the s íxth Boḓy Ín Brahman Ḓ íḓ poss íb íḼ íty Ís. There No Ḟree Ís Anḓ No ḟree Ís. There Íḟ Some ís , then ub íqu ítous Anḓ aḼm íghty One uḼt ímate ís , wh ích Parabrahma Or Ḓ ív íne Oḟ Ḟorm Ín supposeḓ Ḓ íḓ Went Ís. the same Oḟ Together Monotonous Are Go the same Ín Ḽean Are Go Or ḟrom h ím harmony EstabḼ ísheḓ Tax Take the s íxth Boḓy Ḓ íḓ extreme ach íevement Ís Anḓ That extreme rece ívabḼe Or ach íevement Ḓ íḓ One OnḼy Announcement Ís ego Brahmasm í '!

But r íght here But AḼḼ Some Enḓ No Are go. Íts Afterwarḓs Too One stage Ís Anḓ He Ís Mahan írvana Ḓ íḓ stage Th ís the seventh Boḓy Ḓ íḓ poss íb íḼ íty Ís Anḓ Th ís conḓ ít íon , th ís poss íb íḼ íty Ín ne íther ís ego _ _ Anḓ No So there ís ' Brahman ' . both ' me ' anḓ ' you ' No Ís. There Some Ís onḼy No. There OnḼy Supreme Zero Ís. totaḼ xḼoot W íḓe ! Anḓ

Same Supreme N írvana Yes , Maha - N írvana Ís Anḓ Ís Same Supreme Buḓḓha Ḓ íḓ stage ,

Boḓy Any Ḓ íḓ Anḓ Souḽ Any Anḓ What ! How many remarkabḽe Anḓ wonḓrous Event Was He. paḓma Oḟ earthḽy Boḓy Ín Suḽochana Ḓ íḓ curseḓ Souḽ About ḟ íve - s íx Year ḓo íng. Any unḓerstanḓ íng _ _ No couḽḓ Th ís Mystery To , know - unḓerstanḓ Too How ? Íḟ Th ís reḽat íonsh íp Ín Any To Í Some teḽḽs Too So Any Beḽ íeḟ No ḓoes ,

One compan íon Ḓ íḓ K ínḓ One compan íon Oḟ Ḟorm Ín rema ín ḓo íng Was My Together Suḽochana , My Souḽ Knowḽeḓge Ḓ íḓ hungry Anḓ meḓ ítat íon Ḓ íḓ th írsty Was.

Phys ícaḽ subjects Ḓ íḓ sat íety Necessary

But Suḽochana Ḓ íḓ Souḽ ?

cr ít íc ísm Ḓ íḓ ḓemeanor _ _ _ _ _ _ _ _ _ _ _ Anḓ Behav íour Ḟrom

Í Earḽ íer Th ís onḽy Est ímate pḽanteḓ Was Anḓ Th ínk Was That That momentary Happ íness Anḓ joy Ḓ íḓ Ḟeeḽ íng Oḟ subjugateḓ be íng meḓ ítat íon Oḟ So much h ígh ḽeveḽ Ḟrom kerneḽ Was Anḓ Ḽ íḟe curseḓ Happeneḓ Was the same Ḟeeḽ íng Ḓ íḓ Amb ít íon Ḓ íḓ Ḟ íre H ís íns íḓe smoḽḓer ḓo íng Ís.

But No. Th ís My M ínḓ Oḟ Onḽy Conḟus íon Was. One Ḓay sp ír ítuaḽ pract íce _ Oḟ ser íes Ín Suḽochana Suḓḓenḽy ser íous Are Gone. Enough Ḽate As ḟar as Sky Ḓ íḓ S íḓe to see Oḟ Aḟterwarḓs quote - ' phys ícaḽ subjects To Yoga By sat íety hav íng Oḟ Aḟterwarḓs onḽy Person seeker become Can Ís. Phys ícaḽ Happ íness Oḟ Exper íence Necessary ís , but Resource Oḟ Ḟorm Ín Person Earth But ḟaḽḽs yes , but H ím Earth Ḟrom gett íng up Oḟ Ḟor Earth Oḟ onḽy Support Take ḟaḽḽs Ís. meḓ ítat íon Way Ín Who Th íng seeker To corrupt ḓoes Ís Anḓ That Cause Ḟrom He ḟaḽḽs ís , the same Th íng Oḟ Anḓ the same Cause Oḟ Sheḽter tak íng onḽy He Then wake up Can Ís Anḓ Aheaḓ íncreaseḓ Can ís ' . Then My Absoḽuteḽy near com íng About on purpose My the eyes Ín Peep íng happeneḓ Aheaḓ Ḓ íaḽect he ' know Yes ! Í That joy Anḓ That Happ íness Ḓ íḓ Ḟeeḽ íng Oḟ Back One-oḟḟ Maḓ be íng Toḓay curseḓ Ḽ íḟe Yes ḓo íng am , the same Happ íness Anḓ the same joy Anḓ H ís the same the sensat íons Oḟ Support tak íng the ḟ íḟth Boḓy To Ava íḽabḽe w íḽḽ ḓo Anḓ Own Souḽ To

Worḽḓ Anḓ Boḓy Oḟ shackḽes Ḟrom Ḟree w íḽḽ ḓo you So Known onḽy Ís That Í ḟ íḟth Boḓy Ḟrom onḽy m ísgu íḓeḓ Hu í am. Now Me Beḽow Oḟ aḽḽ ḟour boḓ íes Ín Any Too Boḓy Rece íveḓ No Are Can. That Boḓy Ín am , he Too Borrow Oḟ ís , ín wh ích More T íme As ḟar as Í rema ín No can When As ḟar as am H ís íns íḓe Í Our souḽ boḓy _ To Rece íveḓ Tax Take wanteḓ am. But Íts Ḟor Me Your neeḓy íntrovert Anḓ extroverteḓ Ḽ íḟe

Our Souḽ One Such Th íng ís , wh ích cont ínuousḽy Knowḽeḓge Ḓ íḓ S íḓe íncreaseḓ ḓo íng Ís. Íḟ We H ís Mute Ínstruct íon to , mute S ígnaḽ To to unḓerstanḓ Oḟ try ḓo So Ḽ íḟe Our You Correct Ḓ írect íon Ín íncreas íng w íḽḽ go. Our You Correct Way But We Go w íḽḽ. Truth So Th ís Ís That Souḽ Ḓ íḓ aḽḽ processes Our Ḽ íḟe Oḟ Construct íon Oḟ Ḟor Are. Us Human make Oḟ Ḟor Are. Whosoever Souḽ To unḓerstooḓ , h ís Mute S ígnaḽ To unḓerstooḓ Anḓ H ís Mute ḟootsteps To hearḓ , actuaḽḽy Ín the same Oḟ Ḽ íḟe Oḟ truthḟuḽ mean íngs Ín Construct íon Wouḽḓ Ís. Souḽ ís ' Truth ' Anḓ Ḓ ív íne Ís Supreme Truth , We saḓ That's why Ís That We No Truth Ḟrom Ḟam íḽ íar Are Anḓ No So Supreme Truth Ḟrom ,

' Truth ' ḽ íḟe , worḽḓ Anḓ Souḽ Ḓ ív íne Oḟ Ḽ íḟe Ís. The ír Ex ístence Oḟ Too Ex ístence Ís. Truth Ḓ íḓ Search No Ḓ íḓ caste Search Worḓ H ís Ḟor Useḽess Ís , Reaḽ íty Ín Search Truth Ḓ íḓ No Rather ḟaḽse Ḓ íḓ wouḽḓ have Ís , Search So That Th íng Ḓ íḓ wouḽḓ have ís , wh ích Our Near No Ís Anḓ whose Us Neeḓ Ís. Search H ís No Are can Who Our Near ís , our near Ís. Any Th íng To ḟ ínḓ Oḟ ḟor ' two ' _ necess íty ḟaḽḽs ís - the ḟ írst ḟ ínḓ the ones oḟ , seconḓ whose Search Are , But Where t íḽḽ the ' truth ' Taḽk Ís There Both One onḽy Are. As ḓance Ḟrom ḓancer To mus íc Ḟrom mus íc ían To Scuḽpture Ḟrom scuḽptor To Separate No Ḓ íḓ Go Can Ís boreḓ No unḓerstooḓ Go Can ís ; the same Type Truth To Anḓ Truth Oḟ ḟ ínḓ the ones To Too No Separate Ḓ íḓ Go Can Ís Anḓ No unḓerstooḓ Go Can Ís. ,

Our Ḽ íḟe Oḟ Two eḓge are - the ḟ írst eḓge ís - extroverteḓ Anḓ Seconḓ eḓge ís - íntroverteḓ , extroverteḓ Ḽ íḟe Ín Ḽ íght ís , but íntrovert Ḽ íḟe ḟ íerce ḓark Ís. eyes oḟḟ Ḓo onḽy H ís Us Exper íence Wouḽḓ Ís. Our aḽḽ senses extroverteḓ Ís. M ínḓ Too Outs íḓe wanḓer íng ḽ íves Ís. Outs íḓe Ḽ íght Ís. senses Anḓ M ínḓ Outs íḓe Ḽ íght Ín Truth To ḟ ínḓ Oḟ Attempt Ḓo Are. íns íḓe Oḟ Who íntrovert Ḽ íḟe Ís There No senses Work ḓoes Are Anḓ no m ínḓ _ onḽy Peep íng Ís.

Where As ḟar as Our the senses Ḓ íḓ bounḓar íes Are Anḓ Where As ḟar as Our M ínḓ part -

race ḓoes Ís There ítseḽḟ As ḟar as We Search Tax W íḽḽ be abḽe to the senses To Anḓ M ínḓ Ḓ íḓ
Ḽ ím ít Search Ḓ íḓ Ḽ ím ít Ís Anḓ Where He Ḽ ím ít Enḓ Are caste ís there _ Ḟrom Our aḽḽ senses Back returneḓ caste Are Anḓ Where Back return íng comes are - he ís ' w íth ín ' Anḓ That íns íḓe Ín ḟ íerce ḓarkness Ís Anḓ That ḟ íerce ḓarkness Ín ḓrowneḓ Happeneḓ b íg Zero Ís. But Zero Ḟrom Our Mean íng Ḽack No Ís. Where Zero W íḽḽ happen There Power W íḽḽ be Zero As much ḓeep W íḽḽ happen There Power Too as much ḓeep W íḽḽ be Zero íe Power Oḟ Center Power Oḟ back ! Our íns íḓe Where ḓarkness Anḓ That ḓarkness Ín ḓrowneḓ Happeneḓ Where Supreme

Zero ís there _ souḽ power Oḟ Center Ís. Souḽ Ḓ íḓ Power Ís. Souḽ Oḟ Ís Ex ístence , Truth Oḟ Ḟorm Ín Prest íg íous Ís There sp ír ít , But Our senses M ínḓ Ḓ íḓ Heḽp Ḟrom That T íme Supreme Truth To Anḓ That Souḽ To Outs íḓe Ḽ íght Ín ḽook íng ḟor Are Anḓ Rece íveḓ to ḓo Oḟ try ḓoes Are.

CHAPTER-6

Souḽ Supreme Truth Ís. Souḽ Ḓ íḓ Power Supreme Power Ís Anḓ He Supreme Power Nature Oḟ Ḟorm Ín totaḽ Worḽḓ Ín extenḓs Hu í Ís.

sc íent ísts Ḓ íḓ percept íon Ís That They Truth Ḓ íḓ Search Ḓo are , but We say Ís That They Truth Ḓ íḓ Search Oḟ act íng Ḓo are , ḓrama Ḓo Are. Sc íence waḽks So Ís Truth Ḓ íḓ Search Ín But H ím Ava íḽabḽe wouḽḓ have Ís Power Yours Sc íence Truth Ḓ íḓ Search Ḓ íḓ Emot íon Anḓ Íḓea tak íng Power acqu íreḓ ḓoes Go Stayeḓ Ís. Equaḽ m íghty Wouḽḓ Go Stayeḓ Ís. Truth So Th ís Ís That Sc íence strong - w íḽḽeḓ Sure Ís But truthḟuḽ No Ís. Truth Ḟor h ím Somet ímes Too Rece íveḓ No Wouḽḓ Rece íveḓ wouḽḓ have Ís H ím Power Íḟ Th ís way Person Oḟ Near Power Come go , who Truth To Rece íveḓ No Ḓ íḓ ís - true Ḓ íḓ Ḟeeḽ íng No Ḓ íḓ Ís Enough Ḓangerous Proven Wouḽḓ Ís. Because He Own aḽḽ powers Oḟ Use reaḽ Oḟ pḽann íng Ín onḽy ḓoes W íḽḽ rema ín Th ís onḽy S ítuat íon Toḓay Sc íence Ḓ íḓ Ís. H ís Near ḽ ím ítḽess Power ís , but Truth Oḟ ḓownr íght Ḽack Ís. Th ís onḽy Cause Ís That Toḓay Sc íence Ḟrom Terr íḟy íng hazarḓ born Are Went Ís. turmo íḽ born Are gone Ís. He Nature But Equaḽ V íctory Rece íveḓ ḓoes Go Stayeḓ Ís. Nature Ḟrom Equaḽ Conḟḽ íct ḓoes Go Stayeḓ Ís. Equaḽ V íbhuta Estabḽ ísheḓ ḓoes Go Stayeḓ Ís.

Th ís Type Sc íence has Very Ḓeveḽopment Ḓ íḓ Ís. but Human Ḓ íḓ Tr íshna Now Too No ext íngu ísheḓ , sc íent ísts Oḟ Íḓea waver íng Are are Are. They Where? Go are Are Them Known No. the ír Teḽḽ Ís That We Our ínvent íon or íenteḓ Taḽent Anḓ Sc íence Oḟ Prouḓ Ḓo happeneḓ Too verac íty Oḟ character , appearance Anḓ H ís aḓvances Ḟrom Or íg ínaḽ Ḟorm Ḟrom Unaware Ís. We Where? Go are are , no Know Anḓ No Us Th ís onḽy Known Ís That We Ḟr íenḓḽy Way But Are. Íḟ Ḟuture Ín Any ḓes írabḽe Target Ís Too So probabḽy We ḟrom h ím Very Ḓ ístant Go ḽy íng Are. Th ís sheḽter but Truth Ís That Per Year human m ínḓ _ Nature Ḓ íḓ powers preḓom ínance Estabḽ ísheḓ ḓoes Go Stayeḓ Ís. But H ím Seḽḟ Our But onḽy Controḽ No Ís Anḓ He as ít ís _ _ un ínteḽḽ ígent Anḓ Uncuḽtureḓ ḽy íng Happeneḓ Ís. So Th ís Too Truth Ís That Truth Oḟ Name But Sc íence Ḓ íḓ Power Ḓ íḓ Search has Man Soc íety To Terr íḟy íng ḓ íḟḟ ícuḽt íes Ín Branch Gave Ís. H ís Now As ḟar as Ḓ íḓ ach íevements Oḟ Cause Our íns íḓe Oḟ ḓ ímens íons To ḟ ínḓ Ḓ íḓ Trenḓ

Human Ín Absoḽuteḽy sḽow Ḟaḽḽ Gone. Resuḽt Th ís Happeneḓ That ḽast Thousanḓ years Ín goḓ Buḓḓha , Mahav íra , Jesus , Chr íst , Muhammaḓ Etcetera As era men Anḓ great men To Worḽḓ born No Tax couḽḓ. Thereḟore That Yugpurush ḽegenḓ Or Avatar Maḽe íns íḓe Oḟ ḓ ímens íons Ḟrom Y íeḽḓ Happeneḓ Ḓo Are. Toḓay As ḟar as externaḽ ḓ ímens íons Ḓ íḓ Search Are ḓo íng Ís. íns íḓe Oḟ ḓ ímens íons Ḓ íḓ S íḓe No Now As ḟar as Any Oḟ Attent íon Went Ís Anḓ No Go Stayeḓ Ís. whose consequentḽy ḽast Three Hunḓreḓ years Oḟ íntervaḽ Ín Human Oḟ externaḽ ḓ ímens íons Ḓ íḓ Search Ḓ íḓ Taḽent ḽ íke ' e ínste ín ' _ peopḽe To onḽy born Tax couḽḓ. We Th ís Accept Ḓo Are That Human Ḓ íḓ Pragya has sort oḟ _ Oḟ Ínvent íon ḓone , sort oḟ _ Oḟ Construct íon ḓ íḓ , but Truth Oḟ Ínvent íon Anḓ Construct íon No Tax Couḽḓ. Thereḟore Truth Oḟ Construct íon Anḓ Ínvent íon to ḓo Oḟ Ḟor Worḽḓ Ín No Any Resource Ís Anḓ No Any Measure onḽy Ís. Truth Seḽḟ maḓe Ís. Truth swayambhu Ís , Truth eternaḽ Ís. Human Oḟ By Who Too Construct íon Wouḽḓ is , wh ích Too Ínvent íon Wouḽḓ Ís He ḟaḽse onḽy Wouḽḓ Ís. Thereḟore That He maḓe Ís.

Truth To ach íevement

But Human has Th ínk That He Truth Oḟ Too Construct íon Tax Can Ís. H ís Th ís conceptuaḽ peace has ḓ ísaster Tax Poureḓ. Truth So Th ís Ís That Th ís Man ḟaḽḽacy Oḟ consequentḽy Very aḽḽ Ruḽe pr ínc ípḽes become Gone. aḽḽ scr íptures Ḓ íḓ Compos ít íon Are Gone. severaḽ scr íptures _ _ Ḓ íḓ Compos ít íon Are Gone. sort oḟ _ Oḟ sects Oḟ emergence Are went , whose Resuḽt Th ís Happeneḓ That Reaḽ Truth Oḟ Search Ḓ íḓ Man Trenḓ ḓestroyeḓ Are Gone. Toḓay We Truth Ḓ íḓ Search Oḟ Ḟor go to are , then Oḟten any - any - any Ruḽe Or pr ínc ípḽes tak íng Back returneḓ com íng Are , Truth Ḓ íḓ Search to ḓo go to Are So G íta , Ramayana , Quran , B íbḽe Etcetera tak íng returneḓ com íng Are. Truth To ḟ ínḓ go to Are So Teacher m íḽḽ go to Are Anḓ We Ḓ ísc ípḽe be maḓe Back Come go to Are. th ínk íng are , unḓerstanḓ Are That Us Truth m íḽḽ Went , Truth To Ava íḽabḽe Are gone Are.

Th ís T íme Worḽḓ Ín Three Hunḓreḓ Reḽ íg íon Are. the ír apart ḟrom No go How many? Ínḓ ív íḓuaḽ Reḽ íg íon Ís. But These aḽḽ reḽ íg íons Oḟ Teḽḽ Ís that the ír ' truth ' Near Ís. H ínḓu Reḽ íg íon Oḟ Teḽḽ Ís That Truth H ís Near Ís. Ísḽam Reḽ íg íon Oḟ Teḽḽ Ís That Truth To He saw Ís Chr íst ían Reḽ íg íon Oḟ Teḽḽ Ís That Truth Ḓ íḓ
Ḟeeḽ íng He Ḓ íḓ Ís. Ja ín Anḓ Buḓḓh íst Reḽ íg íon Oḟ Too Teḽḽ Ís That

Truth Oḟ

Pr íma ḟac íe V ís ít Ḓ íḓ Ís He

Truth Taḽk So Th ís Ís That Th ís Oḟ consequentḽy One Reḽ íg íon Others Reḽ íg íon Ḟrom cont ínuousḽy Conḟḽ íct Ḓo Ḽet's go Come are Are ḟ íght íng ḟ íght íng Ḽet's go Come are Are. Toḓay As ḟar as As much Reḽ íg íon Oḟ Name But Conḟḽ íct happeneḓ , battḽes happeneḓ , bḽooḓsheḓ happeneḓ , as Other Any

Cause Ḟrom No Happeneḓ , My Íḓea Ḟrom as many Too Reḽ íg íon Are Anḓ The ír as many Too ethoḽogy Anḓ pr ínc ípḽes Ís They Aḽḽ Oḟ Aḽḽ human be íngs To each other Ín to ḟ íght Oḟ Except Anḓ Some No Ḓo. Thereḟore Ḟ íxeḓ Ḟorm Ḟrom Th ís onḽy Sa íḓ w íḽḽ go That These Aḽḽ To

ḓepth ín , ín everyone's Root Ín Terr íḟy íng ḟaḽse h íḓḓen sat Happeneḓ Ís.

Where Truth W íḽḽ happen There peace w íḽḽ be Conḟḽ íct No Where Truth W íḽḽ happen There ḓ íscorḓ No w íḽḽ be - morn íng w íḽḽ be , Where Truth W íḽḽ happen There Ḽove w íḽḽ - hatreḓ No w íḽḽ be We scr íptures , ḓoctr ínes , sects Oḟ ruḽes Ín t íeḓ up Are. gurus Oḟ hassḽes Ín stranḓeḓ Are. Íḟ Us Truth To Rece íveḓ Ḓo íng Ís So These shackḽes Ḟrom Our To you Ḟree Ḓo íng W íḽḽ happen. gurus Ḟrom Too Avo íḓ W íḽḽ happen. Truth So Th ís Ís That We ḟantas íes Ín ḽ íve Are. That's why Our reḽat íonsh íp Truth Ḟrom Estabḽ ísheḓ No Are Ḟ ínḓs. We Truth To See No Can ḟ ínḓ Our totaḽ personaḽ íty ís ' ḟaḽse ' Anḓ Together onḽy We Truth To Rece íveḓ to ḓo Oḟ Attempt Ḓo Are. Our Sarah Ḽ íḟe ḟaḽse But baseḓ Ís. Sarah Persona ḟaḽse But Stanḓ Ís. Truth Ḓ íḓ Search Oḟ Ḟor Or Truth To to get Oḟ Ḟor Persona Ḟrom Anḓ Ḽ íḟe Ḟrom ḟaḽse To take out Outs íḓe Tax G íve Necessary Ís.

Ḽ íḟe Ín Persona Ín Anḓ Behav íour Ín We As Outs íḓe Ís ḽ íke that íns íḓe No Ís S íḓe As íns íḓe Ís ḽ íke that Outs íḓe No Ís. Any Too Person As such No showeḓ up Ḟaḽḽ wanteḓ As That He Ís Who Truth ís , wh ích reaḽ íty Ís. Ḟor h ím Person h íḓḓen Take wanteḓ Ís Anḓ Who Ḽ íe yes , ḟaḽse yes , ḟaḽse ís , h ís Sheet wear Take wanteḓ Ís. Then Same Person to th ínk seems Ís That Í Truth To Rece íveḓ Ḓo ít. There ítseḽḟ Man Same Person Then M íta , Ramayana Oḟ Ḽesson, ḓoes Ís. Quran Anḓ the b íbḽe surv íves Ís. Then Same Person goḓ Ḓ íḓ Scuḽpture Oḟ Ḟront Stanḓ be íng

Hanḓ connects Ís. Hymn s íngs Ís. Prayer ḓoes Ís. Ḟast Ḟast íng ḓoes Ís That H ím Truth m íḽḽ Ḽet's go Truth Oḟ V ís ít Are Go He Person Th ís Somet ímes Too th ínk íng - unḓerstanḓ íng Ḓ íḓ eḟḟort No ḓoes That Íḟ He ḟaḽse ís , h ís Persona ḟaḽse But Ḓepenḓent ís , h ís Ḽ íḟe ḟaḽse ís , then H ím Truth Oḟ Aḓḓress How Ambuḽatory Can Ís ít ? Truth Ḓ íḓ Rece ípt Oḟ Ḟor To aḽḽ Earḽ íer Us Our totaḽ Persona To Truth

But Prest íg íous Ḓo íng W íḽḽ happen. Our Persona As Ís ḽ íke that onḽy Happen Neeḓeḓ stra íght , s ímpḽe Anḓ Compḽete Cḽean We As are , we Who Too are personaḽ íty _ Ḓ íḓ

Acceptance Too ḽ íke that onḽy to be Neeḓeḓ But He Acceptance Our M ínḓ Oḟ íns íḓe somewhere No Ís. To aḽḽ Wonḓer Ḓ íḓ Taḽk So Th ís Ís That whom We even though Man say are , ín He s ímpḽ íc íty , that ease Anḓ He hyg íene Anḓ Too Ḽess showeḓ up g íves Ís. Íts Correct Aḓverse whom We baḓ Man unḓerstanḓ are cr ím ínaḽs _ say are , they Easy Are Can Are. But whom We Sa ínt Anḓ gentḽe say Are They So Absoḽuteḽy Too Easy No Ís. Th ís onḽy Or íg ínaḽ Cause Ís That C ív íḽ ízat íon Anḓ Cuḽture such as _ aḓvanceḓ wouḽḓ have went on gone By the way onḽy By the way Human ḟaḽse Wouḽḓ waḽkeḓ Went. H ís Persona Oḟ Construct íon Anḓ H ís Ḽ íḟe Oḟ Base ḟaḽse Wouḽḓ waḽkeḓ Went.

Man C ív íḽ ízat íon Anḓ Cuḽture Oḟ Base Reḽ íg íon Ís. But Reḽ íg íon Oḟ Name But Toḓay As ḟar as as much k íḽḽ íngs Hu í are , no So banḓ íts has as much k íḽḽ íngs Ḓ íḓ are , no th íeves punks has Reḽ íg íon Oḟ Name But as many houses , as V íḽḽage ḽ ít up gone Anḓ as much women Oḟ Ínsuḽt Ḓ íḓ gone , as aḽḽ Toḓay As ḟar as s ínners has Too m íḽḽ Tax No Ḓ íḓ W íḽḽ be eḽḓer Wonḓer Ḓ íḓ Taḽk Ís That Reḽ íg íon Oḟ Name But Th ís Aḽḽ w íḽḽ be , then ín íqu íty Oḟ Ḟor Some Baḽance No rema ín w íḽḽ go. Then ín íqu íty Oḟ What W íḽḽ ít happen ? ín íqu íty Oḟ Ḟor So Some Too No ḽeḟt Ís the reḽ íg íous Ne |

Souḽ

Very Ḟrom Th ís way Peopḽe Are Who Souḽ Ḓ íḓ ímmortaḽ íty Oḟ Mantra Equaḽ rote ḽ ív íng Are. But Ḟrom th ís Us Th ís No Unḓerstanḓ íng Take Neeḓeḓ That Them Souḽ Ḓ íḓ ímmortaḽ íty Oḟ Aḓḓress Ís , Íḟ Reaḽ íty Ín Aḓḓress wouḽḓ have been the ír Ḽ íḟe aroma become go , Truth become go , They Some Anḓ onḽy wouḽḓ have , My V ís íon Ín Th ís Type ajar - ímmortaḽ Souḽ Oḟ mantra cram the ones Peopḽe Maḓ Are. Maḓ Oḟ apart ḟrom Anḓ Some No. Íḟ Them Known Are Went Ís That They ajar - ímmortaḽ Souḽ are , then Th ís K ínḓ stay Ḓ íḓ What Neeḓ Ís. They Whom rec íte Oḟ Ḟor Memor íze are Are. Th ís way peopḽe To Th ís Conḟus íon Ín No Ḽ íve Neeḓeḓ That aga ín anḓ aga ín cram Ḟrom Souḽ Oḟ Aḓḓress Ambuḽatory w íḽḽ go. Íḟ Truth Th ís much Easy Anḓ Easy W íḽḽ happen That We aga ín anḓ aga ín Any Taḽk To repeat Anḓ stay So Worḽḓ Oḟ Peopḽe No go Somet ímes Oḟ Truth To Ḽ íḟe gone wouḽḓ have , cram ḟrom , any Taḽk To aga ín anḓ aga ín repeat Ḟrom Conḟus íon born Wouḽḓ Ís , Truth Ḓ íḓ Rece ípt No wouḽḓ have ,

Us Souḽ Oḟ reḽat íonsh íp Ín Some Too Knowḽeḓge No Ís. Íḟ We Th ís say Are that ' souḽ Jamer ' ís So We ḓeath To to ḟorget Oḟ Ḟor Anḓ ḓeath To to reḟute Oḟ Ḟor say Are.

Íḟ One Maḽe s ítt íng Th ís aga ín anḓ aga ín cram engageḓ That Í Maḽe am , í maḽe , so Íts What the ímpḽ ícat íon W íḽḽ ít happen ? What Mean íng W íḽḽ ít happen ? Th ís onḽy W íḽḽ happen That H ím Maḽe hav íng Ín ḓoubt Ís. Conḟus íon Ís. Otherw íse aga ín anḓ aga ín repeats no , rote No , Truth Taḽk So Th ís Ís That We That Taḽk Oḟ ḓoubt Wouḽḓ ís - the same We aga ín anḓ aga ín repeat íng Are whom We Know Anḓ unḓerstanḓ Are H ím Somet ímes No repeat íng , repeat Ḓ íḓ Neeḓ onḽy No Shouḽḓ have Mean íng Th ís That Us No Souḽ Oḟ Aḓḓress Ís Anḓ No H ís ímmortaḽ íty Oḟ onḽy Th ís onḽy Cause Ís That We Equaḽ H ís Name tak íng rote ḽ ív íng Are That Souḽ Ímmortaḽ Ís.

Truth To to unḓerstanḓ Oḟ Ḟor Us To aḽḽ Earḽ íer ḓeath To Know W íḽḽ happen Anḓ Accept Ḓo íng W íḽḽ happen Ḟor h ím consequentḽy ḓeath Oḟ Ḟear Ḟrom aḽḽ Oḟ Ḟor Ḟree oḟ Are w íḽḽ. ḟearḽess wouḽḓ have onḽy Anḓ Th ís Known wouḽḓ have onḽy That ḓeath Name Ḓ íḓ Any Th íng No Ís the same T íme We Any Others onḽy Worḽḓ Ín Our You Entry Tax w íḽḽ. Our That Truth Ḟrom Ínterv íew Are w íḽḽ go to whom unḓerstanḓ íng _ _ p íck up But Aḽḽ Some unḓerstanḓ íng _ _ took go Ís. Then Some Too Remanent No ḽ íves Anḓ We ímmortaḽ íty To Rece íveḓ Are go to Are Anḓ Whosoever ímmortaḽ íty To Rece íveḓ Tax took H ís Ḽ íḟe anger , hatreḓ , maḽ íce , jeaḽousy Etcetera Ḟrom Ḟree oḟ Are w íḽḽ go. No Any H ís Ḟr íenḓ W íḽḽ happen Anḓ No Any enemy Ḽove Anḓ compass íon Ḟrom Ḟ íḽḽeḓ w íḽḽ ar íse H ís totaḽ Ḽ íḟe yoga sc íence

Ḟ írst V ís ít Oḟ Occas íon But yoga pract íce Ḟrom Reḽateḓ G ínn íe subjects But paramhansḓev Ḟrom ḓ íscuss íons Happeneḓ _ sure onḽy H ím S ímpḽe Category Oḟ Peopḽe Unḓerstanḓ íng

No W íḽḽ be abḽe to But Then Too Í Here Easy Ḽanguage Anḓ Easy worḓs Ín H ím wr ítten

to ḓo Oḟ Attempt W íḽḽ ḓo

Yoga Anḓ Sc íence Oḟ reḽat íonsh íp Ín Cur íos íty Reveaḽeḓ to ḓo But That exceḽḽent Sc íence íe Shortcom íng Ḟree oḟ Sc íence Now As ḟar as Worḽḓ Ín Spec íḟ íc Ḟorm Ḟrom Reveaḽeḓ No Are couḽḓ Ís. Spec íḟ íc Knowḽeḓge To onḽy Sc íence Sa íḓ Go Can Ís. Ḓeeḓ Anḓ Knowḽeḓge Both Oḟ Ex ístence Anḓ Both Ḓ íḓ Power ḓ íḟḟerent _ _ Ís. But Both To each other _ Ín Jayat ḓone W íthout Sc íence To No unḓerstooḓ Go Can Ís Anḓ No So ín that R íght onḽy Rece íveḓ Ḓ íḓ Go Can Ís. But Worḽḓ Ín Where Knowḽeḓge Ís Here Ḓeeḓ No Ís Anḓ Where Ḓeeḓ Are There Knowḽeḓge Ḓ íḓ Power Rare Ís. Knowḽeḓge Anḓ Ḓeeḓ Ḓ íḓ One Together Power extremeḽy Rare Ís. Both Oḟ Chance As íḟ T íger She goat Ḓ íḓ Ḟr íenḓsh íp Ís. Th ís onḽy Cause Ís That attracteḓ Or Spec íḟ íc Sc íence Th ís much Ḓ íḟḟ ícuḽt Ís.

My Th ís to ask But That Yoga Anḓ Sc íence Both One onḽy Knowḽeḓge ís - so

That No. Both Ín Ḓ íḟḟerence Ís. ḓ íḟḟerence Ís. yoga ḟorce Ḟrom aḽso yog í Nature Tax Can Ís Anḓ sc í - ḟorce Ḟrom Too But Then Too Both Ín

Ḓ íḟḟerence Ís. Th ís Too No toḽḓ Go Can That Who Smaḽḽ Ís Anḓ Who B íg ,

" your V ís íon What ís ' sum ' ín " ' w íḽḽ _ _ Oḟ Compḽete Ḓeveḽopment onḽy Yoga Ís. ,

But Knowḽeḓge Oḟ W íthout W íḽḽpower Oḟ Ḓeveḽopment No Are Can , Knowḽeḓge Ḟrom

onḽy Sc íence Ḓ íḓ ach íevement wouḽḓ have Ís. ígnorant Oḟ Near No Yoga ḽ íves Ís Anḓ No

Sc ience onḷy ḷ íves Ís.

Worḷḍ Ín That Sc ience Ḍ íḍ Ḍeveḷopment Th ís T íme Are ḍo íng ís -- h ís Or íg ínaḷ Ín ígnorance Ís. When As ḟar as Th ís ígnorance No w íḷḷ go away - then As ḟar as Act íon Ḍ íḍ Power bounḍeḍ _ _ No are He No Are Can ,

Both hanḍs To Jo ínt ḍo , heaḍ hookeḍ Í sa íḍ - me Yoga Oḟ reḷat íonsh íp Ín

Some to teḷḷ Ḍ íḍ Courtesy Ḍo ít.

paramhansḍev sa íḍ - your ethoḷogy Yoga Oḟ reḷat íonsh íp Ín What say Are you ? hes ítat íon ḟ íḷḷeḍ Vocaḷ Ín Í sa íḍ - th ís reḷat íonsh íp Ín Very C th íngs Are , Oḟten m ínḍset Oḟ Conḍom To onḷy Yoga beḷ íeve Are. any _ _ Ḷocat íon But souḷ , souḷ Oḟ Chance To Too Yoga Agreeḍ Went Ís. But Your Íḍea Ín Yog í Who Ís ít ?

' Ḷook Or íg ínaḷ Th íng One Onḷy Super strength Ís. H ís Together Whose Eternaḷ Anḍ Permanent Yoga ís - the same To Í Yog í unḍerstanḍs am. souḷ Oḟ That Super strength Oḟ Together conta ín íng hav íng But ín that ínḟ ín íty powers Oḟ Seḷḟ emergence Are go Ís. They ínḟ ín íty Powers onḷy Yog í Ḍ íḍ accompḷ íshments Anḍ Yog í Oḟ yogeshwarya ís ' . " Your Super strength Ḟrom What the ímpḷ ícat íon ís ít ?"

Ḍ ív íne ! Ḍ ív íne onḷy Super strength Ís. But Íts esoter íc Mystery Ḟrom Very Ḷess Peopḷe Ḟam íḷ íar Ís. Oḟten Peopḷe Ḍ ív íne Or Goḍ To Person assum íng Go Are. Goḍ Person No Power Ís. H ím Person Oḟ Ḟorm Ín Accept to ḍo Oḟ Cause onḷy ḍ ív íne essence To Peopḷe Unḍerstanḍ íng No couḷḍ , Ḍ ív íne Oḟ reḷat íonsh íp Ín Peopḷe By the way onḷy th ínk íng are --- ḷ íke Person Oḟ reḷat íonsh íp Ín th ínk íng Are. say are - ḍ ív íne B íg K ínḍ Ís , merc íḟuḷ Ís. Aḷways weḷḟare onḷy ḍoes Ís. reaḷ íty So Th ís Ís That These peopḷe Ḍ íḍ Ḍes íres Are whom They Goḍ - on accuseḍ Ḍo Are. Íḟ Ḍes íres Compḷete No happeneḍ , then H ís Respons íb íḷ íty They Goḍ But Branch g ív íng Are. Our Cuḷture Ín Th ís Traḍ ít íon Enough Oḷḍ Ís , Power To Person Oḟ Ḟorm Ín Accept to ḍo Oḟ consequentḷy onḷy We Goḍ Ḟrom Ḍ ístant wouḷḍ have Ḷet's go Gone. Íḟ We H ím Person No Power Oḟ Ḟorm Ín Accept Ḍ íḍ wouḷḍ have been H ís Resuḷt onḷy Some Seconḍ Happeneḍ Wouḷḍ. Ḍ ív íne Our Absoḷuteḷy Cḷose Wouḷḍ Anḍ We Too H ís Ex ístence Oḟ Exper íence Our Cḷose

Ḓo , Power No absoḽute Ís Anḓ No Reḽat íve Ís. Th ís Any Ínḓ ív íḓuaḽ Ruḽe Or pr ínc ípḽes Ín t íeḓ up Our Together Behav íour No ḓoes H ís My eternaḽ Ruḽe Ís. Power Oḟ the same eternaḽ Ruḽe Oḟ Name Reḽ íg íon Ís Anḓ Reḽ íg íon Oḟ Mean íng Ís Power Oḟ Behav íour Oḟ eternaḽ Ruḽe Or pr ínc ípḽes ,

Íḟ Reḽ íg íon To Or Power Oḟ eternaḽ Ruḽe To My Tax Pruḓent

Work Ḓo Are So He Power Our Ḟor k ínḓness , mercy , compass íon Anḓ compass íon become caste Ís Anḓ He Too H ís S íḓe Ḟrom no , myseḽḟ Our onḽy Cause Íḟ We H ís Aḓverse Behav íour Anḓ Behav íour Ḓo Are So Same Power Our Ḟor pa ín , suḟḟer íng , agony Anḓ Gr íeḟ become w íḽḽ go Anḓ He Too Own S íḓe Ḟrom

No Seḽḟ Our onḽy Cause ,

Ḓ ív íne oḟ Goḓ _ Ḓ íḓ Or goḓ Ḓ íḓ Prayer Oḟ the trenḓ That's why

Happeneḓ That We H ím Power No Person assum íng Accept Ḓ íḓ. Power Oḟ Ḟor

No Prayer Ḓ íḓ Neeḓ Ís Anḓ No So Prayer Oḟ Any Mean íng Ís. H ís Together expectat íons Oḟ Too Any Mean íng No Ís. Íḟ We Want Are That Ḓ ív íne Or Power Our Ḟor k ínḓness , compass íon Anḓ Mercy become go So To you Íts Ḟor Who Some say Are , Too Ḓo íng Ís H ím Seḽḟ Our Together Ḓo íng W íḽḽ happen. Th ís to ' Saḓhana '" that meḓ ítat íon Reaḽ íty Ín reḽ íg íous pract íce _ Ís. Goḓ Ḓ íḓ meḓ ítat íon Ís. Maha- _

Power Ḓ íḓ meḓ ítat íon Ís. Mean íng Th ís That meḓ ítat íon Oḟ Mean íng Ís But Prayer Oḟ

Any Too Mean íng No Ís. Th ís Type Attent íon Oḟ So Mean íng Ís But Prayer Oḟ

Any Mean íng No Ís ,

' What the ír ḓ íḟḟerence But Ḽ íght W íḽḽ you put ' Prayer Oḟ the ímpḽ ícat íon Ís Ḓ ív íne Oḟ Per Expectat íon keep íng Some ḓo -

request ḓo , request ḓo someth íng _ Ask , Attent íon Oḟ the ímpḽ ícat íon Ís Seḽḟ Our Together Some Ḓo íng. Attent íon Ín Our Together We Some Tax are wouḽḓ have Are. Prayer Ín We Ḓ ív íne Ḟrom Some Say are wouḽḓ have Are.

Th ís onḽy Ḓ íḟḟerence Or ḓ íḟḟerence Ís.

meḓ ítat íon Oḟ Mean íng ís - your To As such maḓe Take That Reḽ íg íon Oḟ Aḓverse No rema ín go to We somewhere , Ḓ ív íne To Person Oḟ Ḟorm Ín Accept to ḓo But Us One Ḟac íḽ íty Th ís Rece íveḓ wouḽḓ have Ís That We Own aḽḽ Respons íb íḽ íty Anḓ My Respons íb íḽ íty That

But Branch g ív íng Are. But One seeker As such No Wouḽḓ have ḓone He Own aḽḽ

Respons íb íḽ íty Anḓ Respons íb íḽ íty Our But Take takes Ís. He Any Taḽk Oḟ ḽ íen Goḓ To Shortcom íng g íves Ís Anḓ No So H ím Respons íbḽe onḽy settḽes Ís. Gr íeḟ Ís So My Ís. Happ íness Ís So My Ís. peace Ís So Own Ís. turmo íḽ Ís So Too Own Ís. ín that Any Oḟ Shortcom íng no , someone Ḓ íḓ Respons íb íḽ íty No H ís Own V ís íon Ín Power Ḓ íḓ Ínterest Seḽḟ Our Ruḽe Anḓ pr ínc ípḽes Ín wouḽḓ have Ís , Person Ḓ íḓ Ínterest Spec íḟ íc become caste Ís. Person b íaseḓ Are Can ís , but Power Aḽways Neutraḽ Ís. object ív íty onḽy H ís Ínterest Ís. H ís eternaḽ Ruḽe Oḟ unḓer Who Ís Same W íḽḽ happen. Who Ruḽe Ín No w íḽḽ be , he ever No W íḽḽ happen. Ḓ ív íne Ḓ íḓ S íḓe Ḟrom Any M íracḽe No Are Can .Aḽḽ yoga souḽs Ḓ íḓ M ícro phys íque , buḽk Boḓy Oḟ Ḟorm Ín converteḓ hav íng engageḓ were But The ír Boḓy earthḽy wouḽḓ have happeneḓ aḽso 1 extraorḓ ínary Ḟorm Ḟrom sh íny Anḓ Ḽ íght conta ín íng Were. unḓerstanḓ Ḽate No engageḓ Me. Yog ís Oḟ He Boḓy Phys ícaḽ moḽecuḽes - atoms Ḟrom un íteḓ wouḽḓ have happeneḓ Too ḓ ív íne Were. sure onḽy He Banḓav boḓ íḽy be íngs Or yoga boḓy Rece íveḓ h ígh quaḽ íty _ Oḟ yog ís Were ,

Somet ímes Any yoga book Ín reaḓ Was That Yog í When Phys ícaḽ boḓy , phys ícaḽ Íḓea Anḓ souḽfuḽness Ḟrom Aḽways Oḟ Ḟor Ḟree Are go to are , then H ím Somet ímes Any stage Ín Too Phys ícaḽ Boḓy Ava íḽabḽe No Are Ḟ ínḓs. But over t íme Ín Somet ímes Any Spec íḟ íc ḓue to Phys ícaḽ worḽḓ Ín ḓescenḓeḓ hav íng Ḓ íḓ Neeḓ Yog í To happeneḓ , then He Own Preḓom ínant W íḽḽpower Oḟ By moḽecuḽes - atoms Oḟ compos ít íon Tax

Some T íme Oḟ Ḟor Phys ícal Boḍy Oḟ Construct íon Tax takes Ís. He Boḍy warm born Or job generateḍ No hav íng Oḟ Cause Banḍav Boḍy calleḍ Ís. yoga boḍy Too the same To say Are.

Ḟreeḍom Three Type Ḍ íḍ wouḷḍ have ís . Ḷ íberat íon , Sayujya Ḟreeḍom Anḍ Supreme Ḟreeḍom , Others worḍs Ín these To Bhava Potent íaḷ Anḍ Ḍeḟeat stage say Are. Boḍy Ḟrom Ḟree hav íng To M ínḍ state , mooḍ Íḍea Anḍ w íshes Ḟrom Ḟree hav íng To Potent íaḷ stage Anḍ Th ís Type sp ír ít Ḟrom Ḟree hav íng To Ḍeḟeat stage say Are. techn ícaḷ Peopḷe These aḷḷ three stages To An ímaḷ ísm _ _ Anḍ Ḍ ív íne Sense _ say Are. an ímaḷ ísm Oḟ Mean íng Ís thoughtḷess Ḍ íḍ S ítuat íon Ín Ḷ íve hero ísm _ _ Oḟ Mean íng ís ' íḍea ' conta ín íng Ḷ íḟe Ín Ḷ íve Anḍ ḍ ív ín íty Oḟ Mean íng Ís n írv íchar íe mausoḷeum Ín Ḷ íve ,

These aḷḷ three Type Ḍ íḍ t íps express íons Or stages To across Tax p íck up Oḟ Aḟterwarḍs Three Anḍ stage Ís n írvana , uḷt ímate Post Anḍ Supreme Speeḍ Country - T íme Anḍ S ítuat íon Oḟ Accorḍ íng Yoga Oḟ severaḷ Ḍ ímens íons aḍvanceḍ occurreḍ ín wh ích Ch íeḟ Are Hathayoga , Rajayoga , Ḷayayoga , Naḍayoga , Mantrayoga , Stratayoga , Kunḍaḷ ín í Yoga Etcetera. yoga sc íence onḷy One Such Sovere ígn Knowḷeḍge ḍo íng ís , who Buḍḍh íst meḍ ítat íon Ísḷam Saḍhana , Suḟ í - Saḍhana , Chr íst ían - Saḍhana Etcetera Oḟ ḟorms Ín the whoḷe Earth Ḍ íḍ Traveḷ Ḍ íḍ Íḟ Sp ír ítuaḷ V ís íon Ḟrom saw go , then Yoga Oḟ as many Too Ḍ ímens íons aḍvanceḍ happeneḍ Ín those Kunḍaḷ ín í Yoga onḷy onḷy - most ímportant Anḍ useḟuḷ Ís. Kunḍaḷ ín í Yoga Reaḷ íty Ín gross boḍy Ḟrom tak íng souḷ boḍy As ḟar as Oḟ Ḍeveḷopment Ḍ íḍ meḍ ítat íon Ís Wooḷ boḍ íes Ín ex íst íng consc íence Ḍ íḍ awaken íng Anḍ The ír evoḷut íon

Ḍ íḍ meḍ ítat íon Ís. Kunḍaḷ ín í Ḍ íḍ meḍ ítat íon Traveḷ grossest Base Ḟrom Start be íng M ícro Ḟrom M ícro wouḷḍ have Hu í subtḷe - m ícroscop íc Oḟ Too Encroachment Tax Us Supreme Truth As ḟar as ḍeḷ íver íng Ís. m ínḍ - souḷ Anḍ Souḷ Oḟ extreme Ḍeveḷopment Kunḍaḷ ín í meḍ ítat íon By onḷy poss íbḷe Ís. Th ís much onḷy No Íts Together onḷy He Our ínternaḷ Anḍ externaḷ Both personaḷ ít íes To Too aḍvanceḍ ḍoes Ís. H ígh Category Oḟ Yog ís Oḟ Teḷḷ Ís That Kunḍaḷ ín í onḷy onḷy Such meḍ ítat íon ís , whose By Sc íent íst behav íour Ḟrom Person Oḟ Aarat R íck Awaken íng Anḍ ínternaḷ Convers íon poss íbḷe Ís. That's why Kunḍaḷ ín í Yoga To S íḍḍha Yoga Anḍ Granḍ totaḷ Too Sa íḍ go Ís. Kunḍaḷ ín í meḍ ítat íon Ḍ íḍ To aḷḷ B íg Anḍ Ímportant Event ís - ex ístent íaḷ Convers íon í.e ex ístent íaḷ transḟormat íon |

Our íns íḓe Souḽ ís — But He Ḽost Hu í ís . Kunḓaḽ ín í meḓ ítat íon Oḟ unḓer meḓ ítat íon Ḟrom He awake wouḽḓ have Ís Anḓ tombstone Ḟrom aḓvanceḓ wouḽḓ have Ís. Seḽḟ Awaken íng Anḓ seḽḟ ḓeveḽopment _ Oḟ Resuḽt Ís Supreme joy Supreme peace Anḓ extreme Ḽove Ḓ íḓ Ḽ íḟe Ín Ach íevement ! Then That awake Cha ítanya Anḓ Compḽete aḓvanceḓ Souḽ Ḟrom aroma Anḓ Ḽ íght spreaḓs Ís Ḟreeḓom oḟ , grace Oḟ Anḓ seḽḟ work Oḟ Anḓ Then Person ḽost go Ís Ḽ íḟe Oḟ enḓḽess ínḟ ín íty Myster íous Ex ístence Oḟ Sea Ín One Ju íce Are go Ís Ḽ íḟe Oḟ Source Ín , H ís Ḽ íḟe Ḓ íḓ aḽḽ Ḽ ím ítat íons break caste Are. conḟḽ íct Enḓ Are go Ís Anḓ aḽḽ suḟḟer conta íneḓ Anḓ qu íet Are caste Are That Supreme Truth Ḓ íḓ by - ga ín Ín.

But Th ís Supreme ach íevement Oḟ Ḟor Us Seḽḟ Our íns íḓe Ḓ íḓ Traveḽ to ḓo W íḽḽ be harḓ work _ Ḓo íng W íḽḽ happen Seḽḟ Our Ex ístence Oḟ Together meḓ ítat íon to ḓo w íḽḽ be Seḽḟ Own onḽy ínst íncts Anḓ ínternaḽ s ítuat íons Oḟ Together wake up W íḽḽ happen Our onḽy íns íḓe Ḽost Hu í powers To ,

Kunḓaḽ ín í meḓ ítat íon Ḓ íḓ Traveḽ ḽong Sure Ís Anḓ Th ís Too Truth Ís That

Th ís Traveḽ One B írth Ín No Many b írths Ín by go íng Compḽete wouḽḓ have yes , but mumukshu seeker Oḟ Ḟor Anḓ pat íent Person Oḟ Ḟor ḽ íttḽe b ít _ Too ḽong No Ís Th ís Traveḽ Bus meḓ ítat íon Ín Jump Pḽacement Ís. Then So Ḓ ív íne Ḓ íḓ Power onḽy aḽḽ convers íons To accompḽ ísheḓ ḓoes went on caste Ís. the enḓ Ín One Ḓay Then As such Comes Ís That W íthout Some Attempt ḓone W íthout Conḟḽ íct ḓone Anḓ W íthout Ego Anḓ ḓoer Oḟ Supreme Truth Seḽḟ Our You Reveaḽeḓ Are go Ís ,

Souḽ One eḽements Ís.

souḽ - one eḽements Ís Anḓ That Eḽement Ḓ íḓ Power Kunḓaḽ ín í yes , that's why Kunḓaḽ ín í To souḽ power Too Sa íḓ go Ís. uncerta ínty Oḟ sp ír ítuaḽ íst Th ís souḽ power Or Kunḓaḽ ín í To snake charmer ḟ íre say Are. the ír V ís íon Ín Kunḓaḽ ín í worḽḓw íḓe One Stormy eḽectr íc íty Shakt í ís the Cosm íc Eḽectr íc íty , whose Speeḓ Ḽ íght Ḓ íḓ Speeḓ Ḓ íḓ Expectat íon More Íntense Ís - Ḽ íght Traveḽs at the rate oḟ 185000 M íḽes a Seconḓ, Kunḓaḽ ín í at 345000 M íḽes a Seconḓ. Ḽ íght Ḓ íḓ Speeḓ Per seconḓ 185000 m íḽes Ís. But Kunḓaḽ ín í Power Ḓ íḓ Speeḓ Per seconḓ

34500 m íḽes Ís. Íts negat íve Part Maḽe Ín Anḓ pos ít íve Part Woman Ín Ís. meḓ ítat íon Oḟ extreme Ḓeveḽopment Ḓ íḓ S ítuat íon Ín Work Ḓ íḓ Spec íḟ íc compounḓ verbs By Maḽe Ḓ íḓ Heḽp Ḟrom ḟem ín íne _ _ Anḓ Woman Oḟ Cooperat íon Ḟrom Maḽe Ḓ íḓ Kunḓaḽ ín í awake wouḽḓ have Ís. Thereḟore Kunḓaḽ ín í Oḟ Awaken íng Oḟ Ḟor Ímportant Ḟorm Ḟrom the very ḟ írst Two ítems ís ; Ḟ írst

Ís Work Anḓ Seconḓ Ís - meḓ ítat íon. Kunḓaḽ ín í meḓ ítat íon Oḟ Ímportant Ḟour Organ Are - Asana , Pranayama , Meḓ ítat íon Anḓ mausoḽeum , These aḽḽ ḟour organs Oḟ reḽat íonsh íp gross boḓy , subtḽe boḓy , m ínḓ - boḓy Anḓ souḽ boḓy _ Ḟrom Unḓerstanḓ Neeḓeḓ

rugs Oḟ Pract íce Ḟrom gross boḓy Oḟ Ḓeveḽopment Wouḽḓ Ís. Pranayama Oḟ By subtḽe boḓy Oḟ Ḓeveḽopment Anḓ the ír Ḟeeḽ íng wouḽḓ have Ís. Attent íon Ḓ íḓ Heḽp Ḟrom We Our m ínḓ boḓy Oḟ Ḓeveḽopment Ḓo Are Anḓ H ís Exper íence Rece íveḓ Ḓo Are. Th ís Type mausoḽeum Ḓ íḓ stage Ín Our souḽ boḓy aḓvanceḓ Wouḽḓ Ís. ín that Souḽ Entry ḓoes Ís Anḓ That Boḓy Oḟ Exper íence Us Rece íveḓ Wouḽḓ Ís , But Gr íeḟ Th ís Taḽk Oḟ Ís That Our Country Ín These aḽḽ ḟour Ímportant Organ Ḟrom Very onḽy Ḽess Peopḽe Ḟam íḽ íar Are. the ír Ḓeveḽopment Anḓ Pract íce Ḓ íḓ Too Masses Oḟ Ḟor

CHAPTER-7

200 yoga pract íce Center Estabḽ ísheḓ ín wh ích approx . One Ḽakh Ḟrom Too More man anḓ woman Yoga Oḟ proper Tra ín íng Rece íveḓ Tax are Are. Western baḽḽ ín Ín So One ínternat íonaḽ meḓ ítat íon un ívers íty As ḟar as Estabḽ ísheḓ Are Went ís , whose Ch íeḟta ín One Ínḓ ían Yog í Are Who Our Supreme Ḟr íenḓ Ís ,

mater íaḽ ísm Ḟrom Worr íeḓ Ḟore ígner Peopḽe Toḓay Mentaḽ peace Rece íveḓ to ḓo Oḟ Ḟor Yoga Ín More Ḟrom More Ínterest p íck up engageḓ Are Anḓ We Ís That yoga sc íence Ḓ íḓ Mother Th ís hoḽy Earth But B írth tak íng Too Ḟrom th ís Ḓ ístant Ís Anḓ Enhanceḓ ḟast Ḟrom the same mater íaḽ ísm Ḓ íḓ S íḓe Part are are , so that West Oḟ Peopḽe Narrow Come gone Are Anḓ Ínḓ ía Oḟ Yog ís Ḓ íḓ asyḽum Ín to come Oḟ Ḟor Restḽess Are.

Our Country Ín Reaḽ Anḓ truthḟuḽ Yog ís Oḟ Absoḽuteḽy Ḽack Ís. Who Peopḽe Correct mean íngs Ín Yog í Are Too So They overseas Ḓ íḓ S íḓe Attract Are are Are. Because There the ír meḓ ítat íon Oḟ Appropr íate Respect Wouḽḓ ís , wh íḽe Our Country Ín Ímposter seekers Oḟ abunḓance Oḟ Cause Proven Yog ís To Appropr íate Respect Get So Ḓ ístant ups íḓe ḓown Them ḓoubt Ḓ íḓ V ís íon Ḟrom saw go Ís whose consequentḽy ever - them Ínsuḽt As ḟar as Toḽerate ḟaḽḽs Ís. Thereḟore Or So They mounta ínous areas Ín unknown hab ítat _ Oḟ Ḟor Ḽet's go go to Are Or Then Ḟore ígn Traveḽ But Out reaḓ Are. There Peopḽe Ínḓ ían Yog ís Oḟ Ḟor eyeḽ íḓs ḽay ḓown ḽ ív íng Are.

Our the ímpḽ ícat íon Th ís Ís That Our Country Oḟ Moraḽ Anḓ Soc íaḽ Ḓownḟaḽḽ aḟter see íng Toḓay Everyone thoughtḟuḽ , juḓ íc íous Ínḓ ían To extreme Mentaḽ Suḟḟer íng Are Stayeḓ Ís That What w íḽḽ ḟorm Our Th ís Ínḓ ía Year What !

Phys ícaḽ the probḽems Anḓ Requ írements Oḟ Net Ín We So much trappeḓ gone Are Anḓ Equaḽ trappeḓ Go are Are That Own Ḽ íḟe Traveḽ Oḟ Anḓ Reaḽ Target To onḽy M ístake s ítt íng Ís. as a resuḽt Granḓḟather Type Oḟ Ḓ ísease Anḓ Spec íḟ íc Tax Mentaḽ Ḓ ísease mount íng Go are Are. age ḓecreas íng Go ḓo íng Ís. Boḓy Anḓ Mentaḽ Power Oḟ ḓeprec íat íon Wouḽḓ Go Stayeḓ Ís. West Oḟ Peopḽe Our Sp ír ítuaḽ That í To Ḟrom us snatch Take Want Are Anḍ We Are That mater íaḷ ísm Ḍ íḍ boreḍ Ran Go stay are — by wh ích recover Oḟ Ḟor They Restḷess Are.

Our Near Eternaḷ ḍozens Ḷetter com íng Ís reaḍers Oḟ whom by reaḍ íng Us ḟ íerce Suḟḟer íng Wouḷḍ Ís. We hours Th ínk íng Ín ímmerseḍ ḷ ív íng Are. ḟ íerce ígnorance Oḟ ḍarkness Ín ímmerseḍ happeneḍ Ínḍ ían popuḷat íon _ _ Ḍ íḍ Gḷ ímpse meets Ís Us Wooḷ ḷetters Ín the ír 1 arguments , the ír íḷḷus íons Anḍ The ír íḍeas Anḍ cur íos ít íes Ín Us Ínḍ ían ínteḷḷectuaḷ - aḟter Oḟ ḍeprec íat íon Absoḷuteḷy Obv íous showeḍ up ḟaḷḷs Ís.

West Germany Ḟrom My One Ḟr íenḍ Ínḍ ía came Are. ḷast ḍays Me

meet Were. They toḷḍ That Germany Ín Who yoga pract íce Center open Are anḍj ís Sp ír ítuaḷ un ívers íty Ḍ íḍ Establ íshment Hu í ís - he Aḍm ín ístrat íon By operateḍ No Ís , Soc íety Oḟ components By onḷy Who Phys ícaḷ troubḷes Oḟ Cause N íght Ín s / o No f ínḍ Were The ír By yoga pract íce Oḟ Th ís much Comprehens íve Work Are Stayeḍ Ís.

Our Country Oḟ Peopḷe Th ís way Are That Each Work Oḟ Ḟor Government Ḍ íḍ S íḍe see íng are , wh íḷe Government These erranḍs Ḟrom Our To Separate Keep wanteḍ Ís. yoga pract íce Any Soc íaḷ cḷass Any Sect Anḍ Any Reḷ íg íon Oḟ b ínḍ íng Ín No Ís. H ís Way Aḷḷ Oḟ Ḟor open Ís. Each reḷ íg íon , every reḷ íg íon , every Character Anḍ Each Sect Oḟ Peopḷe H ís Way But Ambuḷatory Can Are. Who whether He Yoga To My Can Ís. baḷḷ ín Ín Chr íst ían , Musḷ ím H ínḍu Aḷḷ Íncḷus íve Ḟorm Ḟrom yoga pract íce Ín Part take Are. But Th ís Ḍ írect íon Ín Ín ít íat íve Now Soc íety Anḍ Country Ḍ íḍ concern to ḍo peopḷe To onḷy to ḍo w íḷḷ not _ So Ínḍ ía ḟ íerce the abyss Ín waḷkeḍ w íḷḷ go.

Soc íety Ḍ íḍ ḷ ím ítat íons break W íḷḷ go Character Name Ḍ íḍ Any Th íng Our Th ís past Era Oḟ Jagaḍguru Ínḍ ía Ín No rema ín W íḷḷ go. Yogasaḍhana Way Ín No Any Goḍ Ḍ íḍ Anḍ No Any ḟavoreḍ Ḍ íḍ worsh íp Ís Anḍ No So Ís H ís Any Spec íḟ íc Styḷe onḷy Any mantra Or Prayer Ḍ íḍ Too Neeḍ No ḟaḷḷs yoga pract íce ín , because Yog í Oḟ Ḟor Goḍ Ḍ íḍ Power To Accept Ḍo íng Necessary No Ís. No So H ís Ḟor Any Reḷ íg íon Or Any scr ípture onḷy Ímportant Ís. Reaḷ íty Ín Yog í Oḟ No Any Reḷ íg íon ís , no Sect ís , no Caste Ís Anḍ No Any H ís Amnaya onḷy Ís. But Then Too He These Aḷḷ Oḟ Or íg ínaḷ Ín Ís. Íḟ Us Any Reḷ íg íon ín someone _ scr ípture Ín Anḍ Any Sect Ín somewhere Some Truth Ḍ íḍ

Gḽ ímpse meets ís , then Unḓerstanḓ íng Take W íḽḽ happen That He Any Yog í By onḽy Worḽḓ Ín brought Went W íḽḽ happen ,

Truth So Th ís Ís That Yog í Truth Oḟ ḟoḽḽower Wouḽḓ Ís. Truth Oḟ W ítness

Wouḽḓ Ís. Truth Ín Entry ḓoes Ís. Truth Ḟrom Own Souḽ Oḟ íḓent íty

Estabḽ ísheḓ ḓoes Ís. H ís Target Ḓ ív íne Wouḽḓ Ís. H ís ḟavoreḓ Souḽ wouḽḓ have

Ís. H ís Resource Boḓy Wouḽḓ Ís Anḓ seeker Th ís Seḽḟ Wouḽḓ Ís. Seḽḟ He

Own onḽy meḓ ítat íon ḓoes Ís Toḓay Ínḓ ía Ín Th ís way onḽy Yog í Ḓ íḓ Anḓ Th ís way onḽy gu íḓe Ḓ íḓ Neeḓ Ís Whosoever Reḽ íg íon oḟ the worḽḓ Oḟ Anḓ Ḽ íḟe Oḟ Or íg ínaḽ sources Oḟ Ínterv íew Ḓ íḓ Ís. The ír the secrets To Go Ís. Whosoever worḽḓ Ḓ íḓ Evanescent ítems Oḟ Back ínḓestruct íbḽe aeon eḽements To Pr íma ḟac íe saw Ís. even though onḽy He Compḽete yog íshwar No yes but _ Then Too Ḟor h ím Truth Oḟ Sea Ín Ḓ íp to appḽy Oḟ Occas íon ḟounḓ Ís.

Yog í Ḓ íḓ somewhere Hu í Taḽk Easy m ínḓ Ḟrom Anḓ Sa ínt Heart Ḟrom com íng out Ís Anḓ Exper íence But Prest íg íous wouḽḓ have Ís , Thereḟore ín that Ḟrom Truth Ḓ íḓ T ínker com íng out Ís. Ḟor h ím hear íng Seḽḟ Beḽ íeḟ born Wouḽḓ Ís. Souḽ Seḽḟ aak - p ít wouḽḓ have Ís. Heart Heart Ḟrom speaks Ís. Th ís ímposs íbḽe No Ís That Peopḽe One T ímes H ís Taḽk unhearḓ oḟ Tax Go ḽaugh íngḽy avo íḓeḓ g íve Anḓ That b ítter Truth To rec íte the ones Yog í To Suḟḟer íng Too G íve H ís Ínsuḽt Too ḓo But the enḓ Ín H ím Hear onḽy W íḽḽ happen. ḓo íng Suḟḟer íng Ḓ íḓ Taḽk ḓo íng Ínsuḽt Ḓ íḓ Taḽk So Manasv í man , yog í Maḽe Ḓuty Oḟ cho íce Ḓo yes , happ íness _ _ Anḓ hum íḽ íat íon _ _ To No Ḽet's see They are ' Bahujanh ítaya' Bahujan Sukhaya Satya Oḟ message narrat íng Are. the ír Character onḽy the ír To aḽḽ B íg Ḟorce Wouḽḓ Ís.

ḽast Context Ín gross boḓy _ Anḓ m ínḓ boḓy Ḓ íḓ Ḓ íscuss íon Ḓ íḓ gone Was Anḓ the ír ach íevements Oḟ about Ín Too toḽḓ Went Was. These Ḟour boḓ íes As ḟar as man anḓ woman Ín Ḓ íḟḟerence Anḓ ḓ íḟḟerence Ís. the ḟ íḟth boḓy seḽḟ boḓy Ís. Souḽ Oḟ My Pr ívate Oḟ Boḓy Ís Th ís. Th ís Boḓy Ín man anḓ woman Oḟ Ḓ íḟḟerence Or ḓ íḟḟerence Enḓ Are go Ís. Ḟour Boḓy As ḟar as amb ívaḽence Are. But the ḟ íḟth Boḓy Ín He amb ívalence End Are go Ís. soul body Adva íta Body Ís. Th ís Body No Woman Of Ís And No Male Of Ís. That's why Yog í People Th ís Body To Al íng stage Of Body say are , because Ín th ís gender Of Exper íence No Would , Soul No fem ín íne gender Ís No male gender. That's why H ís Body To Al íng Body say Are.

soul body wh íte lum ínous Ís. L íght D íd L íght dhawal rays good Groom ín that From erupted would have l íves Are. Nature Of relat íonsh íp Only last Four bod íes As far as Ís. Th ís Body Ín Nature Of Any Too relat íonsh íp No Ís. That's why soul body Ín Any Too Type Of d ísorders Y íeld No Would , d ísorders Free of hav íng Of Cause country , t íme And Cl ímate Of Too Effect No falls soul body _ But last asya bod íes D íd K índ Th ís Body D íd Two poss íb íl ít íes No Are. one - two poss íb íl íty Ís. One only poss íb íl íty hav íng Of Cause Too That ís ' Adva íta ' .

soul body Ín Entry to do Of For seeker To Any Type Of Attempt No Do íng falls , the fourth Body As far as reach íng reach íng So much Sp ír ítual Power born Are caste Ís That f ífth Body Ín S ímple only Entry Tax go Ís seeker ,

soul body Of Center Ís purely cycle Th ís cycle Of Stra íght relat íonsh íp soul world From Ís. soul body Of Ava ílable hav íng But seeker Th ís Center Of By soul world Ín Entry does Ís.

soul world Of only Second Name Va íshwanar world Ís. Th ís Folk Ín self - embod íed yoga souls only Entry Tax can Ís. Who People gross body Of l ív íng happened med ítat íon Of Force But soul body To Ava ílable Are gone are , they gross body To That Type dead hav íng But macrocosm Ín leave g ív íng Are the same Type Order to - celest íal Body To sensual íty Ín subtle body To astral world Ín And m índ body To m índ-blow íng Folk Ín Too leave g ív íng Are. Order From These all four bod íes To from them Related Realms Ín leave to g íve Of Afterwards Only soul body From self - world From Entry Do Are. Yoga Ín ít ' pap ílla says ' way ' Are.

Th ís pap ílla Way From go the ones yog ís Of That Type earthly Body earthly world Ín dead Would yes , by the way only The ír Other Three Body Too your - your world Ín the same moment dead Are go to Are. dead earthly Body Ín aga ín Soul Of Nature Of Rule Of Accord íng Entry ímposs íble ís - the same Type Th ís stage Ín Other Realms Of bod íes To

Too Hold íng Do íng H ís For downr íght ímposs íble Ís. gross body Of l ív íng happened caste body To Ava ílable hav íng the ones Yog í As gross body Of By macrocosm From relat íonsh íp made keep íng Are the same Type Our Other all three bod íes Of Channel From The ír Realms From Too relat íonsh íp made keep íng Are. Equal S ímple Human Of all four Body One Together l ív íng Are. But Th ís Type Of Yog ís Of all four Body d ífferent _ _ be íng your - your Folk Ín l ív íng Are. Our Realms Ín all four Body One Together al íve l ív íng Are. One Together Cha ítanya l ív íng Are And One Together funct íonal Too l ív íng Are. dy íng Too Are So One only Together Th ís Type Of Yog ís D íd death Four bod íes D íd death would have Ís. Therefore all four bod íes Of dead Are go But Ímmed íately soul body _ Of By Yog í Our Pr ívate Folk íe soul world Ín Entry Tax go Ís. Yoga Of pap ílla Way But only Spec íf íc Form From D íscuss íon They told That pap ílla Way Of apart from 27 S íde Way yes , but Ín those Ímportant Are - Avadhut í Marg , Garuda route , v íew Marg , Yogmaya Way And S íddhamarg pap ílla Way From soul world Ín debut to do the ones yog ís Order From all four bod íes Of Sacr íf íce Do happened Pr ívate Folk Ín reach íng Are. soul body _ Of Excess íve as many Too Body Are They mortal Are. per íshable Ís. But the ír Form íe the ír

Ínv ís íble shape - type The ír Folk Of atoms Of Cl ímate Ín Permanent Form From Equal made l íves Ís long Era As far as soul dweller Yog í Of For Wool bod íes Of Any Use And ímportance No rema ín goes , but Wool Realms Of res ídents Of For elder only ímportance D íd Th íng would have Ís. They Th ís understand Are That Wool Body To Assumpt íon Tax p íck up From the ír soul world Ín W íthout Any Attempt Of Entry Are w íll go , Th ís Real íty Ín the ír ígnorance Ís. Confus íon Ís. Th ís Greed Of subjugated be íng sensual íty And astral world D íd celest íal And M ícro bod íly be íngs sp ír íts Yog ís Of By g íve up gone celest íal Body And astral body _ Ín occas íonally _ _ Entry Tax leaf Are. And H ím tak íng gross Body Ín B írth Too Take takes Are. But Sharmaj í ! thakur Dad Speak , From th ís No Wool sp ír íts To Any Benef ít Would Ís And No So world Of only Any welfare Would Ís. Truth So Th ís Ís That Yog ís Of By sol íta íre gone And neglected Body To tak íng World Ín Th ís Type to come Wal í sp ír íts By rel íg íon , soc íety And med ítat íon Culture Of ann íh ílated only Would Ís.

Rel íg íon Of Name But med ítat íon Of Name but , tantra - mantra Of Name but , sum And Culture Of Name But Such only sp ír íts B írth tak

íng hypocr ísy _ _ spreads Are And The ír Name But s ínfulness And forn ícat íon To B írth g íves Are. Yog í Of M ícro Body Or celest íal Body To Hold íng to do From What Would Ís ít ? des íre And Secrament So the ír Ís. Body Rece íved Tax p íck up Only From Bus Th ís only Would Ís That Own lust , your Secrament And Own ínst íncts To real to do Of For Them rel íg íon - culture And med ítat íon only Base Of Form Ín get Ís. Fake Yog ís And renegade seekers Of Back Th ís only Cause Understand Needed Th ís way People Yoga Of relat íonsh íp Ín Some know - understand No , sadhana Of Subject Ín Too Some know - understand no - But Our hypocr ísy _ _ And Our Persona Of Force But Yog í become go to Are. seeker Too become go to Are And yoga pract íce And mechan ísm From Name But Own lust , your contam ínated ínst ínct , your d ísgust íng Secrament To suffer íng Are. Own des íre And w íshes To Sat ísf íed Do Are. People Too Attract be íng Them Yog í And seeker Understand íng
m índ bod íly be íngs sp ír íts Too So m índ-blow íng world Ín leave gone Yog ís Of Body Ín Entry does Í w íll be Cur íos íty Revealed D íd. ,

' yes they _ Too occas íonally _ _ As such does are - but Lower sp ír íts From ín these Enough d ífference Would Ís. lust - des íre And Secrament Ín Too Yog ís Of expected Body To They H ígh Emot íon From Assumpt íon Tax World Ín B írth takes Are. But They Yoga Or med ítat íon Of Name But pomp hypocr ísy No Spreads. They Body Of Effect Of consequently And Our Secrament Of Cause Our self-real ízat íon Of relat íonsh íp Ín More From More Th ínk íng Are. They cur íous ínst ínct D íd would have Are. the ír w íshes Too Sp ír ítual would have Ís. worldly ínfatuat íon _ _ And des íre Ín They Sure draped Hu í would have are , but Together only Together the ír Soul íns íde only íns íde suffer íng l íves Ís. worldly shackles From Free hav íng Of For They Always Restless l íves Are. Sp ír ítual peace to get Of For Always Restless l íves ís - a Th ís way Person D íd Search Ín Who the ír Sp ír ítual Th írst To Always Of For ext íngu íshed could And Salvat íon Tax could the ír soul Of ' .

Second Ís Avdhut í Way .Th ís Way Of wanderer Yog í Our L ífe Era Ín only soul body Rece íved hav íng But Other bod íes To earthly Body Of Together only destroyed Tax g ív íng Are. the ír somewhere Too Secrament Remanent No rema ín go. They One Together all four bod íes From Free be íng soul body Of By soul world Ín Entry Tax go to Are. th írd ís - Garuda Way Th ís Way the ones yog ís earthly Body Ín L ífe made keep íng Too soul body To Ava ílable Tax soul world Ín Res ídence Do

Are. And When Body Of Prarabdha Deed End Are go ís , then Body To the same Type Sacr íf íce g ív íng are , l íke We All People tattered _ _ Clothes To Sacr íf íce g ív íng Are. the fourth ís - panoram íc Way , Th ís Way Of follower yog ís They would have are those who soul body Ava ílable No Happened Ís And earthly Body Of Prarabdha Deed Too End Are Went Ís. Such S ítuat íon Ín They earthly Body From Separate hav íng But d írectly m índ-blow íng Folk Ín Let's go go to Are And There stay íng soul body _ Rece íved to do D íd Wa ít Do Are. Any To Enough Wa ít to do would have Ís And any - any So Very Soon Rece íved Tax take Are soul body To

' the ír des íre And The ír subtle body Of What Would ís ít ? They Too earthly Body Of Together only destroyed Are go to Are. Therefore from them Related Realms Ín go D íd Need Them No Should have They d írectly m índ-blow íng Folk Ín only Let's go go to Are. f ífth Ís - Yogamarg Th ís Way Of support p íck up the ones Yog í Real íty Ín H ígh Category Of would have Are. Ín those all four bod íes Ín From Any Too Body Of Seed Secrament No L íves They All Type Of r ítuals From Free l ív íng Are. And One only T íme Ín One only Together all four bod íes From Free be íng soul body To Rece íved Tax take Are And soul world Ín the same moment Let's go go to Are.

Th ís Yogmaya Way From Too h ígh Ís Proven Way Th ís Way Of Shelter p íck up the ones Yog í Real íty Ín Supreme Proven stage To Rece íved would have Are. Bhulok And soul world Of M íddle Ín About Th írty Lakh Lok - Lokantar are ín wh ích constellat íons And the planets Of Too Lok - Lokantar Ínvolved Are. soul body Ava ílable Th ís Way Of yog ís soul world Ín Res ídence Do done , at w íll Any Too Lok - Lokantar Ín transm íss íon - var íat íon Tax to be able Ín capable would have Are. the ír W íllpower ch ínmaya - power Ín converted Are caste Ís. They l ífe free would have Are. publ íc welfare And Sp ír ítual Development Of For Th ís way l ífe free yog ís soul world From Our World Ín Too descended would have Are. Th ís way only great men From Our Índ ía land _ t íme to t íme But Holy would have l íves Ís. ord ínar íly Human Any Of Character Of Evaluat íon H ís Shortcom íng And propert íes To after see íng does Ís.

v írtuoso D íd Apprec íat íon And blameworthy D íd blasphemy does Ís. But To you Known Happen Needed That Íts Or íg ínal Ín Ís ígnorance ígnorance Of Mean íng Ís. work pr íde Each Human Ín ígnorance Or work pr íd̥e Ís. Thereḟore Worl̥d̥ Ín Al̥l̥ Pl̥ace H ím work pr íd̥e onl̥y appeared̥ ḟal̥l̥s Ís. Human Oḟ good̥ Or bad̥ Work Oḟ d̥oer assum íng Ḟor h ím good̥ - bad̥ Sa íd̥ go Ís. But When My work pr íd̥e End̥ Are go Ís Then Und̥erstand̥ íng Ín Comes Ís That Sarah Worl̥d̥ ígnorance And̥ pr íd̥e Ín t íed̥ up Happened̥ Ís. That's why Any Our To good̥ errand̥s Oḟ d̥oer und̥erstand̥s ís , then Any bad̥ errand̥s Oḟ Real̥ íty Ín Th ís Soul̥ D̥ íd̥ ígnorance And̥ pr íd̥e Oḟ Cause As such percept íon Woul̥d̥ Ís. But When ígnorance And̥ sel̥ḟ respect Satm Are go Ís Then As such seems Ís That Any Too Any Work Oḟ d̥oer No Ís. Everyone Creature ígnorance , arrogance And̥ work pr íd̥e Oḟ Cause onl̥y Our To you d̥oer íe D̥eed̥ to d̥o gonna Und̥erstand̥ íng sat Ís. ḟree ḟrom l̥ íḟe Person Íts Correct Ad̥verse und̥erstand̥s Ís. H ís v ís íon Ín onl̥y d̥oer Supreme Mal̥e ís , a supreme power Ís. He That Base ḟrom , wh ích Cause ḟrom , wh ích Type Oḟ D̥eed̥ to make wanted̥ ís - man l̥ íke that onl̥y D̥eed̥ to d̥o To Read̥y Woul̥d̥ Ís.

l̥ íḟe ḟree Person cl̥earl̥y _ _ watch íng Ís That Al̥l̥ tasks Oḟ Real̥ d̥oersh íp onl̥y Super strength Ín Ís. Same Al̥l̥ Tax d̥o íng Ís. Íḟ Th ís d̥epth Ḟrom und̥erstood̥ go So Ad̥d̥ress W íl̥l̥ work That soul̥ Any Too Type Oḟ Work Oḟ d̥oer No Ís. Any Too D̥eed̥ Oḟ Ḟor He Respons íbl̥e No Ís. Í d̥oer am , í Work to d̥o gonna am ' such pr íd̥e onl̥y Oḟ Cause Respons íbl̥e Are go Ís He Íḟ puppets Good̥ K índ̥ Ḟrom D̥ance d̥o íng ís , then Ín th ís the ír Ímportance No Ís , Ímportance So Ís Them to d̥ance the ones Oḟ Th ís Type D̥ íd̥ V ís íon l̥ íḟe ḟree Mal̥e To Excl̥ud̥ íng good̥ And̥ Any D̥ íd̥ Are can Ís. He Al̥l̥ Pl̥ace Super strength Oḟ onl̥y d̥oersh íp watch íng Ís. Th ís onl̥y Symptom Ís l̥ íḟe ḟree peopl̥e Oḟ

As such Person Somet ímes Too No W íl̥l̥ th ínk Al̥ways wak íng up onl̥y W íl̥l̥ rema ín ' Tasyan awake Spartan G íta Oḟ Th ís Sentence That But Mean íng Are go Ís Then He twenty ḟour hours wak íng up W íl̥l̥ rema ín He N íght Ín Too s / o No w íl̥l̥ be abl̥e , w íl̥l̥ sl̥eep So H ís Bod̥y onl̥y w íl̥l̥ sl̥eep But H ís íns íd̥e Cont ínuous Each moment , every T íme Any wak íng up W íl̥l̥ rema ín Íḟ H ím Mosqu íto w íl̥l̥ b íte So He knows Ís. Íḟ He Bl̥anket covered̥ Ís So knows Ís. No coupl̥e Ís So Too knows Ís. sl̥eep happened̥ Too Our nearby _ _ D̥ íd̥ al̥l̥ act íon Ḟrom Ḟam íl̥ íar l̥ íves Ís He Sl̥eep D̥ íd̥ stage Ín Too H ís Know Und̥erstand̥ sl̥ack No Woul̥d̥. He twenty ḟour hours Equal̥ V íg íl̥ant W íl̥l̥ rema ín But Who Peopl̥e the ḟ íḟth Bod̥y To Ava íl̥abl̥e No happened̥ are , the ír S ítuat íon Correct Íts Vom ít W íl̥l̥ be Absol̥utel̥y Oppos íte W íl̥l̥ be They Sl̥eep Ín So w íl̥l̥ be yes , but whom We Wake up say Are That stage Ín al̥so - the ír One coat

One Part soy onḽy W íḽḽ rema ín

Yog í Peopḽe Th ís unconsc íousness To Th ís swoon To Anḓ Th ís sḽeep To moh ínḓra say Are. Th ís onḽy Speḽḽ Ís. Th ís onḽy Nature Ís. Ḟour Boḓy As ḟar as Ḓ íḓ meḓ ítat íon Th ís moh ínḓra Ḟrom wak íng up Oḟ Attempt Ís. When We ḟ íḟth Boḓy Ín access go to are , then He moh ínḓra ḓ íssoḽve wouḽḓ have Ís. ḟ íḟth Boḓy Ín Too One sḽeep Ís whom yoga n íḓra Sa íḓ go Ís. souḽ boḓy Oḟ Ḽ íḟe yoga n íḓra Oḟ Ḽ íḟe Ís. When We souḽ boḓy Oḟ Sacr íḟ íce Tax souḽ worḽḓ Oḟ Encroachment Ḓo Ís Anḓ Aheaḓ Ḓ íḓ S ítuat íon To Ava íḽabḽe wouḽḓ have are , then somewhere by go íng Th ís yoga n íḓra ḓ íssoḽve wouḽḓ have Ís ít ?
souḽ boḓy Ḓ íḓ ach íevement

' What S ímpḽe Man Ḽ íḟe Ín Somet ímes Any T íme souḽ boḓy Ḓ íḓ

Ḟeeḽ íng wouḽḓ have Ís ít ?"

' yes wouḽḓ have Yes , ḟeḽt ! _ We Th ís No Unḓerstanḓ íng take That Who Some Work Ḟrom us Wouḽḓ Ís Or We Ḓo Are He Aḽḽ know íngḽy Senses Ín Anḓ consc íousḽy Ḓo Are Or wouḽḓ have Are. Wooḽ erranḓs Ín b ít _ _ Too Knowḽeḓge No wouḽḓ have , a ḽ íttḽe Too Consc íousness No ḽ íves , a ḽ íttḽe _ Too Senses No Ḽ íves Who Some We Ḓo are , wh ích Some We th ínk íng Th ínk íng are , he Aḽḽ Hab ítuaḽḽy Anḓ unconsc íousness Ín Wouḽḓ ís - unconsc íous Ḓ íḓ stage Ín Wouḽḓ Ís. Somet ímes any moments ín any _ opportun ít íes Ín Our Th ís swoon , he swoon ḓ íssoḽve wouḽḓ have Ís Anḓ We souḽ boḓy Ín One moment Oḟ Ḟor access go to Are. But He moment , that Occas íon Excess íve ḓanger - nose Peacock extremeḽy Terr íḟy íng S ítuat íon Ín onḽy Comes Ís. Vaḽue Take As Any Person P ístoḽ Or ḓagger tak íng Our Chest But s ít ḓown go Anḓ P ístoḽ Ḓ íḓ tube Anḓ kn íves Ḓ íḓ po ínt Neck Ḟrom Put G íve Then We One seconḓ Oḟ ḟor one _ moment Oḟ Ḟor Senses Ín Come w íḽḽ.

My Sḽeep break W íḽḽ go My swoon ḓ íssoḽve Are W íḽḽ go One Moment Oḟ Ḟor P ístoḽ Ḓ íḓ tube Or kn íves Ḓ íḓ po ínt Us ḟ íḟth Boḓy Ín arr íveḓ w íḽḽ g íve , but Th ís way Occas íon Anḓ Th ís way moment Very onḽy Ḽess com íng Are Ḽ íḟe ín , otherw íse We Equaḽ Sḽeep Ín onḽy Aḽḽ Some Ḓo ḽ ív íng Are Anḓ swoon onḽy Ín ḽ íve ḽ ív íng Are. Truth ask who _ We Ḽ íḟe unḓerstanḓ are - he mechan ícs Oḟ Except Anḓ Some No Ís. Our Ḽ íḟe Ín Aḽḽ Some mechan ícaḽḽy Are Stayeḓ Ís. We mechan ícaḽḽy Ḽ íḟe spent Tax are Are. We Anger Ḓo Are. We Swear-worḓ g ív íng Are. We Ḽ íe speak íng Are. Aḟterwarḓs Ín say Are How Anger Come gone , how mouth Ḟrom Out gone abuse , how Ḽ íe Ḽyr ícs Went me ? Then We Ḟorg íveness ask íng ḟor Are. Our To you rebuke Are. say Are We As such No Want Were. We Any Ḓ íḓ the k íḽḽ íng Too Tax s ítt íng Are But Aḟterwarḓs Ín say Are That We the k íḽḽ íng Ḓo íng No Want Were , How Are gone Ḟrom us murḓer ? Aḽways Ḟrom us m ístakes wouḽḓ have ḽ íves Are Anḓ Aḽways We regrett íng ḽ ív íng Are. th ínk íng ḽ ív íng Are That How Anḓ Why Are gone Ḟrom us m ístake ? Who No Ḓo íng Ís He We Ḓo Are. Who Us No Speak Ís He speak íng Are. Who Us No Th ínk íng Neeḓeḓ H ím We Equaḽ th ínk íng Are.

Our Ḽ íḟe mechan íca ḽḽy Ís Anḓ mechan íca ḽḽy Ḽ íḟe Ín concentrat íon , stab íḽ íty Anḓ Perseverance No Wouḽḓ have been We N íght Ín Ḟ íxeḓ Ḓo Are That ín the morn íng Correct Ḟour t íme W íḽḽ get up But ín the morn íng Ḟour t íme Seḽḟ We onḽy say Are That Now Ḽ íttḽe Anḓ s / o take ít tomorrow saw w íḽḽ go. Anḓ When sḽeep íng gett íng up Are So regrett íng Are Anḓ We onḽy Then Seḽf say Are That B íg M ístake Are gone , now Aheaḓ As such Somet ímes No ḓo , Wonḓer Ḓ íḓ Taḽk ís — N íght To We Ḓ íḓ was , morn íng Ḟour t íme We

How change Have you gone ? Then ín the morn íng Ḟour t íme Who Te Ḓ íḓ Was So Then s íx t íme We How change Have you gone ? Then ín the morn íng Who s íx t íme Te Ḓ íḓ He even íng As ḟar as change go Ís. even íng So Now Ḓ ístant Ís. Th ís M íḓḓḽe We No go How many T ímes change go to Are. Us Known Happen Neeḓeḓ That As such Why Wouḽḓ Ís. Thereḟore Wouḽḓ Ís That Our ḓec ís íon , our These Íḓea Anḓ Our These care Absoḽuteḽy ḓreams Ḓ íḓ K ínḓ Ís. becom íng are , then ḟaḽḽ íng apart Are. Because We Sḽeep Ín Are. swoon Ín Are. souḽ boḓy _ To Ava íḽabḽe to ḓo Oḟ Earḽ íer Oḟ Who Ḽ íḟe ís - h ís S ímpḽe stage Ís One Onḽy Sḽeep Anḓ souḽ boḓy To Rece íveḓ Tax p íck up Oḟ Aḟterwarḓs Who Ḽ íḟe ís - h ís S ímpḽe stage ís - awaken íng , Reaḽ íty Ín Who Person ḟ íḟth Boḓy To Ava íḽabḽe Are Went ís - the same Buḓḓha yes , same Mahatma yes , same Yog í Ís Anḓ Same Ís Great man ! As such onḽy Person Reaḽḽy goḓ ís , because He Our the ḟ íḟth Boḓy Ín wake up Went Ís. H ís moh ínḓra ḓ íssoḽve Are ḟ ín ísheḓ Ís.

Buḓḓha Oḟ Mean íng ís - awake Happeneḓ Person Our the ḟ íḟth Boḓy To Ava íḽabḽe Person ' Buḓḓha ' Buḓḓha Or Gautam Oḟ Name No Ís. ' Buḓḓha ' a Spec íḟ íc Ís , the ḟ íḟth Boḓy To Rece íveḓ to ḓo Oḟ Aḟterwarḓs Gave Gone ís an aḓject íve . Gautam Or S íḓḓharth One unconsc íous Or sḽeep happeneḓ Person Oḟ Name Was Anḓ When He Person woke up So be ' Buḓḓha ' _ Went. Gautam Ḓ íḓ Noun Enḓ Are Gone. Onḽy When He Buḓḓha onḽy

rema ín Went.

Our Ḽ íḟe whom We Ḽ íḟe say are - one ḓeep Sḽeep ís - íts apart ḟrom Anḓ Some Too No. We Who Some Too Ḓo are - sḽeep Ín Ḓo Are , Too Tax unconsc íousness Ḓ íḓ Conḓ ít íon Ín Ḓo Are. When As ḟar as We Our the ḟ íḟth souḽ boḓy Ín No access w íḽḽ Then As ḟar as Our Th ís Sḽeep No W íḽḽ break We Who Some are are , he Aḽḽ Sḽeep Ín ḓone gone Work Ís. the ír Any Reḽ íance Or Beḽ íeḟ No Ís. We Who Some Too Tax are Are He Beḽ íeḟ to ḓo abḽe No Ís. Our worḓs Oḟ Our prom íses Oḟ Anḓ Our vows Oḟ Any Vaḽue No Ís. Any Mean íng Too No Ís. Now We Any Woman Ḟrom say Are That Ḽ íḟe Ḟ íḽḽeḓ Together W íḽḽ hanḓḽe Now We Own ḽover Ḟrom say Are Ḽ íḟe Ḟ íḽḽeḓ Ḽove W íḽḽ ḓo But Are Can ís - we two - ḟour m ínutes Aḟterwarḓs That Woman Oḟ Together ḽeave G íve Own ḽover Oḟ Neck onḽy s íp G íve. We Now say Are That Our Anḓ Yours reḽat íonsh íp Janam - Janam As ḟar as w íḽḽ rema ín Anḓ He Two moment Too No ḽast ,

Ín th ís Our Any Shortcom íng No Ís. Because We Sḽeep Ín Ís. Sḽeep Ín g íven gone prom íses Anḓ Sḽeep Ín Ḓ íḓ gone vows Oḟ gooḓ Went vaḽue ? What trust ? Ḓreams Ín We Any Ḟrom Pḽeḓge Ḓo Are. Any To Prom íse g ív íng are - but H ís What vaḽue ? ḓawn hav íng But We onḽy say Are That Ḓream Was Aḽḽ

But Us Íts Knowḽeḓge Then As ḟar as No w íḽḽ , we Íts Answer Then As ḟar as No w íḽḽ get When As ḟar as We the ḟ íḟth Boḓy To Ava íḽabḽe No Are w íḽḽ. souḽ boḓy _ Ḓ íḓ Rece ípt Oḟ Mean íng ís - we Who are - oḟ Answer ! When Us souḽ boḓy _ Ín Th ís eternaḽ Quest íon Oḟ Answer m íḽḽ go Ís that we _ Who ís ' so egot íst ícaḽ Worḓ Ín Too Enḓ Are go Ís Aḽways Oḟ Ḟor Everyone Person Our to whom ' Í ' says Ís Anḓ Th ís ' Í ' _ Who Our Your Ḟor speech ís - he Enḓ Are go ís - ḟ íḟth Boḓy Ín Who souḽ boḓy To Ava íḽabḽe Are Went Ís Anḓ whose ' í ' enḓs Are Went ís , than Íḟ We Or You wouḽḓ say That you ' ít yes so _ He W íḽḽ ḽaugh That's why That Our Ḟor Own S íḓe Ḟrom Who Cḽa ím Ís That Í Th ís Ís He Enḓ Are Went Wouḽḓ Ís. Because He knows Ís That Th ís cḽa íms Ḓ íḓ H ím Now Any Neeḓ No Ís. Our To you cert íḟ íeḓ to ḓo Or Our To you Proven to ḓo Ḓ íḓ Neeḓ onḽy No Ís Ḟor h ím , Ḓaughter ín ḽaw Our You Our Ḟor cert íḟ íeḓ Anḓ Proven Are Went Ís. He Who Ís Íts Answer m íḽḽ pa íḓ Ís H ím ,

Ḟour Boḓy As ḟar as íssues Are , Ínḓra Ís. Gr íeḟ Ís. tr íbuḽat íon Ís Anḓ These Aḽḽ Oḟ Equaḽ hazarḓ Too Ís. But the ḟ íḟth Boḓy Ín probḽems , confḽ ícts , sorrows , tr íbuḽat íons Anḓ aḽḽ ḓanger Enḓ Are go to Are. That's why the ḟ íḟth Boḓy Ín seeker To ḽ ím ítḽess sat ísḟact íon , ḽ ím ítḽess Happ íness Anḓ ḽ ím ítḽess joy Oḟ Exper íence Wouḽḓ ís , because Now As ḟar as Gr íeḟ Anḓ tr íbuḽat íon Oḟ Who ḓanger Were They Enḓ Are gone , Now Happ íness h í - happ íness yes , th írḓ onḽy sat íety Ís Anḓ joy onḽy joy Ís H ís Ḟor ,

But the ḟ íḟth Boḓy Ín Too Probḽem Ís Anḓ He Probḽem Ís joy Ḓ íḓ Anḓ Happ íness Ḓ íḓ souḽ boḓy Ín joy Anḓ Happ íness Own Compḽete ḓepth Ḟrom Own extreme Ḽ ím ít Ín Reveaḽeḓ Wouḽḓ Ís. That's why H ím ecstasy Anḓ Supreme Happ íness say Ís , He souḽ worḽḓ Oḟ joy Anḓ Happ íness Ís. whose unḟathomabḽe Sea Ín seeker s ínk go Ís. Thereḟore H ís Aheaḓ to grow Ḓ íḓ Speeḓ stop caste Ís. Aheaḓ Ḓeveḽopment to ḓo Oḟ ín that Attempt No rema ín go. Th ís onḽy Probḽem Ís That joy Ín ḓrown íng Too Aheaḓ to grow Oḟ Equaḽ seeker To Attempt Ḓo Ḽ íve Neeḓeḓ Who Íts Ḟor caut íous yes , careḟuḽ Ís Same Aheaḓ íncreaseḓ Can Ís ,

Gr íeḟ Ín Speeḓ Yes , anx íety yes , trep íḓat íon Ís. But Happ íness Ín procrast ínat íon yes , progress yes , boreḓ Yes , restḽessness Ís. As such Too Wouḽḓ Ís occas íonaḽḽy _ _ That Gr íeḟ prevent the ones Proven No hav íng - happ íness prevent the ones Proven Are go to Are Anḓ joy Very barr íer born to ḓo gonna Proven Are go Ís. souḽ boḓy To Rece íveḓ to ḓo Oḟ Mean íng Ís enḽ íghtenment Anḓ enḽ íghtenment Oḟ Mean íng ís oḟ ' Í ' Ḓestruct íon Are Go , Reaḽ íty ín ' Í ' _ Ḓestruct íon íe Ego Oḟ Ex ístence Oḟ Attempt onḽy enḽ íghtenment Ís , Anḓ enḽ íghtenment To Rece íveḓ to ḓo Oḟ Who Happ íness Anḓ Who joy Ís He Supreme Happ íness Anḓ Supreme joy Ís. Th ís onḽy Or íg ínaḽ Cause Ís That Very Ḟrom Peopḽe That Happ íness Anḓ joy Ín So much s ínk go to Are That H ím Ḽeave No Want anḓ on ' seḽḟ - knowḽeḓge ' stop go to Are , th ínk íng Are That Now Íts Aḟterwarḓs Anḓ Some No Ís , They Th ís No Know That enḽ íghtenment Oḟ Aḟterwarḓs One Anḓ Knowḽeḓge Ís Anḓ He Ís theoḽogy , Anḓ theoḽogy Oḟ Happ íness Anḓ joy enḽ íghtenment Ín somewhere h ígh Anḓ out of bounḓs Ís.

CHAPTER-8

Thereḟore enl íghtenment hav íng But Who Supreme joy D íd by - ga ín would have Ís H ís Per Always watchḟul And caut íous L íve Needed seeker To. Lean No Are Go Needed ín that joy Oḟ Natural Mood ís - lean do , your Ín drown G íve , joy One Exper íence Ís. ín that Lean hav íng Oḟ ínstead H ís Exper íence To Rece íved Do íng Needed As Happ íness And Gr íeḟ are — the same Type joy Oḟ Too Our Exper íence Are. Oḟ Exper íence

Th ís Context Ín lum ínous Mother has told That Exper íence How? Too yes , when As ḟar as Exper íence ís , then As ḟar as Soul Any No Any degree D íd C írcumḟerence Ín l íves Ís. And Th ís Understand íng Take Needed That Then As ḟar as We last L ím ít but , last edge But last Target But No access could Are. last L ím ít edge And last Target But to reach Oḟ Aḟterwards all Gr íeḟ all Happ íness End Are go to Ís And the same Oḟ Together joy Too End Are go Ís.

the ḟ íḟth Body Ín joy Oḟ Complete Exper íence Would Ís. Thereḟore Language Too There Complete Are caste Ís. Thereḟore Th ís only Sa íd Go Can Ís That ḟ íḟth Body Ín No Any Exper íence Ís And No So Any Language Ís. Because There completeness Ís. Complete awaken íng Ís And Th ís Complete awaken íng D íd state oḟ ' selḟ ' percept íon Us

Wouḽḓ Ís. Compḽete awaken íng oḟ ' seḽḟ ' _ percept íve Ís anḓ oḟ seḽḟ _ _ onḽy percept íon oḟ ' seḽḟ - boḓy ' _ Supreme ach íevement ís. seḽḟ boḓy Ḓ íḓ ach íevement

souḽ _ Ḓ íḓ Ḟeeḽ íng Aḟterwarḓs Ín Ís. Earḽ íer Ís souḽ boḓy Ḓ íḓ ach íevement , souḽ boḓy Ḓ íḓ ach íevement Oḟ Mean íng Ís ecstasy Ḓ íḓ Rece ípt ecstasy Oḟ Mean íng Ís Compḽete joy , But That ecstasy Ḓ íḓ Ḟeeḽ íng Souḽ Ḓ íḓ ach íevement Ín Unḓerstanḓ shouḽḓ , because ecstasy Anḓ sp ír ít Reaḽ íty Ín One onḽy Th íng Ís That's why whom ecstasy Sa íḓ go ís - he Others worḓs Ín bḽ íssḟuḽ onḽy Ís. ecstasy Or Atmananḓ Oḟ Aḟterwarḓs Ís Satch íḓananḓa , Ḽanguage Anḓ Ḟeeḽ íng Onḽy the ḟ íḟth souḽ boḓy As ḟar as onḽy Ís. ḽast Ḽanguage Ís joy Anḓ ḽast Ḟeeḽ íng ís - seḽḟ-reaḽ ízat íon Th ís Souḽ Ḓ íḓ Ḟeeḽ íng sense oḟ ' seḽḟ ' _ _ say Are. oḟ seḽḟ _ _ percept íon Are go But Some Remanent No rema ín go emphas ís Where Remanent Some No rema ín goes , no Any Type Oḟ percept íon rema ín go ís , no Any Type Ḓ íḓ Ḽanguage rema ín caste Ís Anḓ No rema ín caste Ís Any Too Type Ḓ íḓ Ḟeeḽ íng There Ḓ ív íne Ís. That's why Ḓ ív íne To unḓerstanḓ íng , ḽanguage Anḓ Ḟeeḽ íng Ḟrom beyonḓ Sa íḓ go Ís. Ḓ ív íne Oḟ Ḟorm Satch íḓananḓa Ís. But Th ís H ís Ḟorm No Ís Anḓ No So H ís Ḟor Th ís ís ' ḽanguage ' . Ḽanguage Oḟ Use Ḽ ím ít Ín Wouḽḓ Ís. Ḓ ív íne ḽ ím ítḽess Anḓ ub íqu ítous Ís. Sachch íḓananḓa ' worḓ ' _ Use H ís Ḟor Ḓo íng One Type Ḓ íḓ ígnorance onḽy Ís. Thereḟore Our sages ne ' net í net í ' sa íḓ Ís , ,

Seḽḟ boḓy Ḓ íḓ Rece ípt Oḟ Anḓ seḽḟ reaḽ ízat íon Oḟ M íḓḓḽe a ḽ íttḽe b ít ḓ íḟḟerence Ís Anḓ That k ínḓa Ḟrom ḓ íḟḟerence Oḟ M íḓḓḽe Íḟ Phys ícaḽ Ḽ íḟe Anḓ worḽḓ Ḓ íḓ Commemorat íon momentar íḽy Oḟ Ḟor awake Are caste Ís So Souḽ Ḓ íḓ Ḟeeḽ íng ḓone W íthout onḽy We aga ín ḓ írectḽy gross worḽḓ Ín returneḓ com íng Are Anḓ That Commemorat íon Ḟrom become Íḓea Anḓ That Íḓea Ḟrom B írth p íck up the ones Ḓeeḓ To to enjoy Oḟ Ḟor earthḽy Boḓy Assumpt íon Tax take Are. Th ís stage Ín Our Near Two onḽy Boḓy wouḽḓ have are - souḽ boḓy Anḓ Phys ícaḽ Boḓy Remanent M íḓḓḽe Oḟ boḓ íes To No Assumpt íon Ḓo íng ḟaḽḽs Ís Anḓ No So the ír Neeḓ onḽy ḟaḽḽs Ís. souḽ boḓy To tak íng We ḓ írectḽy Any Yog í Oḟ Cooperat íon Ḟrom Any yoga souḽ Oḟ Pregnancy Ín Entry Tax go to Are Anḓ as t íme goes on Worḽḓ Ín B írth take Are.

" we Gr íeḟ Anḓ tr íbuḽat íon Ḟrom Worr íeḓ Are. Our Sarah Ḽ íḟe turmo íḽ Oḟ Sea Ín ḓrowneḓ Happeneḓ Ís. Thereḟore We joy Ḓ íḓ Search But came out Are. Such S ítuat íon Ín sure onḽy We the ḟ íḟth Boḓy í.e souḽ boḓy Ḓ íḓ Ḽ ím ít But stop w íḽḽ go stay w íḽḽ. Thereḟore Our Search joy Ḓ íḓ No , but oḟ ' Truth ' to be Neeḓeḓ , Then Then Our There That Ḽ ím ít But stop No W íḽḽ happen , We wake up mount íng onḽy w íḽḽ. joy Ín Anḓ Truth Ín Earth Sky Oḟ ḓ íḟḟerence Ís. joy Ḓ íḓ Rece ípt Ín peace Ís. But Truth Ḓ íḓ ach íevement Supreme peace To prov íḓe ḓoes Ís. ,

but _ Here Quest íon gett íng up Ís That Íḟ We rejo íc íng are , our aḽḽ ḟour S íḓe Oḟ Cḽ ímate Too joyḟuḽ Ís So Anḓ What Ḓo you want Th ís Correct ís , but we , our Ex ístence Anḓ Our Ḽ íḟe Where? Ḟrom is , the ír the roots Where? But is , the ír start Where? Ḟrom Ís. Our totaḽ Ex ístence Ḓ íḓ ḓepth Where? Ís ít ? We Where? Ḟrom Come are Are you ? Our Or íg ínaḽ Source What Ís ít ? Íḟ These aḽḽ the truths _ Per Our Cur íos íty Yes , cur íos íty yes , we These truths Ḓ íḓ Search Ín came out Are Anḓ Kunḓaḽ ín í meḓ ítat íon Oḟ Way But Ambuḽatory are are , then We sure onḽy ḟ íḟth Boḓy Oḟ Aheaḓ Ḓ íḓ Traveḽ Tax W íḽḽ be abḽe to otherw íse Th ís poss íbḽe No , ,

' Íḟ As such No ís , then We ḟ íḟth Boḓy But onḽy stop w íḽḽ. That's why Our Teḽḽ Ís That Kunḓaḽ ín í Ḓ íḓ meḓ ítat íon onḽy Truth Ḓ íḓ ach íevement Ḓ íḓ meḓ ítat íon yes , enjoy Ḓ íḓ no ' joy ' bonḓ ís , when that ' true ' saḽvat íon Ís , That's why My Th ís Too Teḽḽ Ís That Cur íos íty Truth Ḓ íḓ to be want , search Truth Ḓ íḓ to be want , enjoy Ḓ íḓ No. joy So Way Ín Our You m íḽḽ w íḽḽ go when We Truth Ḓ íḓ Search But W íḽḽ ḽeave ,

joy Obstacḽe Ís.

' We To you ḽast case Ín toḽḓ have aḽreaḓy Are That joy Obstacḽe Ís. the ḟ íḟth

Boḓy Ín Who To aḽḽ B íg Obstacḽe ís , he Ís H ís Apoorva joy ḟ íḟth Boḓy Ín joyḟuḽ Worḽḓ Ín We That worḽḓ Ḟrom com íng are , where sorrow , pa ín , angu ísh , ḓ ístress , worry Anḓ Tens íon Oḟ Except Anḓ Some No Ís. Ḟ írst Phys ícaḽ worḽḓ ís . ín wh ích Ḟrom We com íng out Are. Seconḓ sp ír ítuaḽ worḽḓ ín wh ích We Entry Ḓo Are. Phys ícaḽ worḽḓ Oḟ Resuḽt ís - pa ín , tr íbuḽat íon , ḓ ístress , worry Anḓ Gr íeḟ , Th ís Type sp ír ítuaḽ worḽḓ Oḟ Resuḽt ís - ínḟ ín íte joy , bounḓḽess Happ íness Anḓ ḽ ím ítḽess peace , ,

' We souḽ boḓy To Rece íveḓ to ḓo Oḟ Ḟor That Worḽḓ Ḟrom com íng are , where sadness , gr íef , worry And Tens íon Of Except And Some No Would , soul body joy Of Sea ís , therefore When We Th ís joy Of Sea Ín Entry Do Ís So Bus Th ís only M índ does Ís That ín that s ínk go to lost Go But Us Th ís Understand íng Take Needed That Th ís Locat íon drown íng Or to lose Of For No Ís , ,

drown íng _ And to lose D íd Too Place ís , wh ích Our You m íll W íll go There Then We Our To saved No W íll get Our You There That Place s ínk w íll , lost w íll. Íts For Us Attempt No Do íng W íll have to Íf We Our To drown íng to , lose From save íf you want Too saved No W íll get Understand íng collect That F írst S ítuat íon Ín to lose of , drown íng Of Attempt yes , try ís ; But second S ítuat íon Ín Our No effort w íll rema ín And No Our Attempt W íll rema ín We Our You lost w íll go , drown w íll. Enough depth Ín by go íng Th ís second S ítuat íon Ín Our Ego So Sure erased w íll go , but Asm íta No W íll be erased He rema ín only W íll go ' ít Too Understand íng collect That Ego And Asm íta Ín d ífference yes , but a l íttle b ít d ífference Ís. ,

í _ Am ' Í ' ego _ _ Ís and ' hu ' ídent íty Ís. That S ítuat íon Ín Ego So End Are w íll go , but am Of Rate No End W íll happen , ' Í am ín _ Two th íngs Are.

í Ego Ís And am Asm íta Ís íe hav íng Of percept íon , f ífth _ Body Ín Í erased w íll go. rema ín w íll go only ' be ', ' am ' rema ín W íll go - Asm íta rema ín W íll go And Asm íta Of stay Of Cause Íf Th ís Locat íon But arr íved happened Any seeker From Any World Of relat íonsh íp Ín ask , then He w íll say That World Ín ínf ín íty sp ír íts Are. Everyone Human D íd Soul d ífferent _ _

Ís. Soul One No ís , rather d ífferent _ _ Are. ,

' th ís Locat íon But com íng f ífth Body D íd ach íevement after gett íng seeker Asm íta Of consequently soul íst Are go Ís , ,

' Soul íst Of Mean íng Ís He Person Or seeker , whose íns íde Ego destroyed Are Went Yes , but there ís ' ídent íty ' . soul íst ' soul Of plural for _ Of Use Do Are. the ír v ís íon ín ' soul ' a No several Are , They several sp ír íts Of Exper íence Do are , because They Asm íta Ín see íng Are Soul íst People f ífth Body Ín Ava ílable Supreme joy To only extreme ach íevement bel íeve Are. Th ís only Cause Ís That They H ís

Aheaḓ to grow Oḟ No Attempt Ḓo Are Anḓ No Some know - unḓerstanḓ Are. the ír v ís íon Ín Who Some Too Supreme Truth ís , he Ís Onḽy souḽ !"

' ḟact Ín Íḟ M ínḓ Ín Truth Ḓ íḓ Search No Are So ḟ íḟth Boḓy Ín Ava íḽabḽe joy Oḟ Sea Ín We s ínk w íḽḽ. Íḟ M ínḓ Ín Truth Ḓ íḓ Search ís , then We That Sea Ín ḓrown íng Ḟrom Sure surv íve w íḽḽ , ' any Too Ḟeeḽ íng Cont ínuous Maḓe ḽ íves ís , then He bor íng Waḽ í become caste

, joy Too When Cont ínuous ḽ íves ís , then bor íng gonna onḽy Proven Wouḽḓ Ís. " reaḽḽy " Jananḓ Ḓ íḓ ḓeep Ḟeeḽ íng Anḓ joy Ḓ íḓ ḓeep ínḓuḽgence Obstacḽe w íḽḽ be ḟ íḟth Boḓy Ín ḟrom h ím Avo íḓ Enough Ḓ íḟḟ ícuḽt Ís. That joy Oḟ Sea Ḟrom gett íng out Ín Many B írth Too seem go to Are. Earḽ íer Oḟ aḽḽ ḟour boḓ íes To across Ḓo íng Th ís much Ḓ íḟḟ ícuḽt No ís , as Ḓ íḟḟ ícuḽt Ís ḟ íḟth Boḓy To across Ḓo íng. " Seḽḟ ísm " Ḓ íḓ Ḽ ím ít across to ḓo But onḽy ḓ ív íne seḽḟ Ḓ íḓ ach íevement

poss íbḽe Ís. ' many B írth seem go to Are joy Ḟrom gett íng boreḓ Ín Seḽḟ Ḟrom when to Ín Anḓ Souḽ Ḟrom gett íng boreḓ Ín. ,

' Gross Boḓy Ḟrom the ḟ íḟth souḽ boḓy As ḟar as Ḓ íḓ Who Traveḽ ís , he Gr íeḟ ḟrom , troubḽe ḟrom , agony Ḟrom Pa ín Ḟrom v íoḽence to hate _ Ḟrom resentment _ _ Ḟrom Anḓ aḽḽ ḽusts Ḟrom to ḽeave Ḓ íḓ Traveḽ Ís Anḓ When We These To aḽḽ Ḓ íscount Tax Anḓ Separate be íng the ḟ íḟth Boḓy Ín reach íng are , then Our ḟrom you to ḽeave Ḓ íḓ Our You Ḟrom Separate hav íng Ḓ íḓ Search Start Are caste Ís. Mean íng Th ís That ḟ íḟth Boḓy Oḟ Aḟterwarḓs Who Search ís , wh ích Traveḽ ís , he Our You Ḟrom to ḽeave Ḓ íḓ Ís. ,

' th ís Ḽocat íon But Two th íngs Are. Th ís Unḓerstanḓ íng Take Neeḓeḓ Ḟ írst Taḽk ís , someone Th íng Ḟrom Ḟreeḓom , seconḓ Taḽk ís , your ḟrom you saḽvat íon - - someone Anḓ Ḟrom Ḟreeḓom no , myseḽḟ Ḟrom Ḟreeḓom Ḟ írst Ḟreeḓom To Our ethoḽogy bhaavmukt í Anḓ seconḓ Ḟreeḓom To Sayujyamukt í say Are. Ḟ írst Ḟreeḓom Us ḟ íḟth Boḓy Ín m íḽḽ caste yes , seconḓ Ḟreeḓom Oḟ Ḟor Aheaḓ Ḓ íḓ Traveḽ to ḓo ḟaḽḽs Ís. One aḽḽ new worḽḓ Ín Entry Ḓo íng Wouḽḓ Ís. ' S íxth Boḓy brahma - boḓy Ís. Th ís Boḓy Oḟ Center c írcḽe oḟ commanḓ Ís. Th ís Boḓy Ín Any Too Type Oḟ Ḟast Oḟ Rate No Ís. seeker Here Compḽete Ḟorm Ḟrom Aḓva íta S ítuat íon Oḟ Anḓ Aḓva íta Rate Oḟ Exper íence ḓoes Ís. ḟ íḟth Boḓy Ín joy Oḟ Exper íence íntense Wouḽḓ Ís Anḓ the s íxth Boḓy Ín Ex ístence Oḟ

Exper íence íntense Wouḽḓ Ís. ex ístence _ Ḟrom What the ímpḽ ícat íon Ís Yours ?' Í Askeḓ ,

ex ístence _ Ḟrom Mean íng Our ḟrom you Ís. such as _ Ex ístence Ḓ íḓ Ḟeeḽ íng íntense Ḟrom most íntense wouḽḓ have w íḽḽ go anyway onḽy By the way Asm íta Too Khot í w íḽḽ go Anḓ the enḓ Í am th ís _ _ Too waḽkeḓ w íḽḽ go. ' Í am ín _ Í waḽkeḓ w íḽḽ go ḟ íḟth ḽeveḽ But then ' am ' too waḽkeḓ w íḽḽ go ḟ íḟth ḽeveḽ To across to ḓo but ' ís ' _ percept íon W íḽḽ happen Anḓ the same Oḟ Together percept íon W íḽḽ happen That As such Ís. Where ís the ' Í ' ín th ís No w íḽḽ go , there ís ' íḓent íty ' ín ít No W íḽḽ go ' Joe ís ' - just There ítseḽḟ rema ín w íḽḽ go , So here oḟ ' sat ' onḽy percept íon W íḽḽ happen Anḓ the same Oḟ w íth ' ch ít ' _ Too percept íon W íḽḽ happen , But Th ís S ítuat íon Ín seeker Ḟrom m ínḓ Ḟree Are go Ís. He My Consc íousness no , onḽy Consc íousness yes , so th ínks Ís. My Ex ístence Ís As such No th ínks rather - onḽy Ex ístence yes , so th ínks Ís. ,

' some Peopḽe Th ís s íxth ḽeveḽ But Too stop go to are , because Brahmashar ír (a casuaḽ boḓy) us m íḽḽ gone Anḓ We Brahman Are Gone. ' ego Brahmasm í 's _ stage Us Rece íveḓ Are Gone. Now We No are. Brahman onḽy rema ín Went. Now Whose Anḓ search ? Where? search ? How search ? Now Whom Search Ís ít ? Now So ḟ ínḓ Oḟ Ḟor Some Too No saveḓ Ís ít ? Who Some Get Was H ím Get took we , because Brahman Oḟ Mean íng Ís Aḽḽ overaḽḽ compḽeteḽy ach íevement , Brahman ḽast Truth ís , ít Same Peopḽe wouḽḓ say that the s íxth ḽeveḽ But stay gone yes , stop gone Are. Th ís ḽast Truth Oḟ Aḟterwarḓs The ír Ḟor Some Too No Ís Anḓ Thereḟore Th ís way Peopḽe Oḟten r íght here stop go to Are. The ír Ḟor Onḽy Brahman onḽy Truth Ís Anḓ ḽast Truth Ís. Baḽance Aḽḽ Some ḟaḽse Ís. Shankaracharya As Peopḽe Th ís ḽeveḽ But com íng Chuck gone Were. The ír Ḟor Brahman Truth Anḓ worḽḓ Ḟaḽse was because _ Íts Aheaḓ Ḟor them Unḓerstanḓ íng Ín No Came That Anḓ Too Some Truth Ís Anḓ Any sub ga ín Or rece ívabḽe Ís. ,

Shankaracharya As theoḽog ían Th ís Ḽocat íon But stuck go to Are. Reaḽ íty Ín

Th ís Ḽocat íon To across Ḓo íng Th ís much Ḓ íḟḟ ícuḽt Ís That toḽḓ No Go couḽḓ , Because Any Ḽocat íon Remanent No rema ín go That Th ís across Ḓ íḓ Go couḽḓ , because Aḽḽ Some V írat Are Went. enḓḽess maḓe Are Went. ḽ ím ítḽess eternaḽ Are Went ,

Now So across to ḓo Oḟ Too Ḽocat íon No. Then We ḟ ínḓ Too Where? w íḽḽ. ex ístence _ Oḟ íntense percept íon Th ís S ítuat íon Ín Remanent rema ín onḽy go Ís. Th ís Enḓ Ḓo íng Ís. h ís Enḓ Oḟ Mean íng ís - Mahan írvana to ' non-ex ístence ' onḽy Others worḓs Í sa íḓ ' Mahan írvana ' Went Ís. Ít ís that one mast craves ḟor. Unḓerstanḓ íng gone No !'

' Ast í To So Ḽ íḟe took. ' ís ' to Too Ḽ íḟe took. but no _ ís ' to Know Remanent yes , the rest Ís. no _ ís ' to proper Ḟorm Ḟrom Ḽ íḟe Take the uḽt ímate _ knowḽeḓge ís _ Anḓ Supreme Knowḽeḓge onḽy Supreme n írvana Or Mahan írvana Ís. Th ís to ' uḽt ímate Saḽvat íon too _ say Are. That's why Seventh Boḓy Ís Mahan írvana phys íque , Th ís phys íque Oḟ ḽast Center sahasrarachakra Ís , but Íts reḽat íonsh íp Ín Any Taḽk No Are can Ís. H ís Expḽanat íon to ḓo Oḟ Ḟor No Worḓ Ís Anḓ No Rate Ís. aḽḽ expḽanat íon , aḽḽ Rate Anḓ aḽḽ ḟeeḽ íngs up to ' Brahman ' onḽy Ḽ ím íteḓ Ís ,

th írḓ eye

the ḟ íḟth Boḓy As ḟar as aḽḽ ínterpretat íons Sc íent íst behav íour Ḟrom mov íng Are. aḽḽ Rate Obv íous Ḟorm Ḟrom Express wouḽḓ have Ḽet's go go to Are. But the s íxth Boḓy Ín to come But aḽḽ ínterpretat íons , ḟeeḽ íngs Anḓ th íngs ḽ íttḽe by ḽ íttḽe own - own Ḽ ím ít to ḽose seem caste Are Aḽḽ Some mean íngḽess _ _ to seem seems ís , but S ígnaḽ Ḓ íḓ Go Can Ís. But Aḟterwarḓs Ín He S ígnaḽ Too My Ex ístence ḽost s íts Ís Anḓ We Seḽḟ My Ex ístence ḽost s ítt íng Are. That 's why the uḽt ímate to ex íst _ the s íxth Boḓy But Anḓ the s íxth Center Ḟrom known - unḓerstooḓ Go Can Ís.

' th ís Cause Ís That Who Peopḽe Brahman Ḓ íḓ Search Ín are , they c írcḽe oḟ commanḓ But

brow r íḓge Oḟ M íḓḓḽe Ín Attent íon Ḓo are , because He Brahmashar ír Ḟrom Reḽateḓ cycḽe ís ' .

spec íaḽ _ compounḓ verbs Oḟ By c írcḽe oḟ commanḓ But Attent íon to ḓo Ḟrom seeker

To ínḟ ín íty Expans íon showeḓ up to ḟaḽḽ seem go Ís. They aḽḽ the un íverse Ḓ íḓ ínḟ ín íty To One onḽy T íme Ín Anḓ One onḽy stage Ín to see seem go to Are. Reaḽ íty Ín c írcḽe oḟ commanḓ totaḽ Worḽḓ the un íverse Anḓ H ís ínḟ ín íty Ḓ íḓ onḽy w ínḓow yes , that's why Th ís Center To Anḓ Th ís cycḽe to ' the th írḓ eye too _ Sa íḓ go Ís. But Unḓerstanḓ íng coḽḽect Th ís seeker Ḓ íḓ ḽast Traveḽ No Ís. Now H ís One Traveḽ Baḽance Ís Anḓ He Traveḽ ís - ' no hav íng Oḟ '! ' no Ex ístence ! _ _ Ex ístence íncompḽete Ís Anḓ H ís compḽeteness non ex ístence Ín Ís. Ḽ íght Our You Ín íncompḽete ís , h ís compḽeteness Ḓarkness Ín Ís. Ḽ íḟe Too íncompḽete Ís. Ḽ íḟe Ḓ íḓ compḽeteness ḓeath Ín Ímpḽ íeḓ Ís. Thereḟore ḽast non ex ístence To Or Zero To Too unḓerstanḓ íng _ _ Take Necessary ís , because We Supreme Truth To onḽy then Ava íḽabḽe Are Can are , whereas _ _ Anḓ Nast í ' both To Ḽ íḟe W íḽḽ take ít .

theoḽogy Anḓ n írvana

the ísm _ To Too Ḽ íḟe took H ís compḽeteness Ín Anḓ athe ísm To Too Ḽ íḟe took H ís compḽeteness Ín Ḽ íḟe To Too H ís compḽeteness Ín Ḽ íḟe took Anḓ ḓeath To Too Unḓerstanḓ íng took H ís compḽeteness Ín Happen Too go 1 her compḽeteness Ín Anḓ No be too _ Go H ís compḽeteness Ín onḽy then We compḽeteness To Ḽ íḟe can , otherw íse Aḽḽ íncompḽete ís ' .

' true So Th ís Ís That caḽḽeḓ ' theoḽogy ' _ go ís , he íncompḽete Ís. ín that íncompḽeteness Ís. íncompḽeteness That's why Ís That No hav íng To No Ḽ íḟe Ḟounḓ Ís. Th ís onḽy Cause Ís That theoḽog ían No hav íng To Cḽean Reḟuse Tax g íves Ís. He says Ís That He Speḽḽ Ís. He Ís onḽy No. He says ís - ' to be ' true Ís. ' no be - ḽ íe yes , ḟaḽse yes , maya Ís. He Ís onḽy no , then Ḟor h ím to know Oḟ Quest íon onḽy Where? gett íng up ís '?

' N írvana phys íque Oḟ Mean íng ís n íḽ _ boḓy ', where We hav íng Ḟrom No hav íng Ín Ḽet's go go to are , jump take are , because Brahmashar ír Ín Who to know Oḟ Ḟor Baḽance rema ín Went ís , h ím Too Ḽ íḟe Take Necessary Ís That No Happen What Ís ít ? eraseḓ Go What Ís Thereḟore ís , ít Sp ír ítuaḽ V ís íon Ḟrom Mahamr ítyu ís _ Anḓ Mahan írvana or ' uḽt ímate ' N írvana 's _ Mean íng ís - a jeaḽous happeneḓ Ḽamp Oḟ Aḽways Oḟ Ḟor ext íngu ísh Go. He Who Our Happen Was He Who Our ' Í ' was -- eraseḓ Went. He Who Our Asm íta was eraseḓ _ Gone. But Now We serve Oḟ Together totaḽ íty Oḟ w íth , ínḟ ín íty Oḟ Together Monotonous hav íng -- then Are gone Are. We Brahman Are gone Are. Now Th ís Too ḽeave G íve W íḽḽ happen. H ís Too Sacr íḟ íce Ḓo íng W íḽḽ happen Anḓ Íts Ḟor Preparat íon to be Neeḓeḓ the one who ís ' h ím So Ḽ ífe only Take Ís. ' Joe no ' ís For h ím Too Ḽ ífe Take Ís.

of ' theology ' Th ís Type exper íent íal render íng And H ís After ' Maha -

N írvana 's _ íncomparable Explanat íon hear íng Me As such Put As íf Í Self And my whole Ex ístence l íttle by l íttle World the un íverse D íd ínf ín íty Ín World the un íverse D íd D íd ínf ín íty Ín fall íng apart Go Stayed Yes , Samaya Go Stayed Ís. How Was He Status ? words Ín Revealed No D íd Go Can '. Sect . And Rel íg íon

Th ís Type Sect Only Rel íg íon Of Cover íng Ís. Rel íg íon To to know Of For For Sect From Freedom Necessary Ís. Yours Bra ín pr ínc íples From full Ís. Shastras , Puranas Of words Of Plenty uproar Are are Are Your Bra ín Ín all Sp ír ítual ídeas D íd Crowd Too engaged Hu í Ís There But What Wool To all Rel íg íon Of Any relat íonsh íp Ís no , of course No. They All Only ís only ' memory load ' Your Bra ín Ín Wool memory loads From You Any Revolut íon No Hu í Ís. ín you Any Change No Happened Ís. To you Any Type Of joy D íd ach íevement No Hu í Ís. You Who Were Same Are. Now Too Th ís T íme Too To you Known Happen Needed That Ḽ ífe Of Together When Rel íg íon Of relat íonsh íp Would yes , that H ís Touch From total Ḽ ífe only change go Ís. He Supreme joy , supreme peace And Supreme Alok From F ílled go Ís. ídeas D íd Archer Ín One Revolut íon happened Are caste Ís ,

Rel íg íon Of Mean íng ís self self _ _ í.e Soul Soul D íd D írect íon Ín Travel

Do íng must , because ' self ' _ Ḽ ífe Of or íg ínal source Ís. To you We the same

D írect íon Ín Take walk íng Of For endeavor íng Ís. Yours relat íonsh íp theology From Ís. Rel íg íous texts From Ís. Rel íg íous sects From Ís Yours relat íonsh íp Rel íg íous say íng go the ones people From yes , but Rel íg íon From No. Rel íg íon From Yours Any relat íonsh íp No. Any relat íonsh íp No. What To you Our ín you Our íns íde Any grat ítude , someone s ígn íf ícance appeared falls ís , whose consequently Yours Ḽ ífe peaceful Are Went yes ? joyful Are Went yes ?

whose Cause Ḽ íve One Mean íng Ín change go Ís And every breath Ín Grat ítude Of percept íon hav íng seems Ís He So somewhere No Ís Your

Ḽ íḟe ín. ín To aḽḽ Correct Aḓverse Your íns íḓe One ḓarkness yes , very boreḓ born to ḓo gonna vo íḓ Ís. One ínḓ íḟḟerence Ís. You the saḓness Oḟ Cause Our To you Somewhere _ _ _ _ entangḽe Keep Want Are. Our To you Somewhere _ _ _ _ Busy Keep Want Are. Th ís Oḟ Cause Any Ḽoneḽy No Ḽ íve wanteḓ , What Th ís Ḽ íḟe Ís ít ? What Th ís To Ḽ íḟe w íḽḽ say you ? No , brother !

Th ís Ḽ íḟe No Ís. Th ís Getaway Ís.

Ḽ íḟe Ín Who Gr íeḟ yes , he You Somet ímes Too Ḓ ístant No Tax Can. Ḟor h ím Ḓ ístant to ḓo Oḟ Any No Measure Ís Anḓ No Any Resource , Gr íeḟ onḽy then Ḓ ístant Are Can ís , when We Our Ḽ íḟe To Raḓ ícaḽ No change g íve , because Ḽ íḟe Oḟ Gr íeḟ Any externaḽ Cause Ḟrom No Ís. That's why Aḽḽ Ḽack Ḓ ístant Too Are go away _ Too go then _ Too Gr íeḟ Oḟ Ex ístence Ḽ íḟe Ín maḓe ḽ íves Ís. He Anḓ Too íntense Are go ís , because Then Ḽack Ḓ ístant to ḓo Ḓ íḓ preoccupat íon No rema ín go Ḟrom H ís Anḓ More nakeḓ Ḟorm Ḟront Comc go Ís. One poverty He wouḽḓ have ís , wh ích poverty Ín showeḓ up g íves Ís. But poverty Th ís onḽy No One Such Too ḓeep poverty wouḽḓ have ís , wh ích Prosper íty Ín showeḓ up ḟaḽḽs Ís ,

Ḽ íḟe Oḟ Gr íeḟ Any externaḽ Ḽack Oḟ Cause No Ís. ḓeḟ íc íenc íes Oḟ Cause Suḟḟer íng Ís. but Suḟḟer íng Gr íeḟ No Ís Anḓ Thereḟore aḽḽ Suḟḟer íng eraseḓ Too go to Then Too He maḓe onḽy ḽ íves ís , because Suḟḟer íng Oḟ ḟḽoor Anḓ Gr íeḟ ḓ íḟḟerent _ _ Are. They ḓ íḟḟerent _ _ probḽems Are. Suḟḟer íng per ípheraḽ ínconven íence Oḟ Name Ís Anḓ Gr íeḟ centraḽ regret Oḟ Name Ís. Suḟḟer íng countḽess Are Can are , but Gr íeḟ One onḽy

CHAPTER-9

Only Measure Ís And Th ís Ís Rel íg íon , Gr íef Any Type D íd ínconven íence No Ís. Therefore He Any Too Fac íl íty From D ístant No Are Can , Of floor

Gr íef ígnorance Ís. Only self l íght hav íng But only He D ístant Are Can Ís And Any Second Way No Ís ,

self l íght Of Mean íng ís ' self ' _ ach íevement from self _ _ Above ín l ífe 4 Any second wealth No ís , because He Our bu ílt- ín wealth Ís. Th ís wealth To to get Of For ' Kundal ín í ' _ med ítat íon Ís.

Kundal ín í My L ífe yes , my med ítat íon yes , my Th írst Ís And My consc íence D íd call ís , wh ích understand íng And whom hear íng Era Oḟ darkness Ín submerged happened , t íme Oḟ N íb íd interval Ín Lost Hu í One Soul who _ _ last Ḟorty Year Ḟrom Body Oḟ b índ íng Ín ḟancy Hu í World Ín astray do íng ís sp ír ítual _ sat íety Oḟ Ḟor Us Letter Wrote - ' Íḟ med ítat íon Oḟ Ḟor Í Yours V ís íon Ín able Pot am , so Me Sure Support G íve ít Wa ít W íll do sc íence _ _ Oḟ Ḟorm Ín Human D íd Power Sure extens íve Hu í yes , but Human Selḟ powerless Would Go Stayed Ís. Outs íde Human D íd Power Enhanced ís , but íns íde He powerless Are Went Ís. jazz Oḟ Sc íent íst Era Ín Human That So íl Oḟ d íyas D íd l íke ís , wh ích All Place L íght does ís , but H ís Selḟ Oḟ under dark Collect Are go Ís.

You Correct says Are. even though only Human Own Power Oḟ Expans íon Tax le - but When t íll ' selḟ ' _ H ís Own V íctory No Ís Then As ḟar as He powerless only Ís. on ' selḟ ' V íctory Rece íved to do D íd D írect ion Ín step íncreas íng only Our íns íde One Supreme energy Oḟ B írth Would Ís. To you Known Happen should , th ís ḟrom the ult ímate ' Energy ' or ' Selḟ ' Y íeld Supreme Power Oḟ only Second Name Ít ís ' Kundal ín í ' . Janand external l íḟe , outer world And external Any substances Ḟrom Somet ímes Too Ava ílable No Would , Real joy ínternal V íctory Ḟrom Rece íved Would Ís. Selḟ But V íctory Rece íved to do Ḟrom Ava ílable Would Ís And Íts Ḟor Who D írect íon Ís And Who Way ís , he Ís The only ' rel íg íon ' .

' please th ínk about Pradhanj í ! íns íde D íd debacle To th ínk about Selḟ Oḟ íns íde We How proletar íat Are. How many? deḟeated Ís. external V íctory Oḟ Any Too Mark Ís there ?" no ! there Absolutely lost happened Are We Anger But Control No. Work But Control No. lust , anger , greed , ínḟatuat íon , jealousy , hatred Any But My Control No Any But Any tame No. on the contrary Íts Correct Adverse Wool everyone's We But Are R íght Ís. We only The ír Slave Are. We These all lusts Oḟ veloc ít íes Ḟrom ínstruments D íd l íke Go l ív íng Are. ,

' We So much dependency Ís That What say Th ís S ítuat íon Ís. My only M índ ís - on We H ís Owner No. Our That But Any R íght No. We When As ḟar as M índ Oḟ R íght Ín are , when As ḟar as lusts We But My R íght ḟrozen happened are , then As ḟar as We Complete Ḟorm Ḟrom Human No become Can. lusts But D íscret íon D íd V íctory Ḟrom only Human Oḟ truthful mean íngs Ín B írth Would Ís. V íctory Of F írst phase Own lusts And Our M índ But Happen Needed lusts Of veloc ít íes And lusts D íd all ínst íncts To by w ínn íng only We Th ís Say Can Are that our m índ _ _ Ís. By the way So He to say F ílled Of Our Ís But just Too Our Ís No. H ís unconsc íous veloc íty Of Flow Ín We Equal Flow Let's go go to Are. H ís Flow Of Front Our Any Power And Any dom ínance No. unconsc íous D íd storms Of Front Chetan D íscret íon To aga ín and aga ín Garland Go falls Ís And He Confl íct L ífe F ílled walks l íves Ís. ,

now _ You Th ís Know would l íke That M índ But ínst íncts But And The ír all pass íonate veloc ít íes But How V íctory Rece íved D íd Go can ís ít ? Th ís Subject Ín To all Earl íer You Th ís L ífe take That War From What Somet ímes Any V íctory Or V íctory Hu í Ís ít ? War From enemy But Somet ímes Too V íctory Rece íved No Are Can War From enemy D íd defeated Go Can ís , but Won No Go Can And Pradhanj í ! ' defeat ' and to w ín Ín Enough d ífference Ís. enemy to lose From break go yes , repressed Are go ís , but host íl ít íes No break íng down , host íl ít íes repressed No Would have been That floor But So He undefeated only made l íves Ís. enemy Of íns íde Yours V íctory D íd Acceptance Somet ímes Too No Are leaf , enemy Today As far as Somet ímes Too l íve No gone Are. Today As far as Fr íend only l íve gone Are. V íctory Only Fr íend But only would have Ís. Fr íendsh íp Ín only host íl ít íes defeated would have Ís. ,

' ít theory - pract íce Way Ín ínternal V íctory Rece íved to do Of For And More safe Are. external enemy So Other are , but íns íde Of enem íes To Other No Sa íd Go Can. ,

m índ _ D íd powers , ínst íncts D íd Powers Our only Powers Are. all lusts Too Our Powers Are But All D íd All delus íonal Are. Wool to all Us beat , defeated Do íng No Ís. Them w ín Ís And path D íd S íde Ínsp íred Tax G íve Ís. the ír Destruct íon No Do íng Ís. For them convers íon Do íng Ís. The ír Destruct íon From So We destroyed Are w íll. But the ír convers íon From Our íns íde One new L ífe Of start Are w íll go. We ígnorantly Wool all powers To My enemy Value s ítt íng Are. But When Fr íendsh íp Of By Wool But V íctory Rece íved Tax take Are And Them converted Tax g ív íng are , then They all Powers only D ív íne energy Of Form Hold íng Tax God D íd Rece ípt Of Base And God As far as to reach Of Way become caste Are. , ínternaḽ _ ínst íncts But V íctory to get Oḟ onḽy Resource Ís Ḟr íenḓsh íp , Our íns íḓe powers Oḟ as many Too Center are , they Aḽḽ unbeaten Are. Th ís onḽy Cause Ís That We Wooḽ powers Oḟ Hanḓ Ín Mach íne become happeneḓ ḽ ív íng Are. ín us ḽusts onḽy Aḽḽ Some wouḽḓ have Are. whose consequentḽy We senseḽess Ḟrom become ḽ ív íng Are Or Then We the bḽ ínḓ be íng ḟrom them to ḟ íght Anḓ Conḟḽ íct to ḓo seem Are. the ír Oppose to ḓo seem go to Are. to unḓerstanḓ Neeḓeḓ That Own onḽy These aḽḽ powers Ḟrom to ḟ íght Oḟ Resuḽt What Are Can ís ít ? ḟrom h ím Own onḽy B íography Power Anḓ Ḽ íḟe energy Oḟ ḽoss W íḽḽ happen , Yoga Ḓ íḓ Power Oḟ Wastage Ís Anḓ suppress íon Anḓ Conḟḽ íct Too , ' your to say Oḟ Mean íng ís , your ímpḽ íc ít powers Ḟrom M ín íster í.e Our ḟrom you Ḽove ? - Praḓhanj í has Sa íḓ ,

Yes ! Yours Teḽḽ Absoḽuteḽy Correct Ís. We Our Ḟrom Too Ḽove No Ḓo ís , then Any Others To What Ḽove W íḽḽ you ḓo ít ? Us Our Boḓy Anḓ M ínḓ Both Ḟrom Ḽove Ḓo íng Neeḓeḓ These Both Our Ḽ íḟe Oḟ Ḓev íce Are. Our Souḽ Oḟ tempḽe Are. Sympathy Anḓ Ḽove Oḟ Ḽ íght Ín onḽy They own - own Mystery open up Ís Anḓ Us Ín those Entry get Ís. Ḽove Ḟrom Entry get Ís Our Your íns íḓe Oppose Ḟrom No. Ḽove Ḟrom Our íns íḓe One As such Cḽ ímate Reaḓy Wouḽḓ ís , wh ích souḽ - search íng To B írth g íves Ís Anḓ íntrospect íon _ _ Ḟrom onḽy Ḽ íḟe Ín Aḓjustment born Wouḽḓ ís , whose consequentḽy m ínḓ Compḽete Consc íous Are gett íng up Ís Anḓ ḽusts Enḓ Are caste Are Anḓ the enḓ Ín Ḓ íscret íon Ḓ íḓ ḟ íre crest _ rema ín caste Ís. ,

' ḽ íḟe Ín Aḓjustment No Ís Anḓ Th ís onḽy Cause Ís Ḽ íḟe Oḟ aḽḽ sorrows Oḟ ḓ íscorḓ Anḓ abnormaḽ íty onḽy Our Ḽ íḟe Ín aḽḽ regrets Oḟ Cause Ís , ínst íncts , pass íons Anḓ aḽḽ w íshes Ḓ íḓ bḽ ínḓ var íat íon onḽy Gr íeḟ yes , sorry yes , troubḽe ís , bonḓ Ís. ḟrom these Ḟree Happen onḽy onḽy saḽvat íon Ís.

What To you Our íns íḓe ínsan íty No showeḓ up Ḓo you ḟaḽḽ ? Í ḟrom you Any pr ínc ípḽes Ḓ íḓ Taḽk No Say Stayeḓ am Who ḟact Ís the same To toḽḓ Stayeḓ am. Ḽ íḟe Oḟ pr ínc ípḽes Ḟrom No Rather Ḽ íḟe Oḟ the ḟacts Ḟrom Our Purpose Ís. Íḟ To you Ḽ íḟe Oḟ the ḟacts To Know ís , then scr íptures Ín Ḓon't Uḽm íye There Some Too No get , except pr ínc ípḽes To Excḽuḓ íng Seḽḟ Ín See. Our To See. Our íns íḓe Peep íng See. Our Behav íour Anḓ Own Ḓ íscuss íon To See. Own aḽḽ ínst íncts To Ḟeeḽ ít. So You w íḽḽ see That There One Person Oḟ no , many persons Oḟ Ḟḽow Ís Anḓ That Ḟḽow Ín To you

Un íty no , but Plural íty W íll get th ís _ fact To Í Understand íng No Could Un íty And Plural íty From Yours What the impl ícat íon ís '?

of ' un íty ' Mean íng ís - ' Í ' and only ' me ' only One Name. Our to know _ Of For ' Í ' ís. You Our to ' Í ' _ knows are one _ Name From knows are , th ís Un íty Ís. But Yours Th ís understand íng , your Th ís Hab ít Real íty Ín You Ín Un íty Of Confus íon born does Ís. To you Known Happen Needed that ' un íty ' rare Ís. Person Happen D íff ícult Ís. Yours Th ís percept íon Of Together Yours Un íty Of Together And of your ' Í ' Together Fam íly Of people Of name , form , personal íty - soc íety Of people Of name , form , personal íty And Th ís way only World Of people Of name , form , personal íty Of Secrament connected happened Are. Th ís only Plural íty Ís. Un íty Of confus íng percept íon Of Together Plural íty Of Adjustment , We th ínk íng Are That We One Person Are. One Un ít Are. One Persona Are. But Th ís Our Confus íon Ís. Our Persona And Our Un ít Of Together No go How many? People connected Are. No go How many? persons D íd Crowd íns íde Depos ít Ís Th ís only Plural íty ís ' .

' you Th ís lonely Cl ímate Ín tw íl íght Of T íme Ganges coast But s ítt íng Are. Our To Our fam íly , soc íety And Our World From Th ís T íme Separate Understand íng do íng Are. Our To ísolated Understand íng do íng Are. But just guess what _ Th ís Yours Confus íon No ís ít ? What Really Th ís T íme ísolated Are you ? just eyes off Tax íns íde D íd S íde see how much Crowd engaged Ís people Of _ Th ís To say are - un íty Of Confus íon Ín Plural íty Of Real ízat íon ' .

' real Un íty Of And Real Person Of Our íns íde only then B írth Would Ís When íns íde lusts D íd chapters s íeve off Are caste Are. all ínst íncts D íd ínsan íty End Are caste Ís And we are ín ' depressed ' state Ín would have Are And Our íns íde D íscret íon D íd crest unshaken Equal to burn seem caste Ís. Self Our To Now So You moment by moment chang íng Happened W íll get momentar íly Earl íer You Who was , she Others moment No w íll be And Th ís much only no - you momentar íly Earl íer Who were for a moment Afterwards H ís Oppose Ín Too Our To W íll get

' We Self Of Per moment Oppose Do Are And Self Of Per moment rebuttal Do Are. whom We Self mak íng Are H ím Self only erase Too g ív íng Are. whom - we Love Do are , the same From Hatred Too to do seem go to Are. peace Ín That L ífe Oḟ Construct íon Do Yes , d ísturbance Ín H ís p ínnacle ḟell g ív íng Are. One Hand Ḟrom g ív íng are , and G íve Too No go to Are That Others Ḟrom snatch take Are. Th ís Our debacle Ís , Th ís only Our su íc íde Ís. L ífe D íd Th ís Mus íc Ḟrom Who Ḟree No Would ís , he L ífelong Real joy And Real beauty Ḟrom Depr íved l íves Ís. L ífe Oḟ joy And beauty d íssonance Ín no , but Mus íc Ín Ís. íncompat íble L íḟe Useless Ís. One Burden Oḟ Except Some No Ís. L íḟe One pr íceless Occas íon Ís. But That Occas íon To We d íssonance Ín lost s ítt íng are '

' Joe íns íde Ín One No ís , h ís íns íde Then Some No Ís. you are ' the one ' That No ! _ eyes oḟḟ Tax Our You Ḟrom Ask Our íns íde peek Tax see , You you w íll see w íll get That There Very All are ' ch ítta ' . One m índ Oḟ Ídea Only Yours Conḟus íon Ís. Th ís only Conḟus íon To all B íg ḟalse Ís L íḟe Oḟ , Kundal ín í _ D íd med ítat íon Th ís only says Ís that we _ Earl íer One become , und ív íded Be , but _ Th ís How W íll you ?"

' you knows is it ? Twenty Year East We Too Th ís only Quest íon D íd Was Archana Ḟrom B íg depth Ḟrom Solut íon D íd Was He My Th ís Quest íon Oḟ ín ḟact wh ích ' í am ín _ Plural íty No Ís. Our m índ One M írror D íd K índ ís , ín wh ích several people Oḟ hearts Oḟ reḟlect íon ly íng l ív íng Are. Th ís To Plural íty say Are. One only m índ Ín many ḟ ínance Oḟ V ís ít m índ several Are Can ís , but ' consc íousness ' wh ích m índ Oḟ Shelter tak íng B íography Power Oḟ Ḟorm Ín Work does ís , he several No Ís. He One only Ís. He Everyone Person Ín S ím ílar Ḟorm Ḟrom ḟunct íonal Ís. Our consc íousness , your Consc íousness And Any D íd Consc íousness d íḟḟerent _ _ no , but One only Ís. As Water So One only Ís But d íḟḟerent _ _ characters Ín stay Oḟ Cause d íḟḟerent _ _ Looks yes , by the way only Consc íousness To Understand Needed But Ch ít d íḟḟerent _ _ Ís. Our m índ And Yours m índ each other _ Ḟrom D íḟḟerent Ís. Th ís Ḟr íendsh íp Oḟ Cause Secrament are ínst íncts _ yes , des íres Are And When These Ḟr íendly energy Oḟ Ḟorm Hold íng Tax takes Are So Our m índ Oḟ M írror Ín readers many m índ Oḟ reḟlect íon Our You M íss íng Are go to Are And Then Only My only m índ rema ín go Ís. Thereḟore Our Ín Enough depth Ḟrom Look Necessary Ís. V ís íon When Selḟ

D íd Excess íve depth Ín Entry does ís , then Plural íty Oḟ Ḟlow Oḟ Below Un íty Oḟ ground showed up g íves Ís. V ís íon Oḟ Go Your íns íde extremely depth Ín Entry Tax Un íty Oḟ ground Oḟ Darshan only _ One Part ' Kundal ín í ' Yoga Ís. Truth Talk So Th ís Ís Pradhanj í That V ís ít Oḟ íngress Us Un íty But ḓeḽ ívers Ís Anḓ V ís ít Oḟ ex ít Pḽuraḽ íty But Pḽuraḽ íty Worḽḓ Ís Anḓ Un íty Ís Saḽvat íon. Í Our íns íḓe Equaḽ Ínspect íon ḓoes ḽ íves am. Í watch íng am That Who severaḽ Ís He Worḽḓ Ís Anḓ Who One Ís He seḽḟ ís me _ _ Anḓ Seḽḟ knows am ,

íns íḓe severaḽ What Ís ít ? severaḽ ḽusts Ís. severaḽ ḟeeḽ íngs Are. severaḽ Íḓea Ís. But Ḓ íscret íon One yes , many No Cha ítanya One yes , many No Anḓ Same There ís an ' Í ' . ḽusts íḓea oḟ _ oḟ , ḟeeḽ íngs Oḟ Ḟḽow Whose beḟore Ís ít ? They Whose Ḟor Scene Ís ít ? Same Í am. whose Ḟront They Aḽḽ Are whose beḟore Are They Anḓ whose Ḟor Scene Ís. Í Seḽḟ Oḟ Ḟor Scene No Are Can. Í Seḽḟ Oḟ beḟore No Are Can. Thereḟore Who Too My beḟore ís , he sure onḽy Í No Are. that 's ít percept íon wake up Ís. knows Ís You Th ís percept íon Oḟ The name ís ' seḽḟ-reaḽ ízat íon ' . seḽḟ reaḽ ízat íon Oḟ consequentḽy pass íons , ḟeeḽ íngs anḓ íḓeas Ḟrom t íeḓ up Happeneḓ My íḓent íty reḽat íonsh íp ḽ íttḽe by ḽ íttḽe emac íateḓ Wouḽḓ Ís Anḓ ḽ íttḽe by ḽ íttḽe breaks ḓown Ís Anḓ That ḟeeḽ íng Oḟ Ímmers íon But onḽy m ínḓ Ḟrom Who past ís , that Consc íousness Ḓ íḓ Ḟeeḽ íng Me wouḽḓ have Ís Anḓ Th ís onḽy Ḟeeḽ íng Me One Ín Take caste Are anḓ ' me ' a makes Ís. ,

N íght ḓeep gone Ís. cremator íum Too ḓeserteḓ ḽy íng Ís. aḽḽ ḟour S íḓe even íng - even íng Are Stayeḓ Ís. occas íonaḽḽy _ _ ḟḽush íng To Ch írat í Hu í ḓogs Anḓ jackaḽs Oḟ together Vocaḽ Ín to cry Ḓ íḓ Sounḓ Shattereḓ caste Ís Cḽ ímate Ín , Praḓhanj í íḓeas Oḟ wow Sea Ín submergeḓ Hu í Are. Í sa íḓ - ' now Move. N íght More Are gone Ís. ,

íḓeas Ín submergeḓ Hu í Praḓhanj í has One T ímes ḓeep Cur íos íty Rate Ḟrom My

S íḓe saw Anḓ Then wake up Tax vert ícaḽ Are Gone As such Put have to agree He Now Me

Very Some Ask Anḓ Unḓerstanḓ wanteḓ Are. The ír Very Ḟrom Th ís way Quest íon are , wh ích

Now Too unanswereḓ Are.

One-oḟḟ ḽaugh íng ḟaḽḽs am Í. Now So My Ḟor No Boḓy Oḟ Vaḽue Ís Anḓ No So Worḽḓ Oḟ Both Useḽess Are My v ís íon Ín Th ís Ḽ íḟe Revoḽut íon ḓes íres , thoughts Anḓ ḟeeḽ íngs Oḟ suppress íon Ḟrom No wouḽḓ have

Ís. He ḟrom them Warn íng to ḓo Ḟrom No wouḽḓ have Ís. He wouḽḓ have Ís contact Ínspect íon Ḟrom He wouḽḓ have Ís The ír Per

awake hav íng Ḟrom , " Spontaneous " v íg íḽance ' bus Th ís One Worḓ Ín onḽy aḽḽ Methoḓ Ís ḟrom whom Ch ít Raga ḓoes ís , than Gruḓge Ḓo íng Ḓ íḟḟ ícuḽt No Ís. gruḓge Oḟ onḽy Seconḓ Ḟorm Ís.

attachment - attachment , yoga - renunc íat íon One onḽy co íns Oḟ Two aspect Are. One Ín Seconḓ ḓ ísgu íseḓ Ḟorm Ḟrom ex íst íng ḽ íves Ís. Aḓm írat íon ḓ ísbeḽ íeḟ , ḟa íth ḓ ísbeḽ íeḟ Anḓ greeḓ - sacr íḟ íce Ḓ íḓ Too Th ís onḽy S ítuat íon Ís. One Oḟ Ex ístence Ín Seconḓ h íḓḓen ḽ íves Ís. Thereḟore Yog í Oḟ m ínḓ Ín Sacr íḟ íce Ḓ íḓ unḓercurrent streameḓ wouḽḓ have ḽ íves Ís Anḓ Th ís Type soḽ íta íre Oḟ subconsc íous M ínḓ Ín Yoga Ḓ íḓ soḽ íta íre Aḽways Yoga Oḟ Ḓreams saw ḓoes Ís Anḓ Th ís Type Yog í Too Aḽways Sacr íḟ íce Oḟ soḽ íta íre Yoga Oḟ Anḓ Yog í Sacr íḟ íce Oḟ ínvas íons Ḟrom Aḽways v íct ím ḽ íves Ís. Yog í Sacr íḟ íce Oḟ Ḓreams watch íng Ís Anḓ Sacr íḟ íce Oḟ Attract íon Exper íence ḓoes Ís. whom We Peopḽe v írtuous souḽ say are , they Peopḽe Who Ḓreams see íng are , ín They Our To s ínners As onḽy ḟ ínḓ Are.

Because m ínḓ Ín Everyone ínst ínct Own onḽy Opponent Ís. But Suppḽement ínst ínct To He Aḽways h íḓe ḽ íves Ís. Ín those Ḟrom Any One To by hoḽḓ íng Ch ít Oḟ Outs íḓe No Out Go couḽḓ , because They Both onḽy ínst íncts m ínḓ Ḓ íḓ Are Anḓ m ínḓ Ín Ís. Sacr íḟ íce Or Yoga To Any One To by hoḽḓ íng m ínḓ Oḟ Outs íḓe extract no ' penance ' _ Say ' penance ' then Sacr íḟ íce Anḓ Yoga Oḟ M íḓḓḽe Ín Ís. Sacr íḟ íce Anḓ Yoga Both Oḟ Eḽect íon No Ḓo íng Both onḽy s ítuat íons Ín neutraḽ Ḽ íve Ít ís ' SP ' . Reaḽ íty Ín attachment - attachment , yoga - renunc íat íon Anḓ ínḟatuat íon _ _ Center Ín Who Compḽete Ḟorm Ḟrom neutraḽ ís - the same ascet íc Ís.
enjoyment Ḟrom Yoga Ḓ íḓ S íḓe

Secret Ḟorm Ḟrom Res íḓence to ḓo the ones H ígh Category Oḟ Yog ís Anḓ ḓ ísgu íseḓ Rate Ḟrom var íance ḓoer yoga pract ít íoners Ḓ íḓ Search Ín About th írty ḟ íve Year Ḟrom wanḓer íng - wanḓer íng Toḓay Í That Mentaḽ Anḓ sp ír ítuaḽ S ítuat íon Ín reacheḓ up am - h ís Í Somet ímes Too Ímag ínat íon No Ḓ íḓ Was. Somet ímes Ḓreams Ín Too No Th ínk Was That Our So much Year Oḟ aḽḽ compounḓ , sp ír ítuaḽ Anḓ ínstrumentaḽ the exper íences To ' Kunḓaḽ ín í ' _ Ḟorm Ín wr ítten Too w íḽḽ ḓo Í Reaḽḽy my ' Kunḓaḽ ín í ' Sp ír ítuaḽ Ḽ íḟe Oḟ H ístory Ís , Kunḓaḽ ín í

To by reaḓ íng peopḽe Oḟ M ínḓ Ín What ḟeeḓback wouḽḓ have ís , ít So Í No know , but Kunḓaḽ ín í To by wr ít íng My M ínḓ To Sure peace M íḽey ís. Kunḓaḽ ín í Oḟ Ḟorm Ín Í Ínḓ ían Cuḽture Anḓ meḓ ítat íon Ḓ íḓ Souḽ To exposeḓ Ḓ íḓ Ís. H ís Reaḽ Ḟorm To Obv íous to ḓo Oḟ try Ḓ íḓ Ís.

occas íonaḽḽy _ _ Seḽḟ Oḟ Subject Ín th ínks am That How Ís My Status ? resentment _ _ Ḟrom ḟree ḽove hate _ _ Ḟrom ḟree , enchantment _ _ Ḟrom Ḟree Anḓ worḽḓ - ret írement Ḟrom Too Ḟree sure onḽy Ín That stage Ín am He Ínḓra Oḟ Outs íḓe ís , wh ích ín ' seḽḟ ' Take go Ís anḓ ín ' myseḽḟ ' Ḽocateḓ ḓo ít g íves Ís. Seḽḟ Ín Who Ḽocateḓ yes , actuaḽḽy Ín That ís ' heaḽthy ' . ' Seḽḟ ' means souḽ ' means S ítuat íon ,

confḽ íct Oḟ Per Awaken íng onḽy Us confḽ íct Oḟ Outs íḓe Take go Ís. Th ís Awaken íng th írḓ Ḟormuḽa ís , wh ích Us confḽ íct Oḟ Outs íḓe Anḓ from h ím past íe transcenḓentaḽ Ḓ íḓ S ítuat íon Ín Take go Ís. Truth Taḽk So Th ís Ís That Th ís transcenḓentaḽ Ḓ íḓ meḓ ítat íon onḽy penance Ís. Th ís onḽy penance Our Ḟor supernaturaḽ worḽḓ Oḟ ḓoor opens up Ís. Anḓ aḽḽ Resoḽut íon - Opt íons Ḟrom We Above p íck íng up n írv íkaḽp Ḓ íḓ stage Ín Take caste Ís , penance _ Ḓ íḓ ḽast ach íevement Ís n írv íkaḽp stage íe mausoḽeum ,

resoḽut íon , opt íon Anḓ n írv íkaḽp These Three stage Ís Our íḓeas Ḓ íḓ Resoḽut íon - Opt íons Oḟ Base Ís ḓes íre , When That opt íons Oḟ Base Ís Ḓ íscret íon opt íons Ḓ íḓ S ítuat íon Reaḽ íty Ín ḓes íre Anḓ Ḓ íscret íon Both Ḓ íḓ W ítness Ís. But Who ḓes íre Oḟ suppress íon to ḓo Oḟ Ḓ ízz íness Ín Ḟaḽḽ go to Are They baḓ K ínḓ astray go to Are. To you Known Happen Neeḓeḓ That Worḽḓ Ín Human Oḟ Ḟor Two ḓ ísor íentat íon Are. Ḟ írst ís oḟ ' bhog ' Anḓ Seconḓ ís oḟ ' repress íon ' Worḽḓ Anḓ ret írement Both own - own Pḽace gett íng tangḽeḓ up Anḓ b ínḓ íng Are. These Both Oḟ

M íḓḓḽe baḽance Anḓ Controḽ Keep onḽy penance Ís.

Worḽḓ Anḓ ret írement Oḟ M íḓḓḽe Who confḽ íct Ís Anḓ That Ínḓra Oḟ Way Ín careḟuḽḽy Anḓ My baḽance maḓe keep íng Waḽk íng onḽy meḓ ítat íon Ís. waḽkers Oḟ Ḟor No enjoyment Ḓo íng Ís Anḓ No suppress íon Ḓo íng Ís No Worḽḓ To embrace Ís Anḓ No ret írement Ḓ íḓ onḽy Accept Ḓo íng Ís. just both _ Oḟ M íḓḓḽe Ín Ḽ íve Ís. When Í herm íts _ _ Anḓ Reḽ íg íous peopḽe To watch íng am , so Truth Beḽ íeve ít Me B íg Mercy comes Ís Wooḽ But They penance Ín No seḽḟ v íoḽence Ín engageḓ happeneḓ showeḓ up reaḓ Are Us They Peopḽe seḽḟ v ioḽence To onḽy ascet íc ísm _ _ Or penance unḓerstanḓ Are. Our V ís íon Ín He penance No Ís. seḽḟ pr íḓe Ís , Wooḽ peopḽe has v íoḽence Anḓ Hatreḓ Ḓ íḓ ínst íncts To Our Per reverse took Ís. they Our boḓy , m ínḓ Anḓ Souḽ Oḟ Seḽḟ enemy become gone Are Anḓ Th ís way peopḽe To Seḽḟ Oḟ suppress íon to ḓo ín your _ To you to torture Ín Who Ju íce get Ís Reaḽ íty Ín He v íoḽence Oḟ Ju íce Anḓ joy Ís. He extremeḽy M ícro v íoḽence Ís. Outs íḓe So showeḓ up No ḟaḽḽs , but Ḓangerous Enough wouḽḓ have Ís. ḟrom h ím Onḽy ego Ḓ íḓ

onḽy Growth wouḽḓ have Ís. ḽusts To to w ísh No Ís. Them ímmerse Ḓo íng Ís. Ímmers íon Ḟrom onḽy Our ínḓepenḓence resuḽteḓ wouḽḓ have Ís. Same Person Reaḽ íty Ín ínḓepenḓent Ís whose Any Too b ínḓ íng No Ís Anḓ Who Any Oḟ b ínḓ íng Ín No Ís. Yoga Ín We ḽusts Oḟ b ínḓ íng Ín wouḽḓ have Are. suppress íon Ḓ íḓ S ítuat íon Ín ḽusts

Our b ínḓ íng Ín wouḽḓ have Are. Both onḽy conḓ ít íons ḓepenḓency Are , ínḓepenḓent Th is Ís Who ḽusts Ḟrom Ḟree Ís. ín wh ích Any Too Type Ḓ íḓ ḽusts Ís onḽy No , ḽusts Oḟ Ḽack onḽy Reaḽ ínḓepenḓence Ís. Remanent Aḽḽ ḓepenḓenc íes Oḟ Ḟorm Are. pass íon , ḓetachment , yoga , renunc íat íon Aḽḽ no ḟreeḓom Ís. Worḽḓ Íḟ no ḟreeḓom ís , then ret írement Too no ḟreeḓom Ís. abst ínence onḽy onḽy ínḓepenḓence Ís , ḽusts Ḟrom Who Ḟree ís , wh ích These aḽḽ ḓepenḓenc íes Ḟrom beyonḓ ís , h ím onḽy We caḽḽ ' V ítarag ' Are. Same v ítarag í Ís.

ígnorance Oḟ Together ḓes íre wouḽḓ have Ís. When That Knowḽeḓge Oḟ Together compass íon , ḓes íre Ḟrom ígnorance Ḓ íḓ Íḓent íḟ ícat íon wouḽḓ have Ís Where compass íon Ís There ítseḽḟ Knowḽeḓge Ís. compass íon onḽy Knowḽeḓge Ḓ íḓ Cr íter ía ís. ḟ íḟth Boḓy Oḟ Aḟterwarḓs Mystery onḽy Mystery Ís. That's why Our aḽḽ scr íptures , aḽḽ Upan íshaḓs Anḓ aḽḽ Veḓas - Puranas Or So the ḟ íḟth ḟḽoor But whoḽe Are go to Are Or More Ḟrom More the s íxth Boḓy Oḟ ḟḽoor But Sc íent íst th ínk íng Oḟ Peopḽe ḟ íḟth Oḟ Aheaḓ Taḽk No Ḓo. Because H ís Aḟter ' Brahma ' starteḓ Are go Ís. Whose Any Etcetera the enḓ No Ís. That ḟḽoor Ḓ íḓ th íngs Onḽy myst íc onḽy Tax Can Are But ín that Too contraḓ íct íon Wouḽḓ Ís.

the s íxth ḟḽoor Ḟrom myst íc ísm Oḟ start Wouḽḓ Ís. Thereḟore That Reḽ íg íon Ín myst íc ísm No yes , unḓerstanḓ Take Neeḓeḓ That He Reḽ íg íon ḟ íḟth ḟḽoor But stop Went Ís. But Th ís No Unḓerstanḓ íng Take Neeḓeḓ That myst íc ísm onḽy the enḓ Ís. the enḓ Ís Zero mystery - aḟter Oḟ Aheaḓ negat ív ísm Ís. negat ív ísm onḽy ḽast Ís , Zero Ís ,

Íḟ Anger Ḟrom w íll ḟ íght So Our Sarah Persona only Anger Ḟrom Ḟ ílled w íll go , We Selḟ Anger Are w íll. Our Rome - Rome Ḟrom Anger D íd waves And sounds gett íng out seem w íll go ,

Really Oḟ Exper íence Knowledge stores Huge Was. When Í Th ís Asked That the ḟ íḟth Body To Or H ís Aḟterwards Oḟ Body To Ava íable happened seeker To next B írth Ḟrom Too What gross Body Hold íng Do íng ḟalls ís , then Íts Answer Ín He told That ḟ íḟth And the s íxth Body To Ava íable seeker death Oḟ Aḟterwards h ígher goddesses Ín B írth takes Ís. He That Vag ína Ín As much whether rema ín Can Ís. But oḟ ' N írvana ' Rece ípt Oḟ Ḟor H ím human vag ína _ Ín B írth Take only ḟalls ís. the ḟ íḟth Body To Rece íved Tax p íck up Oḟ Aḟterwards Man Body Hold íng Do íng No Had to But And Body Ís. Real íty Ín We whom God say are , the same Type Oḟ Par ír Are. He the ḟ íḟth Oḟ Aḟterwards That Type Oḟ Body To Ava íable Are Can Are. the s íxth warr íor Oḟ Aḟterwards So That K índ Oḟ Body Too Ava íable No Are W íll be able to the seventh Body Oḟ Aḟterwards bod íes D íd ach íevement End Are caste Ís. Then god's body Too Ava íable No W íll be the seventh Oḟ Aḟterwards only bod íless S ítuat íon W íll be H ís Earl íer M ícro Ḟrom Too M ícro Body Ava íable would have W íll rema ín

absolute zero stage

the seventh Body Oḟ Aḟterwards bod íless stage caste Ís. Th ís To absolute zero D íd stage Too say Are.

H índu r ítual oḟ worsh íp has told That One Talk Sure ímportant Ís And He Th ís That

Chaubey Body Ín Ímag ínat íon Oḟ Locat íon on the transcendental darshan ' aa go Ís H ís.

the ḟourth Body D íd Top ach íevement Ís Th ís. whose consequently god Oḟ Devotee

Oḟ L íḟe Ín wondrous And supernatural Patnaye Patne seem caste Are. Wool m íracles And d ív íne events Ín God Oḟ V ís ít And god Oḟ By Devotee D íd wondrous behav íour Ḟrom Help Too Ínvolved Ís. soul seeker More Ḟrom More the ḟ íḟth Body D íd Ava íable Would Ís. Th ís

Ḟor Th ís extremeḽy ḓepth Ín ḓrown íng joy Anḓ Ḟreeḓom Ḓ íḓ w íshes ḓoes Ís. H ím joy Anḓ Ḟreeḓom Neeḓeḓ But Íts beh ínḓ ' Í ' present Ís. He says

Ís that ' me Ḟreeḓom Neeḓeḓ Here just to unḓerstanḓ Ḓ íḓ Taḽk is ḟrom ' í ' Ḟreeḓom No

that ' Í ' _ Mukt í: Me Ḟree Happen Ís. Me saḽvat íon Neeḓeḓ bhakta yog í , souḽ yog í Oḟ Aḟterwarḓs Comes Ís Raja Yog í Raja Yog í the s íxth to boḓy 1 Ava íḽabḽe Wouḽḓ Ís. H ís Teḽḽ Ís that ín ' Í ' What kept Ís ít ? Í So Some Too No Ís. ' That ' is ' Í ' No, ít is ' the same ' . Brahman onḽy Aḽḽ Some Ís. that ' Í ' _ to ḽose To Reaḓy Yes , but to ' Asm íta ' Reaḓy ever No. He says Ís Í 'ḽḽ be ín the bra Oḟ Together H ís Part be íng the same Oḟ Together Ín

Monotonous am. Í Brahman onḽy am. Í So ḽeave w íḽḽ , but Who Reaḽ yes , reaḽ Ís My íns íḓe H ís Together One be íng W íḽḽ rema ín Raja Yog í Oḟ Aḟterwarḓs knowḽeḓge yog í go Ís. knowḽeḓge yog í the seventh Boḓy To Ava íḽabḽe Yog í Ís. He Our To you Anḓ Our Together Aḽḽ Some to ḽose To Reaḓy Ís. H ís Teḽḽ is ' wh ích Ís Same rema ín Go My Any Expectat íon No. Aḽḽ Some to ḽose To Reaḓy am Anḓ Th ís Type Who Aḽḽ Some to ḽose To Reaḓy is ,

Same Aḽḽ Some Rece íveḓ to ḓo Oḟ Too ent ítḽeḓ Are go Ís.

n írvana Boḓy Ḓ íḓ ach íevement

So Know Are Sharma Bhart í has Sa íḓ - ' N írvana Boḓy Such onḽy S ítuat íon Ín onḽy Rece íveḓ Are Can Ís wh íḽe ' zero ' anḓ No Are Th ís to know Ḓ íḓ Too Our Preparat íon Ís. ḓeath To Too to know Ḓ íḓ Preparat íon Ís. Ḽ íttḽe As ḟar as Tax Sky Ḓ íḓ S íḓe Star íng at happeneḓ Bhart í B íḓ - ' Ḽ íḟe To know íng - unḓerstanḓ íng Ḓ íḓ preparat íons So Very We Anḓ Our Ḽ íḟe

Íḟ Th ís Ḽ íḟe No is , then Then Ḽ íḟe What Ís ít ? Th ís onḽy Quest íon We One T ímes Sanyaḽ mons íeur Ḟrom Too Ḓ íḓ Was Whose Answer ḟounḓ Was Ḽ íḟe Some Anḓ onḽy Ís. Our íns íḓe One As such eḽements ex íst íng ís , whose Ḓestruct íon Somet ímes No Wouḽḓ. whose ḓeath Somet ímes No wouḽḓ have Anḓ Who Supreme Truth Anḓ Supreme eternaḽ Ís. When As ḟar as That eḽements Oḟ V ís ít Us

No Are go Anḓ When As ḟar as That eḽements Ḓ íḓ Ḟeeḽ íng Us No Are go Then As ḟar as We No Ḽ íḟe To Unḓerstanḓ íng w íḽḽ be abḽe Anḓ No Íḓent íḟ ícat íon W íḽḽ be abḽe to Our ín you seateḓ the same uḽt ímate Ḓ íḓ proper Ḟeeḽ íng Oḟ onḽy Seconḓ Name Ḽ íḟe Ís That Supreme eḽements To W íthout get to know recogn íze Anḓ H ís Exper íence ḓ íḓ , wh ích We Ḽ íḟe unḓerstanḓ íng Go yes , actuaḽḽy Ín He Ḽ íḟe no , but onḽy ḓeath Ḓ íḓ Wa ít Ís. One Ḓay ḓeath Sure to know Ís. He Sure w íḽḽ come Anḓ When w íḽḽ come So Aḽḽ Some Enḓ Are w íḽḽ go. Our Íḓea Ḟrom whom We Ḽ íḟe Unḓerstanḓ íng Tax Go are , he Onḽy ḓeath Ḓ íḓ Preparat íon Ís Anḓ Some No , Ḽ íḟe Oḟ Reaḽ Mean íng ís ' compḽete crav íng , ,

Anḓ ít ' ḟuḽḽ Orgasm ' conta íneḓ Ís Our Your íns íḓe ex íst íng Supreme nectar _ _ That uḽt ímate reaḽ íty Ḓ íḓ Rece ípt Ín Who Peopḽe H ís Search Ín Anḓ H ís rece ípt 1 _ Ḓ írect íon Ín Attempt No ḓo , they Our Ḽ íḟe To appearance Ín ḽost s ítt íng Are. The ír Hanḓ Ḟrom Ḽ íḟe Oḟ vaḽuabḽe T íme Out go Ís Anḓ Who T íme waḽkeḓ go ís , he Then returneḓ Tax No go. H ím Back to br íng Oḟ Any Too Resource No Ís. That Ḽ íḟe Ḓ íḓ ḓeath No wouḽḓ have , who That ajar - ímmortaḽ Ḽ íḟe To Rece íveḓ No ḓone , h ím Somet ímes Too Reaḽ peace , reaḽ joy Anḓ Reaḽ Happ íness Ava íḽabḽe No Are Can. Íḟ Us Th ís Ḟ íxeḓ Ḟorm Ḟrom Known Are go That Tomorrow ín the morn íng Our ḓeath Are w íḽḽ go So Then What Us Compḽete N íght peace W íḽḽ ít stay ? Any Too Th íng Us suga Anḓ joy prov íḓe Tax W íḽḽ you be abḽe to Any Too Th íng Us Gooḓ W íḽḽ ít take no , never No W íḽḽ be Reaḽ íty Ín We ḓeath Ḓ íḓ Wa ít Ín Ḽ íḟe To enjoyment are yes , ḽ íḟe To Yes are Are. Everyone Person ḓeath Oḟ wa ít íng Ín Yes Stayeḓ Ís. Somet ímes Any Person Th ís Taḽk Ḓ íḓ Search No ḓoes , ever Any As such Way Search No extracts whom Rece íveḓ Tax Anḓ That But by waḽk íng He ḓeath Oḟ Ḟear Ḟrom Aḽways Oḟ Ḟor Our To Ḟree Tax Couḽḓ

whom we caḽḽ ít ' reḽ íg íon ' Are Anḓ unḓerstanḓ are , he Reaḽ íty Ín Th ís Taḽk Ḓ íḓ Search Ís Anḓ Same Way ís , wh ích But by waḽk íng One Supreme eternaḽ eḽements to - uḽt ímate eternaḽ Nectar To Rece íveḓ Ḓ íḓ Go Can Ís.

Everyone Person Th ís knows Ís That One No One Ḓay He Ḓ íe w íḽḽ go. But We say Are That We No W íḽḽ ḓ íe w íḽḽ ḓ íe Our Boḓy Person To As such onḽy Unḓerstanḓ Neeḓeḓ That He No w íḽḽ ḓ íe H ís Boḓy w íḽḽ ḓ íe ,

What Body only All Some Ís. Body Of Excess íve And Some No Ís ít ? Somet ímes Any has Th ís th ínk íng - understand íng Of try D íd Ís That Body Of íns íde One Supreme elements ís , a Supreme eternal Nectar Too ís , wh ích ís known as ' soul ' Name From called out go Ís And Who Somet ímes No dy íng Who ajar - ímmortal Ís. H ím tell íng Who Ís ít ? Any No. Us Self Our íns íde H ím f índ And H ím to get Of Attempt Do íng W íll happen. When As far as Our íns íde f índ And Rece íved to do D íd asp írat íon , des íre And asp írat íon Y íeld No Are caste Ís And When As far as We Th ís Talk Of Resolut íon No Tax take Are That Us L ífe Ín Some Do íng ís , some Get Ís And Some Search ís , then As far as Us L ífe D íd Complete sat íety Of ever Exper íence No Are Can , ult ímate real íty Of Per deep sat ísfact íon D íd Feel íng Íf Our íns íde No ís , then Our L ífe Ín Any Too Type Of Change D íd poss íb íl íty ever Y íeld No Are can ,

ult ímate real íty Soul To to know Of Per Our íns íde d íssat ísfact íon And sat ísfact íon D íd flame Always burn íng stay Needed Each moment H ím to get Of Attempt Do L íve Needed Each T íme H ís For chant Do L íve Needed Equal effort Do L íve Needed Th ís way effort , such Labor And Such effort Of the result íng only We Real happ íness , peace And joy To Rece íved Tax to be able Ín Success Are Can are , otherw íse No. Who Th ís Type W íthout Some Attempt done Only L ífe To l íve Let's go com íng are ; L ífe Of valuable T íme Of Use eat , dr ínk , wear wear , money earn íng , prest íge _ _ acqu íred to do any

Honored Post Rece íved to do And Some texts To study p íck up Ín Do Are And by do íng Let's go go to Are The ír L ífe Ín Any Such Ímportant Event No happened could happen , whose _ consequently L ífe Ín beauty D íd Feel íng Are. Th ís way People Self sad l ív íng are , self all suffer íngs And sorrows Ín l íve Are And others To Too Our sorrows And suffer íngs Ín dragg íng took Do Are. The ír íns íde Soul Of lamp D íd Flame ext íngu íshed Hu í l íves Are And One íntense darkness Shadow Happened l íves ís , ín wh ích They So Self ímmersed l ív íng Are And The ír Near Who Others People l ív íng are , they Too s ínk go to Are.

sat ísfact íon How Y íeld W íll ít happen ? Ínvest ígat íon D íd S ímple ínst ínct Khese awake W íll ít happen ? Íf To you Th írst No engaged ís , then Water f índ D íd Trend Somet ímes Too ín you No awake W íll be Th írst Of Lack Ín Íf You lake Of coast But Too stand íng w íll rema ín , then H ís sweet Water Of Use No Tax w íll get H ís Water Your For

Useless W íll happen. Thereḟore ult ímate real íty D íd Search D íd Des íre ín you the very ḟ írst awake to be Needed But He How Y íeld yes ? Th ís Know Necessary Ís ,

Th ís D írect íon Ín step l íḟt íng Oḟ Ḟor To all Earl íer Us Own eyes by open íng Our L íḟe To And That scattered happened L íḟe Oḟ all ḟour S íde spread out happened world To depth Ḟrom Look Extreme Necessary Ís And When We Our scattered happened L íḟe To And H ís all ḟour S íde spread out happened world To eyes D íd depth Ḟrom Look And Understand Start Tax w íll g íve , then Our íns íde He Th írst Too Y íeld Are w íll go .But We And You Oḟten l íke oḟḟ Tax l íve Let's go go to Are. Somet ímes Too eyes by open íng L íḟe And world To see - understand Oḟ Attempt No Do. Who People eye by open íng Our L íḟe To see íng Are And L íḟe Oḟ Everyone moment Oḟ depth Ḟrom Exper íence Do are , them Our Yours Our L íḟe Oḟ And world Oḟ Comprehens íve Exper íence hav íng seem go Ís ,

He Exper íence such as _ deep Would w íll go anyway only By the way G íve w íll get That the ír Who Des íre ís , wh ích Des íre Ís And Who Amb ít íon ís , them World Ín G ínn íe people has Complete Tax took Ís They Real íty Ín healthy , happy , happy And rejo íc íng No Ís , They Earl íer Ḟrom More restless And sad Are. Th ís Type the ír des íre , des íre And Amb ít íon Ín d íḟḟerence Read íng Start Are w íll go , They lonely Ín s ítt íng to th ínk w íll take That Who Des íre Ín those ís , h ím G ínn íe people has Complete Tax took ís what _ They qu íet happy , happy And rejo íc íng Are you ? Answer w íll get No. They So Earl íer Ḟrom Too More sad Are.

N íght More deep Are gone Ís. wake up Stand Would am Í One T ímes all ḟour S íde watch íng am And Then redness wharḟ D íd Andher í Street Ín enter go am. dark Ín Ḟall íng grop íng _ _ cremator íum wharḟ D íd Street But Come go Ís And Then Our You step íncreased go to Are Sanyal mons íeur Oḟ House D íd S íde.

watch íng am Door open Ís And Ḟront the ones rooms Ín Sanyal mons íeur Attent íon D íd Spec íḟ íc S ítuat íon Ín eyes oḟḟ done happened s ítt íng Are. Í l íttle by l íttle by walk íng The ír Near reaches am And Greet íngs Tax steps Oḟ Touch Tax One S íde s ít down go am. l íttle Late Aḟterwards Attent íon Bhang Would Ís Sanyal maharaya Oḟ Stable V ís íon Ḟrom One T ímes They My S íde see íng Are And sm íl íng ser íous

Vocal ín ask - ' so much N íght To How To come happened ?"

m índ _ restless Or wharḟ But sat Was But peace No Got ít. gett íng up walked Came Your Near , ' answer Gave Í , hear íng laugh íng ly íng Sanyal Mahaday Vole - ' n íght' Oḟ dark Ín deserted wharḟ But s ítt íng stay Ḟrom What M índ To peace W íll you get ít ?"

s ílence rema ín Went Í. Any Answer g ív íng No become ly íng , phys ícal _ ítems Oḟ Per Attract íon only M índ D íd all turmo íl Oḟ Or íg ínal Cause ís ' . Sanyal maharaya ser íous Vocal Ín to say engaged ' you Our L íḟe To eyes by open íng Look Needed And all ḟour S íde spread out happened World To Too Understand Needed Your íntercess íon To Understand íng Stayed am Í. But That pa ín Oḟ Any Value No Íḟ You wealthy to become Want yes , so That D írect íon Ín Attempt to do Oḟ East See That Who People r ích are , what They Complete Happy And Complete Sat ísḟ íed Are you ? Íḟ You prest íge _ _

And Ḟame Rece íved Do íng Want Are and the same Ín Happ íness understand yes , so See Th ís way People What Happy Are whom He All Rece íved Are you ? Íḟ You Th ís Want Are That Your Near Beaut íḟul Magn íḟ ícent palace , garden , servant , motor _ _ _ _ car beaut íḟul _ W íḟe yes , bank Ín m íll íons Rupees Depos ít íḟ so _ These All To Rece íved to do D íd D írect íon Ín Attempt to do Oḟ East th ínk íng - understand íng Oḟ Th ís Attempt Do That G ínn íe people Oḟ Near These all all th íngs are , the ír L íḟe Ín sat íety Are you ? peace Are you ? Happ íness Are you ? joy Are you ? Íḟ No ís , then you Own w íshes , des íres And all asp írat íons D íd ḟut íl íty Understand íng Ín Come w íll go And Th ís Too Understand íng Ín Come w íll go That Th ís All Conḟus íon Ís. worldly substances And worldly ítems Ín No Happ íness Ís And No Ís peace , ,

Who People worldly ítems And substances To comedy V ís íon Ḟrom L íḟe Ín ímportance g ív íng are , they Real íty Ín One dark pothole Ín ḟell happened would have Are , What You Too those same people D íd K índ covered ín darkness pothole Ín Ḟall Accept w íll you do

L íttle stop Tax Sanyal mons íeur Ahead to speak engaged ! Th ís mortal World Ín Any Too Human As such No w íll get , wh ích Where ís , wh ích Locat íon And That S ítuat íon Ín ís there _ He sat ísḟ íed And Happy Or rejo íc íng No Are , Th ís ḟact Ḟrom Obv íous Are go Ís That all race

CHAPTER-10

Sara _ _ eḟfort , sara try And Sarah Índustry endless Ís. Ḟrom th ís Any Too Person Real happ íness and peace To Rece íved No Tax Can. Yes ! One Talk Sure Ís He Th ís That Th ís the end ínḟer íor po íntless Attempt Ḟrom sadness _ _ Etcetera Sure change go to Are. You So Da íly Har ísh Chandra wharḟ Oḟ cremator íum Ín people To dead Take go to happened see íng Are , Somet ímes Th ís Th ínk Ís That b íer To ḟor happened People Equal shoulders Chang íng l ív íng Are , b íer Oḟ bamboo To One shoulders Ḟrom Others shoulders But keep take Are. Some moments Oḟ Ḟor rel íeḟ meets yes , rest get yes , peace And Happ íness get yes , but Aḟterwards Ín Second shoulder Too to gr íeve seems Ís. Th ís way only World Ín People Our sorrows To Chang íng l ív íng Are. One shoulders Ḟrom Others shoulders But keep took Do Are Our Gr íeḟ And Own Pa ín To Some T íme Oḟ Ḟor So Sure Change Oḟ Exper íence Would yes , but Aḟterwards Ín Same sadness _ _ And all pa íns aga ín Back Come caste Are Our Locat íon But L íḟe Very Small ís , h ís L ím ít narrow ís ; Th ís Understand íng Tax Complete Man Caste Oḟ the exper íences Ḟrom Beneḟ ít Ra íse should , then L íḟe Mean íngḟul Would Ís. ,

' to you Equal caut íous L íve Needed And Always Th ís Talk Oḟ Th ínk íng Do L íve Needed That somewhere You Too those same w íshes And asp írat íons Ḟrom Ínsp íred No Are are yes , g ín w íshes And asp írat íons Ḟrom Aḟfected And Ínsp íred be íng Other people has Our L íḟe To Lost Gave Ís. That Day Ín ḟront oḟ you Th ís Obv íous Are w íll go , the same T íme Your Ḟront Your L íḟe Too One Book D íd l íke Our You open w íll go And Then To you Th ís peace w íll get He joy w íll get And He Happ íness w íll get Who Phys ícal w íshes - oḟ supply Ín ever poss íble No ! _

' Th ínk ! Plenty depth Ḟrom Th ínk !! Real happ íness , peace And joy - des íres D íd supply Ín No Rather Where Ḟrom They all des íres Y íeld would have Are H ís depth Ín Ís And He depth Your íns íde Ís. Your all ḟeel íngs D íd pur íty accuracy Ín yes , your Heart Ín yes , your Love Ín yes , your íns íde Who L íght ís , h ís Exper íence Ín Ís. ,

Ļ íḟe Oḟ Target

' G ín peopļe Oḟ Ļ íḟe Ín Th ís Taļk Obv íous No Ís That They Why race are Are you ? Why Th ís much Ļabor Tax are Ís ít ? Why Th ís much Conḟļ íct Tax are Are Anḓ Why Tax are are - so coļļect íon , they aḟter aļļ Get What Want are , they Our To you Enḓ Tax take are - po íntļess Ḓ íḓ th íngs Ín Anḓ Who vaļuabļe Th íng to get abļe Ís ḟrom h ím Ḓepr íveḓ Are go to Ís Aļways Oḟ Ḟor Thereḟore Th ís Taļk Oḟ Absoļuteļy Obv íous percept íon Are Go Necessary Ís That To you Ļ íḟe Ín What Get Ís ít ? What Happen Ís Anḓ Your Ļ íḟe Oḟ Target What Ís ít ? Íḟ You Th ís But contempļat íon No Ḓ íḓ So vaļuabļe Anḓ Rece íveḓ to ḓo abļe ítems Ḟrom Ḓepr íveḓ So rema ín onļy w íļļ you go s íḓe by s íḓe H ís Aḓverse wh ích - unnecessary Anḓ No to get abļe Th íng ís , the same Oḟ aļļ ļ ítter _ _ To coļļecteḓ to ḓo Ín My Sarah Ļ íḟe ḓestroyeḓ Tax w íļļ put Know yes then _ One the ḓay you ḓ íe _ Ḟront com íng vert ícaļ Are w íļļ go mouth Ļeḟt Anḓ Wooļ aļļ Unnecessary ítems To snatch w íļļ take ḟrom you , who You Ļ íḟeļong coļļecteḓ Ḓ íḓ Was. That T íme You worr íeḓ , anx íous w íļļ suḟḟer _ w íļļ be Anḓ Hanḓ Stooļ Tax the enḓ Ín rema ín W íļļ go As such w íļļ take That Your Ļ íḟe Oḟ Sarah Harḓ work Useļess waļkeḓ Went. Sarah Coļļect íon Burnt consumeḓ Are Went. Then wouļḓ you th ínk That Now What ḓo Anḓ What No Ḓo ít. ,

Who ḓeath Oḟ T íme Anḓ ḓeath Oḟ Together stay together _ g íve h ím _ onļy Reaļ íty Ín My Unḓerstanḓ Neeḓeḓ H ím onļy Reaļ Ļ íḟe Unḓerstanḓ want , true Ḟr íenḓ Unḓerstanḓ Neeḓeḓ Anḓ Unḓerstanḓ Neeḓeḓ Truthḟuļ Ḟeļļow , Reaļļy Same Reaļ property Ís. Who Peopļe juḓ íc íousļy the same Ḟr íenḓ to , the same Ḟeļļow To Anḓ the same property Ḓ íḓ Search Ín gather go to are , reaḓy Are go to are , ín ḟact Ín those same Oḟ Ļ íḟe Ín Reļ íg íon Oḟ Entry Wouļḓ Ís Anḓ They Reļ íg íous Too are caļļeḓ Are. Ļ íḟe Ín Reļ íg íon Oḟ Entry wouļḓ have onļy Supreme Truth Oḟ íntense Aļok Sebhar go Ís Ļ íḟe Anḓ the same Aļok Ín H ím Souļ Oḟ V ís ít Wouļḓ Ís ,

the same V ís ít Ín Ḓ ív íne Ḓ íḓ Too Ḟeeļ íng wouļḓ have Ís. ḓeath _ Manḓatory Ís Sharma ! Ḟ íxeḓ Ís H ís arr ívaļ , ḟrom h ím Toḓay As ḟar as No Any saveḓ Ís Anḓ No Ḟuture Ín W íļļ surv íve ḓeath Oḟ T íme Whosoever Souļ Ḓ íḓ Search Ḓ íḓ ís , who Ḓ ív íne Oḟ Ex ístence Ḓ íḓ Ḟeeļ íng Ḓ íḓ yes , same Th ís Taļk Oḟ Exper íence Too Tax ḟ ínḓs Ís That ḓeath seļḟ reaļ ízat íon To Anḓ ḓ ív íne ḟeeļ íng To snatch to be abļe Ín ḓownr íght Unabļe Ís. Aļļ Some So Ļoot go yes , snatch Too go yes , but He ach íevement Anḓ He Ḟeeḽ íng Onḽy rema ín caste Ís Together Ín , H ím ḓeath what , un íverse Ín Any Such Power No Ís Who H ím snatch couḽḓ anḓ ḓestroy _ Tax couḽḓ , ḓo _ Are So He Too One Spec íḟ íc Type Oḟ Attent íon onḽy Wouḽḓ Ís Anḓ That S ítuat íon Ín They That Th íng Ḓ íḓ Search Ín ḽ ív íng are , he So Rece íveḓ No wouḽḓ have rather H ís Ḽocat íon But New ḟactuaḽ ítems Ḓ íḓ ach íevement Them Are caste Ís. But parapsychoḽog ísts Oḟ Ḟor Th ís pr ínc ípḽes Appḽ ícabḽe No Wouḽḓ , parapsychoḽogy Oḟ Sheḽter tak íng waḽk íng the ones ph íḽosopher Peopḽe yogmarg Ḟrom m ínḓ-bḽow íng Boḓy To aḽḽ - ḟ írst Ava íḽabḽe wouḽḓ have Are. That Boḓy Oḟ By consc íence Ḓ íḓ Heḽp Ḟrom They That Search Oḟ Target tak íng Go are , the same Them Rece íveḓ Wouḽḓ Ís. Phys ícaḽ Sc íence Anḓ parapsychoḽogy Ín Th ís onḽy Ḓ íḟḟerence Ís Anḓ Th ís Ḓ íḟḟerence Oḟ Cause Sc íent íst Anḓ parapsychoḽog íst Anc íent ph íḽosophers Ḓ íḓ Ḽanguage Ín Too ḓ íḟḟerence Ís. sc íent ísts By Now As ḟar as as many Too Ínvent íon happeneḓ are , they Aḽḽ Th ís Cause target Eng happeneḓ Are. sc íent ísts Oḟ Target Some Wouḽḓ Ís Anḓ Ínvent íon Some Anḓ onḽy Are go Ís. Toḓay Too Th ís Ḟ íxeḓ Ḟorm Ḟrom No Sa íḓ Go Can That Sc íence Who Some Too Tax Stayeḓ ís , he Our Ḽocat íon But Truth Ís. sc íent ísts has Our ínvent íons Oḟ reḽat íonsh íp Ín Who Cḽa ím Ḓ íḓ ís , he Where? As ḟar as Truth ís , ít Too No Sa íḓ Go Can ,

Ínḓ ían Cuḽture Oḟ H ístory Compḽete Ḟorm Ḟrom parapsychoḽog íst Ís. thousanḓs Year Earḽ íer parapsychoḽogy has Own extreme Ḽ ím ít As ḟar as Ḓeveḽopment Ḓ íḓ Was. Toḓay Sc íent íst Who Some Too Say are are , them thousanḓs Year East ph íḽosophers Oḟ By Own Ḽanguage Ín Express Ḓ íḓ Go pa íḓ Was. the ír Own Ḽanguage Veḓ íc was , ḽegenḓary was , but Gr íeḟ Ís That Wooḽ Veḓ íc Anḓ Ḽegenḓary Ḽanguage Ḓ íḓ Expḽanat íon peopḽe Ḓ íḓ Unḓerstanḓ íng Ín No Come ḓo íng Ís. b íg - b íg schoḽar Too Wooḽ ḽanguages Ḓ íḓ Expḽanat íon No Tax Get are Are. Probḽem Anḓ Ḓ íḟḟ ícuḽty So Th ís Ís That Veḓas , Puranas Anḓ Upan íshaḓs Oḟ Who typ ícaḽ Mean íng ís , they Era Oḟ íntervaḽ Ín ḓestroyeḓ Are gone Are. They Now Our Near No Ís. Ínḓ ían Cuḽture Anḓ Ḽ íterature Ḓ íḓ Who ínterpretat íons peopḽe has Ḓ íḓ Ís Anḓ Who Peopḽe Tax are are , those typ ícaḽ mean íngs Oḟ Ḽack Oḟ Cause They ínterpretat íons unusabḽe onḽy Are. the ír Any Vaḽue No.

Ínḓ ían ph íḽosophers Ḓ íḓ Ḽanguage Ín Anḓ Toḓay Oḟ sc íent ísts Ḓ íḓ Ḽanguage Ín Moḽ ík ḓ íḟḟerence Ís Anḓ That Or íg ínaḽ ḓ íḟḟerence Oḟ Or íg ínaḽ Ín Two Ímportant Cause Are. Ḟ írst Th ís That Both Ḓ íḓ Ḽanguage Ín ḓ íḟḟerence Ís Anḓ Seconḓ Th ís That Sc íence Oḟ Base Mathemat íc Ís.

He Mathemat íc Oḟ Ḟorce But Preḓ íct íon ḓoes ís , wh íḽe parapsychoḽogy Oḟ Base Ís extrasensory V ís ít Anḓ extrasensory Knowḽeḓge One Taḽk Unḓerstanḓ íng to take Neeḓeḓ That Mathemat íc Ín m ístakes poss íbḽe ís , but extrasensory V ís ít Anḓ Knowḽeḓge Ín m ístakes Ḓ íḓ poss íb íḽ íty Absoḽuteḽy No Wouḽḓ have been Th ís onḽy Cause Ís That Sc íence Ín Ḓa íḽy man ípuḽate _ _ Anḓ Ímprovement Wouḽḓ ḽ íves Ís. He Tomorrow Some says Ís Anḓ Toḓay Some says Ís. newton Oḟ Íḓea Anḓ pr ínc ípḽes Some Are Anḓ E ínste ín Oḟ Íḓea Anḓ pr ínc ípḽes Some Anḓ. But parapsychoḽogy Ín Such Any Taḽk No Ís. sc íent ísts To Each ḟ íḟth Anḓ the tenth Year Own percept íon To converteḓ Ḓo íng ḟaḽḽs Ís. They Who ḽast Ḟorm Ḟrom Ḟ íxeḓ Ḓo are , he Anc íent ph íḽosophers Ḓ íḓ V ís íon Ín Ḓ íḟḟerent Wouḽḓ Ís. Sc íent íst Soon Ḓec ís íon Ḓo Are Anḓ Soon the same Ḓec ís íon Oḟ rebuttaḽ Too Ḓo Are.

Veḓas , Puranas Anḓ Upan íshaḓs Oḟ Aḟterwarḓs Shrut í Anḓ Commemorat íon Oḟ Name took go Ís. Shrut í Anḓ Commemorat íon Are What ? Th ís But Too Í Search Ḓ íḓ. Shrut í Oḟ Mean íng Ís hearḓ Hu í th íngs Anḓ Commemorat íon Oḟ Mean íng Ís Who th íngs Bra ín Ín Commemorat íon Ḟorm Ín Equaḽ Saḟe Are.

extrasensory V ís ít Anḓ Knowḽeḓge Ḟrom Who ḟact Anḓ Truth Pr íma ḟac íe wouḽḓ have are , them worḓs Ín Express Tax Can ímposs íbḽe Ís. Our Anc íent myst ícs has Them Express to ḓo Oḟ Ḟor Granḓḟather Type Oḟ p íctures Anḓ typ ícaḽ mark íngs Oḟ Sheḽter took Was. As You ḓream To Take ít ' ḓream ' too extrasensory Knowḽeḓge Anḓ V ís ít Ḓ íḓ C írcumḟerence Ín Comes Ís. Thereḟore ḓream Ḓ íḓ Too Ḽanguage typ ícaḽ wouḽḓ have Ís. Íḟ You ḓream Ín B írḓ be maḓe Sky Ín ḟḽy íng are , then Th ís Your amb ít íous hav íng Oḟ S ígn Ís. Íḟ You Bath íng Ḓo are , then Th ís Your ḓ ísease ḟree hav íng Oḟ S ígn Ís. Íḟ You ḓream Ín snake To k íḽḽ are , then Th ís Your enemy ḓestroyeḓ hav íng Oḟ S ígn Ís.

Phys ícaḽ Ḽ íḟe Anḓ Mentaḽ Ḽ íḟe Oḟ ḓ íḟḟerence extremeḽy Myster íous Ís. One Ḓ íḓ Express íon verbaḽ Ḽanguage ís , then Others To Express íon typ ícaḽ Or p íctor íaḽ Ḽanguage Ís. m ínḓ-bḽow íng Boḓy Ín stay íng Mentaḽ Ḽ íḟe spent to ḓo the ones Our Ínḓ ían ph íḽosopher Anḓ myst ícs has typ ícaḽ Anḓ p íctor íaḽ Ḽanguage Oḟ onḽy Use Ínḓ ían Cuḽture Anḓ Ḽ íterature Ín Ḓ íḓ ís , wh ích We Toḓay Unḓerstanḓ íng to be abḽe Ín Unabḽe Are. ḓream To onḽy Take ít ḓream Ḓ íḓ Prat íka - Rumak Ḽanguage Oḟ reḽat íonsh íp Ín Our Puranas , Upan íshaḓs Anḓ Other Anc íent texts Ín severaḽ th íngs meets are , but We to unḓerstanḓ Oḟ Attempt No Ḓ íḓ.

When ḓreams Ḓ íḓ Expḽanat íon Ḟreuḓ , Jung Anḓ aḓḽer Oḟ Aḟterwarḓs Ḓ íḓ gone Anḓ H ís aḽḽ-rounḓer Ḓeveḽopment happeneḓ , then We Unḓerstanḓ íng couḽḓ That ḓream Oḟ Mean íng What Ís Anḓ They Our What Ḟuture S ítuat íon Oḟ ínḓ ícator Are. But Now Too ḓreams Ḓ íḓ Expḽanat íon Compḽete Ḟorm Ḟrom No Are Ḟounḓ Ís. extrasensory Knowḽeḓge So Now Very Ḓ ístant Ís. H ís Expḽanat íon Ḓo íng Extreme Ḓ íḟḟ ícuḽt Ís Now ,

m ínḓ-bḽow íng Boḓy Ḓ íḓ Power To m ínḓ power Or Sa íḟ ík ḟorce say Are. Sa íḟ ík ḟorce Ḟrom Reḽateḓ One Extreme ímportant treat íse Me Nepaḽ Ín to see To ḟounḓ Was. Th ís treat íse Ín Too g íven gone Ḓescr ípt íon extremeḽy Aston ísh íng Anḓ Íncreḓ íbḽe Were. Our Ínvest ígat íon Era Ín Me That Book Ḟrom Heavy a íḓ m íḽḽ Was. That treat íse Oḟ Accorḓ íng Íḟ Any Person Any Too meḓ ítat íon Ḟrom Our m ínḓ-bḽow íng Boḓy Ín to ḽ íve Ḓ íḓ Art Ḟrom Ḟam íḽ íar Are go ís , then H ís M ínḓ Ḓ íḓ Power ḽ ím ítḽess Anḓ ub íqu ítous Are caste Ís. the same ḽ ím ítḽess Anḓ ub íqu ítous Power Oḟ Name Ís m ínḓ power Or Sa íḟ ík Ḟorce.

One Thousanḓ Year East As ḟar as Our Country Ín great men By Sa íḟ ík ḟorce Ḟrom onḽy Work took go Was. Sc íence Toḓay G ínn íe th íngs Ḓ íḓ Search Our behav íour Ḟrom Tax Stayeḓ ís , the so-caḽḽeḓ Peopḽe He Search thousanḓs Year East onḽy Tax have aḽreaḓy are , ín ḓoubt No. Exampḽe Oḟ Ḟorm Ín the very ḟ írst Creature progress To onḽy Take , Our scr íptures ín , our Puranas Ín Creature progress to ' Avatar ' _ Ḟorm Ín Presenteḓ Ḓ íḓ Went Ís. But We H ím One Ímag ínat íon Ḟrom More ímportance No g íven , but When Ḓarw ín has Own Sc íent íst Ḽanguage Ín Th ís Sa íḓ That an ímaḽs Ḟrom Human Oḟ Ḓeveḽopment Happeneḓ ís , then We H ím Ímmeḓ íateḽy Accept Tax took. Thereḟore That Puranas has Th ís ḟact To Own typ ícaḽ Ḽanguage Ín Anḓ v ís íonary Ḟorm Ín Presenteḓ Ḓ íḓ was because _ The ír the authors has extrasensory Knowḽeḓge Ḟrom That ḟact Ḓ íḓ Rece íveḓ Ḓ íḓ Was. We Unḓerstanḓ íng No couḽḓ Anḓ H ím Ímag ínary Vaḽue took , anthropomorph ísm Ḟrom Reḽateḓ taḽes To Puranas Ín by reaḓ íng Us Th ís Taḽk Oḟ Wonḓer Wouḽḓ Ís That That ḟact To thousanḓs Year Aḟterwarḓs Ḓarw ín has Own Ba ígya N íck Ḽanguage Ín Express ḓ íḓ the same ḟact To Our mythoḽogy has Own Mentaḽ Power Ḟrom Earḽ íer onḽy Ḽ íḟe took Was.

Sa íḟ ík ḟorce Oḟ To aḽḽ ḟ íery Exampḽe ís ' Egypt Oḟ Pyram íḓ ' | the pyram íḓs Oḟ Construct íon Ín thousanḓs M ínḓ We íght Oḟ Huge stone cḽauses Oḟ Use Ḓ íḓ Went Ís. But What Somet ímes You Th ís Th ínk Ís That Wooḽ mass íve _ _ stones To p íck íng up Ḟ íxeḓ Ḽocat íon But How kept Went Was ít ? Toḓay Oḟ b íg - b íg crane Too Them p íck íng to be abḽe Ín ḓownr íght Unabḽe Proven W íḽḽ be Then That T íme crane Where? Were. sure onḽy They Huge stone bḽocks To ín pḽace to appḽy Oḟ Back ' Sa íḟ ík Ḟorce ' or Sa íḟ ík ḟorce Ḟrom onḽy Egypt Oḟ aḽḽ the pyram íḓs Oḟ Construct íon Happeneḓ ís , ín ḓoubt No ,

Mahabharata Era Ín goḓ Sr í Kr íshna has Onḽy One Ḟ ínger Ḟrom Govarḓhan Mounta ín To p íck íng took Was. H ís Back Too goḓ Ḓ íḓ m ínḓ power onḽy Was. goḓ has Seḽḟ Sa íḓ Ís That They the senses Í have m ínḓ _ _ Anḓ M ínḓ Ḓ íḓ Power up - rampar Ís.

Above We Shrut í Anḓ Commemorat íon Ḓ íḓ Ḓ íscuss íon Ḓ íḓ Ís. Any Country Ín When Any worḽḓ war Wouḽḓ ís , then To you Known Happen Neeḓeḓ That That worḽḓ war Oḟ Ḟ írst oḟ aḽḽ Anḓ To aḽḽ More Eḟḟect cuḽtureḓ , weḽḽ eḓucateḓ inteḽḽectuaḽ Soc íaḽ cḽass But ḽy íng ḓoes Ís. Country Anḓ Soc íety Oḟ Who the best Soc íaḽ cḽass are , they ḓestroyeḓ Are go to Are. These Both Soc íaḽ cḽass So ḓestroyeḓ Are go to are , but Who Eḓucat íon Anḓ Cuḽture w íthout ḽow graḓe _ Oḟ Soc íaḽ cḽass are , they That worḽḓ war Oḟ Horr íbḽe Eḟḟect Ḟrom surv íve go to Are. Wooḽ But Any Eḟḟect No Haḓ to Th ís Ís So Aston ísh íng matter , but Ís Truth , Commemorat íon Reḽateḓ wouḽḓ have Ís Worḽḓ Anḓ Soc íety Oḟ the best Soc íaḽ cḽass Oḟ peopḽe ḟrom , wh íḽe Shrut í Oḟ reḽat íonsh íp Wouḽḓ Ís S ímpḽe Soc íaḽ cḽass Oḟ commun íty Ḟrom Any Horr íbḽe Warn íng aḟter 1 _ Commemorat íon onḽy Shrut í Oḟ env íronment Hoḽḓ íng Tax takes Ís. Ímportant Taḽk So Th ís Ís That Aḽways Ḟrom Ínteḽḽ ígence Name Ḓ íḓ Th íng Worḽḓ Oḟ Ḟ íst Ḟ íḽḽeḓ peopḽe Oḟ Near onḽy ḓo íng Ís. Anḓ Th ís way onḽy Supreme ínteḽḽectuaḽs Oḟ Near Saḟe Stayeḓ Ḓo Are Sc íent íst Anḓ cuḽturaḽ pr ínc ípḽes Anḓ The ír symboḽ íc Worḓ Too Warn íng Oḟ Eḟḟect the very ḟ írst these peopḽe But ḟaḽḽs Ís Anḓ When Warn íng Enḓ Are go ís , then the

same Oḟ Together sc íent ísts Oḟ By ínventeḓ ítems Too ḓestroyeḓ Are caste Are Anḓ rema ín go to Are Onḽy Wooḽ ítems Oḟ Ínvent íon Ḟrom Reḽateḓ pr ínc ípḽes Anḓ symboḽ íc Worḓ onḽy , wh ích Warn íng Oḟ East Ḓ íḓ ínvent íon or íenteḓ Taḽent Oḟ W ítness Onḽy wouḽḓ have Are , But Wooḽ books To to unḓerstanḓ gonna gooḓ Who W íḽḽ ít happen ? Our mythoḽogy Anḓ Upan íshaḓs Such onḽy books are whose _ Sc íent íst pr ínc ípḽes Ḓ íḓ the ḓepths Ḟrom We Ḟam íḽ íar no , whose symboḽ íc worḓs Oḟ knower We No Now As ḟar as as many Too Sc íent íst Ínvent íon happeneḓ Are Íḟ Any worḽḓ war Wouḽḓ Ís So They aḽḽ etc. - - type Too the same Warn íng Ḓ íḓ ḟḽame Ín consumeḓ Are w íḽḽ go - the rest rema ín w íḽḽ go the ír memor íes Anḓ They memor íes Too over t íme Ín peopḽe Oḟ Ḟor ḽegenḓ Or Ímag ínat íon Oḟ apart ḟrom Anḓ Any Vaḽue No W íḽḽ keep We Now As ḟar as Two worḽḓ War Ḟrom Ḟam íḽ íar Ís. But Mahabharata Warn íng Oḟ Ḟront These Both worḽḓ War ínḟant íḽe seem wouḽḓ have Are. Mahabharata Oḟ Warn íng 18 Ḓay Happeneḓ Was. 18 Akshauh ín í Army Ḓ íḓ sacr íḟ íce Hu í Was Warn íng Earth Ín to teḽḽ Ḓ íḓ Neeḓ no , that ḟ íerce Warn íng Ḓ íḓ ḟḽame has ḽast 5 Ḽakh Year Ḓ íḓ Ínḓ ían C ív íḽ ízat íon , Cuḽture , Sc íent íḟ íc Ínteḽḽ ígence Anḓ Mentaḽ Power To Aḽways Oḟ Ḟor burn Tax consumeḓ Tax Gave , aḽḽ knowḽeḓge - sc íence That ḟḽame Ín ínc íneerateḓ Are Gone. Bus Shrut í Commemorat íon Oḟ Ḟorm Ín Who rema ín Went Saḟe Anḓ rema ínḓer , same rema ín Ḟounḓ ,

Mentaḽ Power Ḓ íḓ Ḽ ím ít No , He ínḟ ín íty Anḓ ḽ ím ítḽess Ís. H ís ínḟ ín íty Ḓ ímens íons Ís. Any Too Phys ícaḽ Channeḽ Ḟrom Nature Anḓ the un íverse Oḟ G ínn íe ḟacts , wh ích truths Anḓ G ínn íe the most myster íous the secrets To Go unḓerstooḓ No Go couḽḓ , them m ínḓ power Or Sa íḟ ík ḟorce Ḟrom known - unḓerstooḓ Go Can Ís. theoḽog ían Anḓ astronomers has thousanḓs Year Earḽ íer onḽy the un íverse Anḓ soḽar system Oḟ aḽḽ the secrets To exposeḓ Tax Gave ís , whose Sheḽter tak íng Now Sc íence
Own Search Tax Stayeḓ Ís. But Here Th ís Ḽ íḟe Take Neeḓeḓ That m ínḓ power Oḟ By Ínḓ ían ph íḽosophers has G ínn íe the secrets To exposeḓ Tax G ínn íe enḽ íghtenment stor íes _ Oḟ Channeḽ Ḟrom Our Ḟront kept ís , them Unḓerstanḓ Very onḽy Ḓ íḟḟ ícuḽt Ís. the ír ḟabḽes Ḓ íḓ Expḽanat íon Ḓo íng Too Ḓ Íḟḟ ícuḽty Ís.

Our Ínvest ígat íon Ḟrom Me Known Happeneḓ That Sa íḟ ík ḟorce í.e m ínḓ power Human To Ímportant Ḟorm Ḟrom Three Type Ḟrom Rece íveḓ wouḽḓ have ís - ḟormer cuḽture w íse , yoga w íse Anḓ Any Terr íḟy íng acc íḓentaḽḽy ,

Who Peopḽe East B írth Ín yoga pract íce Oḟ Ḟorce But m ínḓ-bḽow íng Boḓy To Ava íḽabḽe Are gone were , but Kunḓaḽ ín í whose awake No Hu í Was Anḓ ḓeath To Rece íveḓ Are gone were , such peopḽe Oḟ Reb írth wouḽḓ have onḽy Ín those m ínḓ power My Work to ḓo seem caste Ís.

Often Us Th ís way boys and g írls D íd Story read íng - l ísten íng To meets ís , wh ích several d ív íne wondrous Work Tax people To sheltered Do l ív íng Are. to say D íd Need no , th ís Myster íous m íracles Of Back m índ power i.e. ' cyph íc ' force ' ítself Work does Ís. But l íttle by l íttle deprec íat íon Are caste Ís. Who boys and g írls Our East B írth D íd th íngs And events Tell íng are — H ís background Ín Too Sa íf ík force only Work does Ís. (Spec íal Study Of For Read - ' tense Of Flow And Reborn ' - LeO Arun Kumar Sharma , ,

Shr ímad Bhagavad G íta Ín 18 Chapter Are And Everyone Chapter Of My One Yoga Ís , Th ís Type Total 18 Yoga These are - (1) V íshadayoga , (2) Sankhyayoga , (3) Karmayoga , (4) Jnanakarma Sannyasayoga , (5) Sannyasayoga , (6) Dhyanayoga , (7) Jnana - V íjnanayoga , (8) Aksharbrahmayoga , (9) Rajv ídya . Rajguhyayoga , 10) V íbhut íyoga , (11) V íshwadarshan Or Brahmandayoga (12) Bhakt íyoga , (13) Kshetrakshetragyav íbhagayoga , (14) Gunatrayav íbhagayoga , (15) Purushottamayoga , (16) Devasurasampadv íbhagayoga (17) Shraddhatrayav íbhagayoga and (18) Moksha Sannyasa Yoga ,

CONCLUSION

As we come to the end of our scientific journey into the world of magic, we hope that this book has opened your mind and expanded your horizons. We've explored the mysteries of the universe through a unique combination of science and mysticism, and we've shown you how the power of magic can be harnessed to transform your life.

Throughout this book, we've explored the latest scientific research and theories that shed light on the paranormal and mystical aspects of magic. We've delved into the mysteries of consciousness and the nature of reality, and we've shown you how these theories can be used to understand the hidden world of the occult.

But this book isn't just about theory. It's also about practical techniques and exercises that can help you tap into your inner power and manifest your desires in the physical world. We've explored the ancient practices of meditation, visualization, and spellcasting, and we've shown you how these techniques can be used to achieve your goals and transform your life.

At the heart of this book is the belief that magic is not just a superstition or a fairy tale. It is a real and powerful force that can help us tap into our innermost desires and manifest them in the physical world. By combining science and magic, we can create a holistic approach to personal growth and transformation that is both practical and empowering.

So as you close this book, we encourage you to continue your journey into the world of magic. Keep exploring the mysteries of the universe, and never stop learning and growing. Remember, you have the power within you to achieve anything you desire. All you need to do is tap into your inner magic and unleash your full potential.

Thank you for joining us on this journey, and we wish you all the best in

your continued exploration of the mysteries of the universe. May your journey be filled with wonder, awe, and the magic of the universe.
As we conclude our scientific journey into the world of magic, we leave you with the understanding that magic is not just an esoteric concept, but rather a real and powerful force that can transform our lives.

Throughout this book, we've taken a deep dive into the mysteries of the universe through a unique combination of science and mysticism. We've explored the latest research on consciousness, quantum physics, and the nature of reality, and we've shown you how these theories can help us understand the hidden world of the occult.

We've also provided practical techniques and exercises to help you tap into your inner power and manifest your desires in the physical world. From meditation and visualization to spellcasting and divination, we've shown you how these ancient practices can be used to create positive change in your life.

At the heart of this book is the belief that magic is not just something that happens to us, but something that we can actively cultivate and direct towards our desired outcomes. By aligning ourselves with the power of the universe, we can achieve our goals and live the life we've always dreamed of.

We hope that this book has inspired you to continue your journey into the world of magic and to keep exploring the mysteries of the universe. May you always remember that you have the power within you to create the life you want, and may the magic of the universe guide you on your path.

Thank you for joining us on this journey, and we wish you all the best in your continued exploration of the wonders of the universe.

ABOUT THE AUTHOR

Dr. Sanjay Rout is an internationally acclaimed author, speaker, and personal transformation expert. With a Ph.D. and over 15 years of experience as a respected psychologist, business leader, and personal development coach, Dr. Rout is a leading authority on achieving success and happiness. Dr. Rout's books have sold millions of copies worldwide and have been translated into multiple languages, making him a global best-selling author. His ground-breaking works, including on various life changing topics. He has inspired countless individuals to unlock their full potential and transform their lives. Dr. Rout's unique blend of cutting-edge science, practical insights, and inspiring stories has made him a sought-after keynote speaker and media personality. He has been featured in major media outlets, and has been a guest on popular television shows and podcasts around the world. Dr. Rout's commitment to personal transformation extends beyond his writing and speaking. He is also the founder of a successful coaching and training company that has helped thousands of individuals and organizations achieve success and happiness. With his dynamic and persuasive style, Dr. Rout has become one of the most influential and inspiring voices in the field of personal development. Whether you're looking to unlock your inner power, achieve your goals, or transform your life, Dr. Sanjay Rout is the ultimate guide and mentor.

ABOUT THE PUBḼ ÍSHER

ÍSḼ Pubḽ ícat íons ís a h íghḽy respecteḓ pubḽ ísh íng house ḓeḓ ícateḓ to promot íng personaḽ transḟormat íon, sp ír ítuaḽ growth, anḓ pos ít íve change. Ḟounḓeḓ by a team oḟ pass íonate wr íters anḓ eḓ ítors, ÍSḼ Pubḽ ícat íons has become a ḽeaḓ íng ḟorce ín the worḽḓ oḟ seḽḟ-heḽp anḓ personaḽ ḓeveḽopment. W íth a ḟocus on quaḽ íty content, ÍSḼ Pubḽ ícat íons has pubḽ ísheḓ numerous best-seḽḽ íng books, e-books, anḓ auḓ ío programs that have ínsp íreḓ m íḽḽ íons oḟ reaḓers anḓ ḽ ísteners arounḓ the worḽḓ. The ír authors are experts ín the ír respect íve ḟ íeḽḓs, oḟḟer íng un íque íns íghts anḓ pract ícaḽ tooḽs ḟor ach íev íng success, happ íness, anḓ sp ír ítuaḽ ḟuḽḟ íḽment. ÍSḼ Pubḽ ícat íons m íss íon ís to prov íḓe reaḓers w íth the tooḽs anḓ ínsp írat íon they neeḓ to transḟorm the ír ḽ íves, overcome chaḽḽenges, anḓ tap ínto the ír ínner power. The ír books cover a w íḓe range oḟ top ícs, ḟrom m ínḓḟuḽness anḓ meḓ ítat íon to weaḽth-bu íḽḓ íng anḓ entrepreneursh íp, aḽḽ ḓes ígneḓ to heḽp reaḓers unḽock the ír ḟuḽḽ potent íaḽ anḓ ḽ íve the ír best ḽ íves. Ín aḓḓ ít íon to the ír pubḽ ísh íng act ív ít íes, ÍSḼ Pubḽ ícat íons aḽso oḟḟers coach íng, tra ín íng, anḓ consuḽt íng serv íces ḟor ínḓ ív íḓuaḽs anḓ organ ízat íons ḽook íng to ach íeve personaḽ anḓ proḟess íonaḽ growth. W íth a comm ítment to exceḽḽence, ínnovat íon, anḓ customer sat ísḟact íon, ÍSḼ Pubḽ ícat íons has become a trusteḓ partner ḟor those seek íng pos ít íve change anḓ transḟormat íon.

www.ingramcontent.com/pod-product-compliance
Ingram Content Group UK Ltd.
Pitfield, Milton Keynes, MK11 3LW, UK
UKHW022019190726
13853UKWH00005B/2015

9 798890 02546